Published by

Because Entertainment Inc.

1395 Frances Street, Vancouver British Columbia, Canada V5L 1 Z1

Because Entertainment, Inc.

Copyright Because Entertainment, Inc. © 2012. All rights reserved.

ISBN 978-0-9920275-1-3

Andrew Loog Oldham asserts his moral right to be identified as the author of this book.

Without limiting the rights under copyright reserved above, no part of this book may be reproduced in any form or by any electronic or mechanical means, including information storage and retrieval systems, without prior permission in writing from the publisher, except by a reviewer who may quote brief passages in a review.

STONE FREE

WRITTEN BY

ANDREW LOOG OLDHAM

EDITED BY

RON ROSS

Brian Epstein. Portrait by David Bailey

A dedication to Brian Epstein:

Brian persevered against all odds and got his lads a recording contract—

And that act changed all of our lives for the better.

CONTENTS

PROLOGUE 1

INTRODUCTION 7

ALEC MORRIS 21

DIAGHILEV 37

LARRY PARNES 53

ALBERT GROSSMAN 71

BRIAN EPSTEIN 97

KIT LAMBERT AND CHRIS STAMP 115

JERRY BRANDT 153

ADRIAN MILLAR 175

MALCOLM MCLAREN 201

DON ARDEN 219

PETE KAMERON 253

ALLEN KLEIN 285

IMMEDIATE RECORDS 325

PHIL SPECTOR 365

GOD ONLY KNOWS 381

ACKNOWLEDGEMENTS 391

ABOUT THE AUTHOR 393

PROLOGUE

IT IS QUITE surprising that I did not end up a criminal.

I discovered, though, that I didn't have the bottle at the tender age of ten. It was bad enough the third-rate public school I'd been sent off to was closed by the authorities for stealing our tuition money. Despite its dubious standing as an academic Potemkin village, I'd been impressed with Cokethorpe's converted manor house and the dashing Colonel Elston who tooled around the leafy countryside in a sleek black Rover.

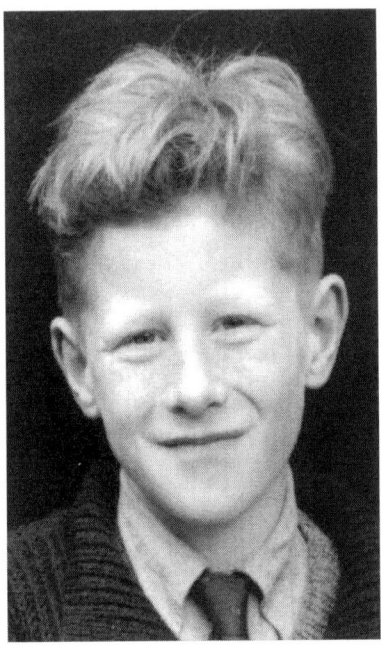

ALO—Ready to bop

My mother had me come home to her flat in London's Swiss Cottage where she enrolled me in the local junior school. On my very first day the neighborhood's aboriginal young hoodlums forced me to nick some sweets from the confectioner's half a block down from the morbid stack of bricks that passed itself off as a school on the corner of Eton Avenue and Winchester Road. I got caught and that was the end of my youthful walk on the wild side.

I learned to cultivate a rich fantasy life stimulated by the cinema and often hummed the theme songs to my favorite films out loud to myself. When the natives caught me at it one day they pushed me into the boys' lavatory for a command performance before forty excessively amused young yobs. I think I was an intelligent youngster but I don't think I'd have grown to have been quite so sensitive had I not been singled out as hilariously different by my Swiss Cottage peers. I did not enjoy playing Oliver to this band of Artful Dodgers.

Despite my distinct lack of talent for larceny I have been guilty in my time of other crimes, among them extortion, blackmail, and grifting. To the extent that I made my living in the music business these misdemeanors were almost expected of me. And over many years I certainly had a post-graduate education in double dealing from both partners and competitors who often swapped roles in the living theater of my life.

After I became sober out of life and death necessity, my moral posture became straighter and my capacity for empathy became more muscular. However, I do awaken in the night from time to time sure I have done something "wrong," which upon open-eyed reflection I have not. I am able to put my feet back on the floor, so to speak, and bid adieu to the passing moment of dread as I count to zen, give thanks, and often start my day before I am quite ready for it, but glad of it nonetheless.

In the spring of 2003 I decided to drive from Connecticut to Vancouver, a long ride during which I could imagine myself as Marty Milner or George Maharis as my fancy struck me. I like cars, although collecting time pieces is almost as rewarding and more practical. If all the autos I have had over the past forty-five years were to be parked in one garage, Jerry Seinfeld would make me an offer. I was looking forward to being on the road again.

When I crossed the border into Canada at Niagara Falls I wasn't surprised to be pulled over by a vigilant protector of the Commonwealth. After all, the back seat of my white BMW was jam-packed with Pelican trunks full of books, teas, and nutritional supplements in the form of various pills and capsules. Proudly displayed on the beemer's back window was a decal of the Colombian flag while the license plates declared the vehicle to be registered in the Constitution State. My scene partner bore a pleasing resemblance to Val Kilmer before middle age increased his middle and I discretely studied him studying me.

"What brings you to Canada?" the script required him to ask.

My reply was somewhat improvisational: "I've come here to finish the writing of a book," I deadpanned.

"What kind of books do you write?" Val inquired, no doubt less interested in the answer than whether I could be trusted to behave myself in his beloved homeland.

"Biographies," says I tersely.

"About whom?" says he with equal economy and surprisingly good English. His expression betrayed no especial interest in my Colombian driver's license with its notable lack of an expiration date and its useful information about my blood type, should I start to bleed while driving.

"About myself," if you please, officer. I fancy he smiled to himself but I was busy trying not to lock eyes with him.

At that point I think he'd decided I was all right but thought he might enjoy chatting a bit.

His next question included a pregnant pause, as the evening breeze on the border swelled gently in time with the background music I was silently providing to our little vignette.

"And what . . . have you done in your life that has you writing books about it?" He was good, this Val stand-in, his tone just the right mixture of sarcasm and friendliness. Good sense prevailed and instead of asking him if he had ever been told he looked like Val Kilmer, I answered him straightforwardly.

"Early in my career I was fortunate enough to manage and produce a British musical group known as the Rolling Stones."

I was now hoping I wouldn't have to explain that I was responsible for "Satisfaction" but not "Brown Sugar." This didn't seem like the time or place for an appraisal of the Stones' catalog.

Val, bless him, had some improvisational chops of his own.

"So could you say that you discovered them?" he asked, whether with genuine interest or sly sarcasm I couldn't discern.

"Yes, you could say that."

The pause that followed was truly priceless. What the fuck was coming next?

"And are they grateful?" Oh yes, he was that good.

"Not recently," I replied truthfully.

"Welcome to Canada, Mr. Oldham."

Cut . . . and . . . print.

PROLOGUE

ALO

INTRODUCTION

THEY SAY A game is only as good as its players and in this, my third book, I am pleased to introduce you to a number of the greatest pimpressarios and hustlers I have ever known or admired. Many of them, like Brian Epstein, Allen Klein and Phil Spector, are household names with whom I was closely associated. In those chapters I attempt to balance an objective view of their lives and accomplishments with my personal perspective and experiences. While the Rolling Stones were leading men in *Stoned* and *2Stoned*, here in *Stone Free*, I cast them more as Mike Todd might have in *Around The World In 80 Days*. On the other hand, the careers of great showmen such as Diaghilev, Alexander Korda and Otto Preminger, whom it was not my privilege to know, are explored for what they may teach those who aspire to the highest echelon of Players.

So while there is a strong element of autobiography in *Stone Free*, there is somewhat less emphasis on what I've done and more on what I've learned. Age has perhaps not only mellowed my strongly held opinions but also inspired a desire to get down in writing a suitable "Summing Up," as W. Somerset Maugham put it so well in one of his own ruthlessly honest memoirs. *Stone Free* examines the relationship between Artist and "Manager" from many more angles than I'd attempted previously, and it is my hope that, however much these early decades of the 21st Century may differ from the fertile mid-20th Century environment in which I thrived, there are certain timeless truths about show business and its Hustle that I can impart to those now considering their own future.

Most of my model hustlers, with varying degrees of accuracy and candor, might prefer that the world and their mothers think of them as entrepreneurs and impresarios. Yet the more self-aware have recognized in themselves much of the unworldliness and vulnerability that characterize the artistes who provide the clay from which these Pygmalions render their visions and appetites in three dimensions. Pimpressarios, no less than artistes, are forced to live with failure as well as success, and an inevitable end to their "lucky streak."

When a storied past has been reduced to the last small swatch remaining from the bespoke lounge suits of life once ordered up by the wardrobe-full, one is sometimes happy to share a pint with the fellow who came in to play bass on that tour long ago. Or maybe not. However, for the hustler who ever embraces the game, that same bass player might lead to the prize behind Door Number Three.

Whatever. The true hustler always lives in the present and the future. The past is too often encumbered by debts, both financial and karmic, and relationships left shattered equally by either success or failure. One convenient point I'm making by anointing the Hustle as a value worthy of creative genius, is that it eliminates the false distinction between a Diaghilev and a Larry Parnes. Such discriminations have always struck me as specious, in that I can equally appreciate the failed product of great intentions in the name of Art and the low-brow million-selling pop informed by genius. I've never been one to condemn productivity outside of marriage.

Thy name be Hustle and Hustle be thy game and, in a dictionary, it is defined neutrally as "to work energetically." Aggressive urgency is more to the point than a wish to deceive or abuse. By contrast, an "impresario" is merely "one who puts on entertainment," while an "entrepreneur" simply "organizes and assumes the risk of a business or enterprise." I've tried the last two, and they don't work without that propulsion that raises the game above the level of Commerce. And I am at pains to point out that a player is not necessarily a grifter, though confidence and his game go hand in hand.

I still get up with a will and enthusiasm to work energetically today to bring about what might become reality tomorrow. It becomes me. I hustle me and I hustle you. And, on some days, the act of hustle is genius, so long as we can agree that genius is, at least for this primer, the extraordinary capacity to put things together, that are just longing to be put together: a singer and

INTRODUCTION 9

a song, a band and a record label, a way of life and a moment in time. The possibilities are endless, but very simple once the hustler creates a sum greater than its parts.

In the music business in which I happily hustled, the game used to be surprisingly simple. While any number of lawyers, accountants, engineers and photographers might have contributed to that product clad in an LP sleeve without a word of text upon its face, they all really did march to the tune that I and the Rolling Stones played on our respective instruments. And they either remained essentially anonymous or we looked elsewhere.

First photo session with the newly formed Stones

Whereas today, the credit given to a multitude of stylists and gurus on any given CD deserves the six point type with which their achievements are immortalized on the "artwork." To quote Norma Desmond, "I am big. It's the pictures that got small." Does anybody buy a CD because the artist praises Simon Cowell for the opportunity? No; as talented and ear-worthy as Mr. Cowell is, his job is basically no different than a shoe salesman who can fit your foot and know what you will be comfortable walking around in. To obsequiously cultivate Simon's good will is as foolish as the woman who believes that Manolo Blahnik makes her legs look good. That such women probably comprise the majority of his clientele may not diminish Mr. Blahnik's considerable talents, but it does make me think somewhat less of him as a hustler. When a hustle is really on, both the buyer and the seller win, proportionate to their respective commitments to the game.

And the movies certainly haven't gotten any bigger since Gloria Swanson tortured Bill Holden. When I was first moved as a child by the garish posters decorating the London tube, the players that defined my interest in the game were amazingly few: screenwriter, producer, director. Now credits can carry a dozen producers, most of them "executive," which should send a chill up the spine of the accountants but doesn't, plus a team of writers, re-writers, and ghost writers paid by a host of on-and-off-shore companies who put up the money based on the executive producers' ability to deliver a "star," rather than a film.

If one were to be so naïve as to be enthralled by "the business" of show these days, the confusing and unnecessary data presented by "reality" TV and the celebrity weeklies should most rightly induce motion sickness. Instead it has created a generation of Britney's, Brittany's and Brittaney's doomed to having their credit ratings mixed in with other young women one fry short of a Happy Meal. And lest you chide me for criticizing those behind the scenes for confusing themselves with stars, Phil Spector and I actually did produce the records on which we quite conspicuously headlined our own names.

I am reminded of a theory of showbiz success that a friend advanced in the '80s, which is now no more relevant than phrenology. He called it the "Debbie Harry theory of stardom," which in its simplest Darwinian formulation suggested that if Debbie Harry had been four inches taller, she would probably have quite naturally become a model, rather than a pop singer, and the world would have missed something quietly revolutionary. Conversely, no young woman with the looks to become a model with any degree of success in those days would have thought to have become a rock singer, nor would she have had any credibility as such if she had. Or at least no more credibility as a musician than Annette Funicello.

The arrogance of young stars today, certain they are equally accomplished as thespians and musicians, is surely the product of their handlers' self-interested input rather than a self-confident appreciation of their own sex appeal. Everyone is so professional at everything now that no one is particularly professional about anything. "Professional" used to mean quite a bit more than, "I make money doing this."

Now to her credit, the music industry's overnight sensation of 2012, the charmingly plus-sized Adele, is the exception that proves the rule. She is, of course, no product of the fashion runway, nightclub scene, reality TV or a talent contest. Her innate vocal talent and sincerity put her in the very good company of women like Petula Clark, Dionne Warwick or Dusty Springfield who went to #1 in her grandmother's day. But while the quick rise to the top was just as thrilling then as now, the long-term expectations were so much lower for those songbirds. In fact, they and their handlers had no long-term expectations as such.

The great good fortune that Ms. Warwick had to be given first whack at Burt Bacharach and Hal David's endless stream of hits has been overshadowed by the apparent imperative to gather 1,000,000 Twitter followers. Television commercials sell more records than radio airplay but no music executive in his right mind believes that the artists who made the tracks are anything more than glorified one-hit wonders.

So when an artist like Adele comes along, who has grown over time and seems to have no more self-destructive vices than a tendency to ask for a second helping, the pressure is enormous and were she someone close to me, something like life-threatening. Her stature as a "real" artist, and moreover one who can generate sustained sales over time where piracy and a mere week at the top of the charts are the norm, makes both her achievement and her vulnerability all the more poignant. No one should be surprised if it takes Adele three years to make another album by which time the "industry" will have become ever smaller and less relevant. Remember that when opportunity knocked for us in the Sixties, we put out a single every twelve weeks and an album every four months. Who knew but that our latest hit might be our last. Oh yes, we all were hustlers but given our presumably short shelf life, we had to be.

The word "hustling" has been degraded by the times, but if I can ascribe purity to such an activity, it is marked by the operator's divine apprehension that he is witnessing the coupling of a singer and a song in the bedroom of a cathouse to which he holds the keys. What to others might seem vulgar or odd, is to the player magical. Today a "hustle" is synonymous with a con, whereas in earlier times it usually was not. Most often, the hustler was a huckster, a Barnum & Bailey-spirited entrepreneur whose simple idea was to find something attractive to his customers, present it as it should be presented to reach an audience, take the money, dream and guess again. Since the 1970s we have all been invited to play God in a world where we should do less, do it better, eat less and walk the dog more. The game used to be less corporate and more cooperative, founded on the fun of getting it done as opposed to fear of failure.

Let me get one thing straight. When Brian Epstein, Mssrs. Lambert & Stamp, and I huckstered and hustled our wares, we ourselves were not important. We were not important, even in our own minds—at any rate not on the all-important first run. That may be hard to believe but it was true and it was wonderful. Wonderfully simple. We did what we did because the people we were blessed to be working with and our mutual "product" made us feel alive. We had formed an alliance with some thing, as well as some one, be it Beatles, Stones or Who, who might not change the price of bread but brought unexpected enjoyment to many strangers' lives.

Our parents, who had struggled to survive a depression and a war, were understandably not about having a good time. Many would like to have imposed the huge debt incurred by victory over the headlines upon the innocent heads of their children, never realizing that entertainments which they had enjoyed as occasional treats were now to be a steady diet for their offspring. Readily available contraception and the mass manufacture of cheap and cheerful clothing for kids might actually have pulled in more teen bread than the soundtracks we created for the movies in their minds, but we were never about the biggest payday so much as the Sound that became a Way of Life. Even back then we sold a lot of jeans.

In the U.S. in particular, revisionist thought tends to conflate the British Invasion with the assassination of JFK, civil rights turmoil, and the Vietnamese war, but at the time, those of us landing on the first beach-head sensed nothing but our good fortune. When the Beatles appeared on the Ed Sullivan Show on Sunday, February 9, 1964, a mere three months had passed since America had lost not only its leader but the hope for the future he inspired. The Fabs changed the national mood, especially for the kids, overnight. All of us who followed them over were blessed by the Beatles' incredible timing.

A little later, there were unfortunate lapses of manners rationalized by egos grown out of bounds, as many who rode the first wave were shocked to find the drugs and drink were taking them and not the other way 'round. Among those privileged to be present in the delivery room, I was perhaps outstanding in equating the hustle with all life had to offer. We lost the plot and the confidence of the acts we had inspired in the first place. But on the first all-potent run there was hardly time for reflection or "enough about me, what do you think about me?" We had the key to the door and it was still opening.

It's important to define the hustler as both what he is and what he is not. A hustler has a certain faith that what he can imagine can be externalized so that as many participants as possible benefit, preferably crediting him as the producer of a singular experience. He clearly distinguishes between production and performance.

The true hustler strives for the unique. An impresario or entrepreneur may have brilliant and profitable insight into a formula that has been successful in the past, but cloning that experience for the public, be it once or a thousand times, won't let him into the club. I'd go so far as to say that the producer or director of a top-grossing remake of an old TV show cannot possibly be a hustler by my definition. And artists who allow themselves to be part of such projects deserve what they get, which is only the more lucrative version of what has-been film actors became when they finally succumbed to TV fifty years ago. They become irrelevant and the soul withers. The hustler has more respect for artists. His payoff is the knowledge that he created something out of nothing, and this includes the wisdom to walk away when the wheel turns.

He is painfully aware that once his hustle is public and successful it follows as night the day that some fortunes will be reversed. Despite the trappings of power, the risk-taker is often the first and hardest hit by this reality. Because he is looking for a partner and not merely a mark, and because he should never be overexposed as the public face of the game, his partners once the hustle succeeds quite naturally begin to wonder if the hustler is really required. A master of psychology, the player will exit gracefully, realizing that the scene where he punches the wall should be off-camera. He may fear that he can never repeat but the burning desire to do so eventually readies him for the next ride. Nothing becomes a hustler less than dwelling on his last play to the point where being right becomes more important than being on.

So the hustler, contrary to popular conception, is concerned with value for money. And he places a high value indeed upon his creation, because he is more essentially creative than capitalistic. As we will note in the studies that follow, the traits that make a hustler lie along a continuum. On one end are the accountants, lawyers, publishers and remix engineers that the play may require for execution. To the extent that these supporting players gain any degree of creative control of the hustle, the hustler loses. And as they gain the upper hand the supporting players may enjoy thinking of themselves as hustlers, but they aren't. They're more like the highly qualified society doctors who performed illegal abortions in the dark old days, abusing their skills and avoiding their reflection in the mirror. Today they more legally, if not necessarily more safely, remake and remodel the features of both men and women who already had the good fortune to be born beautiful.

And on the other end of the continuum is the hustler who takes Pygmalion too far and wishes his creation to become his lover. The selfishness that makes for a great artist will be revolted by such emotionalism and engender a strong desire to kick his hustler to the curb. Pity the hustler married to his star. Be careful what you wish for, as the saying goes.

Ideally, he will live and thrive in the centre of the continuum. He will understand just enough about business to keep from being taken and just enough about artistry and its temperament to inspire his partners. He will struggle to remain true to his own self-identity which, like his play, is unique. But, like all middle paths, the centre of the continuum is traversed with great difficulty, as both internal and external tensions vie to throw him off balance. It is in the nature of the hustler to drive too fast and invite such forces to thwart him. He is lucky indeed if he manages to drive sober on clear nights. The road itself is never straight.

One might say that those of us who succeeded very quickly in the '60s deserved to have our memberships revoked once we began to employ the fatal avoidance tactic of "I don't know, talk to my lawyer." The lawyer, of course, wished for nothing more, and one can almost see him sitting back in his office chair, rubbing his hands together like a Dickensian villain. We were what the MBAs of today like to call "low lying fruit," to be taken for granted and plucked at one's leisure. For many of us, myself included, there was just too much to learn about the world in too short a time with precious few mentors to point the way. But there were moral issues we simply failed to comprehend: we put at risk not only our vision and our talents but the bands that fed us.

Well, no worries on that score today, mate. The machine is now so well-oiled and top heavy with experts that a 21st Century version of Andrew Oldham would have only to put out one attention-grabbing record on his own before he'd be bought, sold, and looking for a new gig. The road to rock 'n' roll ruin, both creative and financial, is littered with a trail of redundant corpses. The biggest difference between yesterday and today is that now the system is not only bloody but efficient. What the industry really needs is a Schindler's list before everyone is marched to a kind of death.

Reliance on the visual image of an artist rather than the artist's sound or physical presence on stage means that the monster that Diana Ross became over a long stretch of time is now born fully formed as the succubus that is Kim Kardashian. Contrary to the Debbie Harry theory, all musical artists are now models, and while I'll allow that a model's profession may not be easy, it is far from a craft. It is convenient to blame drugs, affluence, and isolation for the constant crack-ups, but really it's a matter of character. When would-be hustlers tell aspiring artists they're perfect just as they are because their arse sells jeans and they're entitled to $50,000 gift bags if they show up at the opening of a handbag store, then it's really incumbent on the artist to pull their dim head out of their beautiful butt.

A good artist, with respect to his relationship with his hustler, is like a good dog. He is trainable, and if treated well, willing to please. But if the player confuses his role as a leader with that of a parent or lover, the dog's inner beast will eventually bite. In a sense, the artist's "happiness" is not the concern of the hustler, who should always concentrate on enhancing the artist's productivity. What the hustler can do that the artist almost never can is draw to the game the supporting players, including the public, who buy into the love fest. The hustler is a kind of evangelist; the role allows one to become either the Dali Lama or Jimmy Swaggart. What's important is that everyone come to Jesus.

And not to draw the analogy too fine, it is in their best interests to do so. The performing arts are crucial to our lives, and hustle is how the major player brings art and entertainment unto the populace. The outrageous celebrity gift bags of today are the Beatles' tea sets of yesterday, and strictly peripheral to the daydreams a hustler pursues with frequently maniacal energy. A good hustler is pleased to have this noticed.

Since the urge to create precedes both the hustler and his artist, the art in music is not dead, and the art in artfulness is not dead, either. It is possibly comatose, and it's certainly suffering from corporate delirium and the digital tremors. But, though the sleight of hand is harder to divine, filtered as it is through marketing that often supersedes the product itself, still there is leg room for the talented individual. That is whom this book is about and for: the individuals who once roamed the world as if they owned it, and whose spirit is still abroad today in the soul of every person who'd rather send her television back than watch X Factor.

I wish to make my influences contagious, like some serum composed of technically dead cells that immunize the vaccinated from the scourges of their times. I would like to think such a serum derived from my own legacy might provide some healthy daydreaming and protection as well. An honest hustler dreams, after all, of emulating the hustles of his heroes and that is an enthusiasm to be relished as a thanksgiving meal.

Belief is key. Sometimes we don't know what we believe until we find something to believe in. Before I met Mick and Keith I had only the vaguest comprehension that artists who wrote their own material like John and Paul made a lot more money than those who didn't. But it wasn't until I started dreaming about what the Rolling Stones could become that I understood that they must write their own songs if they were to survive, financially successful or not.

At that point my idée fixe that anyone who could play a musical instrument could write a song compelled me to hustle Jagger and Richards somewhat forcibly (I locked them in), leaning on two fun-loving blues fans to unearth the ability in themselves to eventually create songs like "Satisfaction" and "Gimme Shelter" that utterly transcended their own influences. It's been a long time since the creativity unleashed in that kitchen became first, second nature and then routine,

Keith Richards and Mick Jagger

occasionally threatening to tarnish their legacy. But all of us there at the start share a certainty that the world, as well as us, is a better place for it, though we seldom discuss it any more.

Why should we? The point was to "just do it" and see what happened. I hustled them and they hustled back. For a time our willingness to hustle the world meant we couldn't take a step wrong. I wish more people could experience that feeling.

So the hustler walks the streets of life humming a tune he can't himself play, but he hears an attitude in his mind and when he encounters someone who can hum the tune out loud, the hustle is on. Certain qualities are always useful. It helps to have great hair. But only the manikin dabbling in art would settle for that, and it's the hustler's art and craft to see to it that the performer transforms their shared attitude into a veritable pyramid of solid productivity.

My greatest disappointment is how eagerly today's would-be hustlers and artists settle for the fame and fortune that never lasts. The cart is before the horse and the lunatics are running the asylum. Because people fear tomorrow, yesterday temporarily rules. I'd like to be certain the next time a David Bowie raises his dyed head, the world stands up and applauds as it did for us. What that will take is a new generation of hustlers unafraid of tomorrow. For as Bowie himself once almost said, "Tomorrow belongs to those who can hear it coming." We can be heroes, if just for one day. This book is about and for those heroes. It's a book in which Andrew Ridgeley belongs, because he's the one that convinced George Michael they could do it.

ALEC MORRIS

I WAS AN only child and though my mother raised me by herself she was not exactly a war widow. Swept off her feet by a dashing young American flyer, after whom she named me, Celia found herself alone and with child after her lover was shot down over the Channel. She found a protector and faithful friend in Alec Morris, who while not quite a surrogate father to little Andy, nevertheless provided me with my first male role model. Though he was a businessman and not a showman, Alec embodied many of the qualities against which I would judge success throughout my life.

* * *

The first time I met Alec Morris he was about fifty, I was almost eight and he had just made love to my mother. He had the biggest smile on his face I had ever seen. I wanted that smile for myself before I wiped it off him.

I wanted that smile and would spend the greater part of my life chasing after it. It was the comfortable smile of a comfortable man. The smile of a man at the top without vanity, distinguished by simple choices cannily made, with adherence to the road taken and word given. At the time I had no idea how long it had taken Alec for that smile to become his natural expression.

My mother Celia and I lived in the basement flat of 44 Belsize Park Gardens, which ran parallel to Haverstock Hill and the Hampstead tube station. Number 44 was the first flat we had lived in that my mother owned; in fact it was the first flat proper we had lived in, owned or rented. Life for me so far had been a series of nurseries, boarding schools, and the single rooms my mother rented within others' apartments that I visited during summer holidays and Christmas.

Alec Morris

Alec, his wife and two teenaged children lived a better upholstered life on the bright side of town, in the exclusive enclave known as the Hocroft Estate. Both families tacitly understood the nature of the relationship; it wasn't spoken of, it simply was.

Recently, Alec's daughter Pat wrote me and brought home just how in charge of his domestic bliss Alec must have been: "Celia used to visit a lot," Pat wrote. "She used to come in the kitchen—my mum loved to sit in the kitchen—and yak to Eunice, our lovely maid, and the three of them would chat ever so friendly, and I never knew anything about Celia, or you, either." There is something to be said for traditional English reserve.

Our move to an actual flat that comprised five rooms and a couple of bathrooms was like playing for the crown at Wembley after kicking the ball around in the back yard. I remember other places, but I think they were some of the nurseries I boarded at, a sort of getting me ready for a life on the road.

Only a few years ago, I found out in just how many institutions and foster homes my mother may have lived during her childhood, but she never spoke to me of her past. Both our lives seemed to start from whenever I happened to remember them. And, although I was never foster-homed, my mother's struggles to raise a child while herself unmarried led her to board me from time to time at schools not far removed from those institutions that cared for the orphaned.

I had started my first term at the state school tucked behind a car park that was next to the eastern entrance to the Swiss Cottage tube station. It was the first day-school I had attended and I hated it, much preferring being boarded and away where I had privacy and my mind had wings. Schools in the city seemed dark, grimy and claustrophobic; there was nowhere to run to, nowhere to hide.

Around this time, I became aware of Alec being in my mother's life and somehow instinctively connected him to our better circumstances. I was playing soldiers in the semi-garden that was outside our living room window facing the street. I placed my regiments as though it were jungle terrain; it was all very Kenya and Mau-Mau to me, and was not my favourite game. But it would have to do, as it was preferred that I played outside while my mother and Alec were otherwise engaged inside the flat.

So there I was in the garden, the Mau Maus are moving in on my heroic British warriors, when suddenly a shadow fell across the battlefield. It was Alec, standing out in the street, in silhouette, mysterious in the evening of the day. He simply stood there, waiting on my mum to join him for dinner, smiling and inviting me to size him up; "say something or get over it."

He inspected the gold serpent ring that wrapped around his pinkie with a ruby in each eye; I wanted that as well. He checked his braces. He could keep those. His suit was of a weight and shine that just smiled bespoke and I wanted that, too. It was in a shade of grey a world apart from the universally drab school uniforms I myself wore. His silk shirt was monogrammed, his tie royal maroon with the tiniest old gold motif, while his nails and his diction were both manicured. His shoes were hand-made and polished to a gentleman's high gloss.

Suddenly Alec's life away from my mother took on a new fascination. How he went about getting and keeping was something I wanted to know. I already recognized the difference between the average and the strong. I wanted to spend as much time as possible under that warm smile, preferably while inhaling the rich masculine aroma of Alec's leather upholstered Rolls.

Without condescension, Alec was attentive to Celia's little boy, recalling our previous conversations in a manner that implied he wasn't merely making small talk while cultivating the girlfriend's brat. Although a man of a certain age, Alec was contemporary; his *joie de vive* reflected the self-assurance of a man who had worked very hard and well to get to the top, who accepted his good fortune as well deserved.

My emphasis, both then and now, on his appearance and manner does not mean to imply that he was anything less than serious. Rather, it emphasizes that he was very good at life. He had nurtured his face to the world as an immigrant might. Rather than bemoaning his lack of "breeding" and its advantages, Alec became on his own merits a member of the society he admired. Though as far as possible from the manor born, he embodied a typical upper class British reticence to share the less delicate parts of his experience as a child of a Polish ghetto. All of Alec's complexity and sophistication were conveyed to my boyish mind by the sensuous aroma of his motor's interior; it suggested a world I could now appreciate existed as a reality to aspire to.

The tough times did not show, did not maim his vision, or how he had decided to view the world. He had put the rough luggage aside; and his humble beginnings—doubly hobbled by his Jewish and Polish heritage—now lay beneath a surface that was resoundingly optimistic and British. For an inquisitive, star struck eight-year-old, there was only his present.

Far more than my mother's boyfriend, Alec was the first man in my life, should truth be told. As I craved and was fascinated by alpha creativity, I was blessed to find it often in the men I knew and admired. A nuclear family was something I came to work at.

Alec was the first, albeit bald, well-respected man to acknowledge potential in me, wide-awake to his being and to all the possibilities that stretched out before him; the example that all my future influences would somehow hinge upon.

He had grown up in the East End of London at the turn of the century, grown tired of it by the time he was a teenager and, in 1915, he smuggled himself aboard a ship headed for the United States. There, with skills already acquired in the East End, he got jobs in New York teaching older ladies how to tango and foxtrot. In those ballrooms and dance saloons he met another sly dancer, the actor/gangster/gigolo George Raft, who many years later would be kicked out of the UK for allegedly fronting an American Mafia-backed casino on the south side of Mayfair's Berkeley Square.

Alec always liked to dance. I watched him dance some years later with my mother. He was not actually tall, nor was he thin, but he was both when he danced. And when they danced, I understood how the laws of the dance floor were the same as those of real life. Watching my mother comfortable and safe in Alec's arms, her head resting upon his neck as they glided over and controlled the floor, I noted the same smile and I wanted it more, the smile that said all was well in the world.

After a few years in the States, getting up to everything everywhere, Alec returned to London and joined the now successful family furniture business. When World War Two ended, Alec, his wife and two teenaged children, John and Pat, moved to Hocroft.

I met John about five years later when he, perhaps at a loss for conversation with a much younger lad, took me in his black four-doored Lincoln Continental convertible with zit-red and white leather upholstery, to Stamford Bridge Football ground to see Chelsea play some Northern team. I fell in love with John's car and Chelsea's Jimmy Greaves.

John was the black sheep of the family, which is a bit tough on mum and dad when you only have two kids. He started out blessed and right. He went to public school, was the first Jew on the British National Water Skiing team, and then started on his way down. Before he could bring Alec's investment bank to its knees, Alec got rid of John.

While John may or may not have gone to jail, he most certainly did drive a mini cab and, when he was buried a few years ago, atop his coffin was a photo of him in all his early splendour on water skis, waving the way his father taught him.

Sister Pat, on the other hand, married young, and went to Canada with her husband Denis, where he did very well but at the cost of a heart attack that killed him. The widow Pat returned to England in the Seventies with her kids and, whenever I was back in London, I would visit her in Hendon for a cup of tea and a joint. Later on, we settled for just tea.

I only met their mother, Mrs. Alec Morris, a few times. I imagined her looking at me and wondering whether I was Alec's son; sometimes I hoped as much the same myself. I knew more about Alec and his family than I ever did my own. My mother never mentioned, never said a word about her own mother and father; I have never seen a picture of either of them, never knew my mother's mother's name, and only learned my grandfather's name, Militar Schapofski, when my mother was attempting to frighten me away from drink by informing me that her good-for-nothing father Militar had died near the Sydney racetrack of liver cancer at the age of 42.

But my grandmother never got a word in, was never mentioned even by mistake in casual conversation; or, if my mother ever had such a thing, an unguarded chat. How my grandmother met Militar and what had happened to her, I never found out. That part of my mother's life was something she never shared with me to the end of her days. One wonders if she shared it with the Polish Jew with whom she shared her bed and her hopes for her own son's future. It was not until Celia was almost gone that I quite by accident glimpsed a hint of her hidden past.

The publication of my first volume of autobiography in 2000 reintroduced me to a public that could justifiably have assumed I had disappeared in 1970 with the demise of my record label Immediate. Apart from the satisfaction I derived from the largely favourable press, my new visibility brought with it some unexpected rewards.

In September of that year, a brown manila envelope arrived at my home in Bogotá Colombia from my London publisher. We had received a few of these from the time *Stoned* had been released; they usually included some press cuttings, which were 99% favourable, and some fan letters, which were a little less so.

This dispatch included a letter of a different kind. It was from a Michael Oldham who wrote from down in Somerset, England. Michael had read a review of *Stoned*, which referred to my mother by her given names, Cecilia Olga, as opposed to the diminutive Celia. A huge penny dropped as Michael realized that this Cecilia Olga might just be the sister his father had lost track of after World War II. My mother had mentioned that she even had a brother but once, one day while she was in the mood to share her very personal cache of mementos from the War. Suddenly, a photo of a uniformed fellow dropped out of the papers my mother was holding. Photo-booth sized, it showed a gent with dark hair and wearing a naval uniform.

I reached for the picture.

"Is that my dad?" I asked as my mother hurried to take the photo back. We had been discussing her short-lived relationship with my father, a young American airman named Andrew Loog who had been killed on a mission. This put to pay any notion that I was in fact Alec's boy.

"No," she said with her characteristic reluctance to speak of her own past. "It was my brother."

This was the first I had heard about this relation. She went on to tell me that he had served in the Royal Australian Navy during the war, and after the war she had not stayed in touch. She did not even know whether he was alive or dead, nor apparently did she care. They had never got along that well. Another door shut so far as Celia was concerned.

And that was all there was to it until Michael Oldham's letter arrived. He had planned to surprise his father, my uncle, the brother who had not been worth getting in touch with after World War II, with a copy of *Stoned* as a gift for Father's Day.

Needless to say, I was astonished. Not only was a family I had always believed was on the other side of the world in Australia actually living more or less on my own doorstep, but also that, prior to the publication of *Stoned,* they remained oblivious to the fact that I was both celebrated and notorious as the boy Oldham who discovered the Rolling Stones.

I was to find that my new career as memoirist was the gift that kept on giving. Three years after my reunion with Celia's side of the family, I received an e-mail from a Robert Loog in Louisiana. He asked if I'd like to see a picture of my dad. The photo he sent on was of a very good looking man in his early twenties in whose visage I thought I detected a certain vanity. Appropriately enough, Andrew Loog bore more than a passing resemblance to my own son Max, who was at the time only a few years younger than his grandfather in the photo. One might say that Andrew Sr.'s good looks had skipped a generation, but it was still gratifying to realize all three of us shared the vanity gene.

All of this is by way of indicating that apart from Alec, male influences in my young life were almost altogether missing. Alec's respect for my mother and me, in light

My mother, Celia, who made my world complete for as long as she could.

of his own undeniable status and station as a man of the world, helped to fill an enormous gap. My mother herself felt that gap poignantly, though she would never acknowledge it. Upon arriving in England from Australia, sister and brother had been separated not only from their mother but each other, to live in a succession of foster homes that Celia ever strove to live down. She evidently felt that her brother had been placed in better situations than she and held it against him.

Nevertheless, my uncle sought a reconciliation. After the war, her brother did track Celia down. He rang the doorbell and received no answer, even though he was sure that my mother was staying quiet inside. Her peculiar sense of pride must have been quite hard for her to bear at times.

On another occasion, they met by chance at a funeral for someone they may both have known, but my mother ignored her brother, as the other side of the Oldham family remembers it. I never found out whether my uncle had served in the Royal Australian Navy, or where and who his mother, my grandmother, was. I never even got to speak to my uncle. He had been rushed into hospital in Somerset a week before Father's Day, some five months before Michael contacted me. He never recovered from the heart attack, and never did receive his Father's Day gift.

Is it only when we are young that everything, every building, seems so timeless, strong and clean? Or is it just that when we are older, we find so much that is old and worn out, before we remember that the glass must be half full in order to be half empty, and we jolt ourselves back into positive thought?

Earlier in life we ignore the warts, the imperfections in the world and its people, or perhaps we just blot them out, impervious to the plight of the majority that does not register as the reality of the game, because we think we are winning the game. Which, in a way, we are; except we do not know that we are playing on the team of ignorance. However, Alec made me realize that I had to stop dodging bullets, that I had to get a grip on life. By the time I was twelve and thirteen, he was showing me how I could make choices, how I had to make choices, how I had to get life right.

In the life classes he gave me as he paid my way through multiple schools, he never told me what was what. He just put me in situations where it was apparent. I used to take odd jobs on Saturday mornings and school holidays and, one Easter holiday, Alec told me that I could have a job with a friend of his who had a factory in Kilburn. I did not ask Alec what kind of job; it would have been rude, but it might have also been sensible.

Kilburn represented a war zone; its high street Irish, not yet Aussie, neither one thing nor the other, a riff raff, an average mix, not East End, not West End, just very undecided. But still it seemed quite rough. London was then a horde of peoples, separated not so much, if at all, by church, but more by where they had been born, because where you were born normally determined the parameters of where you would live unless good fortune and hard work allowed you to leap and bound over the board to the top of the hill. It was not all expensive but, unless fate smiled, it was decided.

The job was in a parts manufacturing company, and I was given the task of counting ball bearings. It was on a depressing second floor factory loft on a side-street off Kilburn High Road. It reeked of *Oliver Twist* and I lasted a week. The owner was kind and understanding; he knew I was not cut out for this line of work. One of the lady ball bearing counters even took a shine to the boy from the hill. Perhaps I reminded her of her own child. She helped me go unnoticed, but after a week I had had enough. Alec did not seem disappointed; he just beamed his Buddha look, knowing that I had learned a lesson that would later become a page in the book of life he gave me.

In my little world, Alec Morris was a star, and it was an odd irony indeed that by 1970, as he reached the end of his working days, so apparently did I. By 1970, the Rolling Stones had been doing very well without me for a few years. Marianne Faithfull was living (well, more or less) and recording occasionally; my Immediate Records had gone bankrupt and I had left the UK to live in Connecticut and New York City. I squandered my ability and depleted my means, but managed to get a life I still have when

I met the Latina from Bogotá in the box at the Lyric Theater in London. Oddly, we were watching *John, Paul, George, Ringo and Bert* though I couldn't really tell you why either of us wanted to see it.

By the early Seventies, my mother had somehow fallen out with Alec and had married a Yugoslavian cancer research doctor named Janez Ferluga who played the violin and charmed my mother to absolute bits. "Quite a catch, isn't he, Andy?" smiled my mother when I rolled into London from New York for the wedding.

I was late for the actual service, but managed to catch the reception, as did Alec's daughter Pat. Her dad was put out, but understanding, about my mother leaving him to get married. He realized that she had a future with Janez, something the part of me that fatherised Alec was reluctant to admit. I was hurt on his behalf, but as usual, Alec was right, something we'd all realize much, much later when my mother got Alzheimer's in the early Eighties and Janez cared for her every day, every way, until she died in 2002.

Alec's investment business had basically gone down the drain, thanks in no small part to the malfeasance of his son John. He and Mrs. M had moved from the Hocroft Estate long ago, to a flat behind Marble Arch. He did not really like it there. "Too many tea cloths on the Edgware Road for me, Andy," is how he commented on the influx of Arabs into his hood. Later, in the Eighties, he and his wife moved into a well-to-do Jewish old people's home south of London. It was one of the saddest days of my life, never mind theirs, knowing that he had already climbed the mountains of his life's achievement, and was now coming down the other side fast. Without the Rolls Royce.

I went with my mother to collect some things that Alec was giving away, things he would not have room for in the old people's home. "The walking stick's gone, the walking stick isn't there," my mother hissed under her breath, her mouth clenched into a tight, fake smile as we waved at the chauffeur-driven Rover driving Mr. and Mrs. M to their next and final home.

"He promised me the walking stick," my mother continued hissing until we stopped waving and the Rover moved out of view on this bright, but deadly depressing London autumn day.

What is it they say? Travel first class in this life, or your relatives will after you're gone. I had nothing to say to my mother in response to this walking stick outburst. I didn't care about the fuckin' walking stick; right at that moment I didn't care about my mother. I cared about Alec.

A few times in the next couple of years, I would travel from New York to London to visit Alec, thanks to Freddie Laker's cut price airline. Money was not that good for me. I was not being offered much work, and I should not have been, while the record industry was in pre-CD dire straits and it looked for a moment as if the Rolling Stones catalogue was going to join Gerry and the Pacemakers and Peter and Gordon in the budget-line bins. But they did not, and I got better.

I visited Alec and Mrs. M separately. They spent the remainder of their lives, and their marriage, in different wards. Somebody painfully barmy kept bothering the dreadfully thin Alec, and Alec kept telling him to fuck off. But he did it without raising his voice, using the same strong but calm Zen tones he had used to coax me down from the chair in Belsize Park Gardens all those years ago, when I stood distraught with string around my neck, appalled by his physical intimacy with my mother.

"Fucking mad, Andy, all of them," and then to the botherer, "Later, Bernie, later, I've got a visitor, my son is visiting me, leave me alone for now."

I wasn't his son, but for him to finally describe me so felt very nice. I knew he was deeply disappointed in his own son, both for the young man's lack of character and the reduced circumstances his crime had forced upon his mother and father. Alec had been the most self-sufficient of men, and now old and ill he could no longer afford the independence he'd fought to secure all his life.

With a firmness in his voice that belied the frailty that frightened me when I put my hand on his leg, he made me promise him something.

"Never let it come to this, Andy. Pay attention. Look around, never let it come to this."

It's been close but so far I have not . . . .

DIAGHILEV

I WAS BORN in January, 1944. According to Chinese astrology, I am a monkey, or more specifically, a wood monkey "with a knack for communicating with others." Monkey people, it is said, "tend to stir up trouble simply out of boredom. Lots of fun, they also possess a serious side and influence a good many people throughout their lifetime. Even so, they can easily get discouraged and confused and *must* do things their way! Often pioneers in new undertakings, they are sharp and ambitious and make big deals happen." Famous show biz monkeys include Liz Taylor, Charles Dickens, and George Lucas, so all in all, a pretty good horoscope for a hustler in embryo.

Sergei Pavlovich Diaghilev, circa 1916

I wanted to be in show business from the age of eight. Mother and I were living at 65 Eton Avenue at the time, and when we went to visit family friends, we'd walk to the Swiss Cottage tube station, my attractive hand tightly clasped in hers. Every step of the way, once we started down the stairs to enter the station, I found myself overwhelmed by the strange and gaudy posters pasted on every available tiled surface, each one announcing fresh thrills, gripping dramas, biting excitements and raw emotions flickering four times a day (and six on weekends) at the local cinema or, *viva* Las Vegas, at a theater in the faraway West End. I knew then where I wanted to be, and I still wanted to be there even after I arrived. I still like to be there today.

Long before actual hero worship found its target in Johnnie Ray, Eddie Cochran, Elvis Presley, Buddy Holly and James Dean, the posters were a roadmap to a world it seemed highly unlikely I would ever visit. While my school friends swapped photos torn from *Titbits* of Dirk Bogarde, Diana Dors, Cary Grant and Natalie Wood, I was totally taken with the credits. I was oddly attracted for one so young to the men I would come to think of as an adult as the pimpresarios. For some reason the words "presents" and "produced by" made a far greater impression than "starring in."

I believed at an early age in the profundity of superficiality, and Americans appeared to be the experts. Certainly Britain in the mid-'50s seemed immune to Yank charms. It took my generation growing up a bit to cause the previous generation to bewail that the Empire was truly gone, replaced by cowboys and Coca-Cola. Of course, we had some help with that from Elvis and Cliff.

Nothing so exemplified an England cramped by the lingering memory of a horrible war like a junket to Butlin's Holiday Camp. On its tarry pebbled beaches, Andy Capps flushed with drink and pale from ill-health sat in flimsy deck-chairs, snot white hankies protecting their beet red bald domes from a feeble sun that would burn before it tanned. Of course, even then, Britons in the know were frequenting the beaches of France and Spain, but they don't serve our kind of food there, do they, dearie? Our parents' generation wore their self-rationing as a badge of honour.

So at the same time I was drawn like Alice to walk through the looking glass of the underground movie posters (or less sentimentally, like Ewan MacGregor to the toilet in *Trainspotting*), I was also being pushed. My mother, in her way, was more sophisticated than most, but she had her quirks that seem emblematic of the time. Heating in our drab little rain-swept part of the world was expensive and, either out of intimacy or frugality or both, my mother liked us to share the same bath water, albeit at different times. I can't remember if there was a pattern to who bathed first, but it hardly matters to the ick quotient.

Nicky Haslam, the society interior decorator, once mentioned to me that his father's generation held that "one did not wear brown in town." There were so many many things that "just weren't done." Unless, of course, one was the Duke of Windsor, who left us pretty much bereft of style once he and his trollop were hounded out of the Isles. Nicky, though, is Eton educated, and still counts as clients a cross-section of the aristocracy that ranges from the Prince of Wales to Ringo Starr, so he may not, after all, have experienced the '50s in quite the same way I did.

As time goes by, it was not that long ago. I'd much rather have been left in the cinema alone in the dark than dragged to Butlin's and its putative "fresh air." I became quite the vicarious traveller. Cary Grant and Grace Kelly invited me to eavesdrop on their sun-and-sand meet-cute in Alfred Hitchcock's *To Catch a Thief*, the Riviera's Hotel Carlton no less majestic for being back-projected. Native son that he was, Sir Alfred had the Shakespearean genius to slyly suggest that the Côte D'Azur of our day was as decadent as 16th Century Venice seemed to the Elizabethans. Via *Houseboat*, set in New York, and *North By Northwest*, set in the Great American West, Archibald Leach became my travel agent and Universal Studios my *alma mater*.

Whilst on the subject of Cary Grant, née Leach, let us examine the underbelly of this book. We will find it difficult to discuss the hustlers without their attendant stars and vice versa.

And to the extent that the stars are generally considered to be more interesting than their handlers, it is our mission to prove them indispensable to each other. The stars—the food on the table, the fishes and loaves—and, on occasion, the Red Sea parting.

Let it be said at the outset: stardom is as unpredictable as an Arab Spring. Created upon a falsehood it degrades. Honed from marble, it is a lasting marvel, surviving the ravages of gossip and time, overwhelming successes, total cock-ups and half-baked also-rans. All you have left at the end of the day is the music and the movies, and, of course, the rep.

Cary Grant and Mick Jagger would head most A-Lists as Shaolin masters of the art of survival informed by decorum and aloof indifference. They both transcend and personify the games at which they determined to succeed, as did Nureyev, Marilyn Monroe and Freddie Mercury, except for that small detail called "survival." Grant survived by retiring and Jagger by working. Both Grant and Jagger kept their clothes on, loafered legs casually crossed, and from the appropriate time in their lives, managed their business themselves.

Durable stardom requires an attention to detail that tries the patience and raises the standards of lesser mortals. Cary Grant once phoned hotel mogul Conrad Hilton in Istanbul, Turkey to find out why his breakfast order at the Plaza Hotel in New York was short one half of an English muffin. One likes to think that Conrad made a note to his manager at the Plaza to remind the kitchen that one happy Grant was worth a thousand tourists from Kansas City. Nobody was fired, and reminded of it at a party months or years later, Cary probably offered to buy the storyteller a drink.

As I studied the names on the tube station posters and noted the hierarchy from top to bottom, larger type to smaller, I really had no idea who these people were, let alone what they did. Somehow the posters themselves made what they advertised important and attractive. But as the rabbit hole beckoned Alice, those occasionally peeling billboards on the lavatory-white walls sucked me into a fourth dimension of imagination, while jitters and hope got me high off possibility.

I eventually sorted out that every film credited a producer, writer and director who were in turn associated with a production company, which I came to think of as more essential to the making of the film than any of the individual contributors. As a matter of historical fact, by the time I was old enough to sit in a cinema by myself, the old Hollywood studios had begun to lose much of their power and creativity. Even before television finished off Louis B. Mayer's MGM, box-office favorites such as Burt Lancaster and Kirk Douglas were forming their own production companies outside the studio system and creating new templates for the hustle. Where the traditional studios like Paramount and Warner Brothers bore a certain resemblance to Henry Ford's gargantuan automobile factories, the new "independent" film companies, financed by their founders' star power, were like Renaissance ateliers.

Originally formed to produce the kind of movies Burt Lancaster wanted to star in, notably *Sweet Smell of Success*, Hecht-Hill-Lancaster Productions soon had a tremendous hit with the big-screen adaptation of TV's *Marty*. Reprising his video play, cutting edge writer Paddy Chayefsky pioneered the "slice of life" style of drama that lives on half a century later as the quintessential "torn from the headlines" franchise, *Law and Order*. Once *Marty* won four major Oscars in 1955, the kind of movies Irving Thalberg had made were museum pieces. The studios could no longer afford to produce them and the biggest stars weren't interested in playing in them. Only a tightly knit independent production company with a common vision could compete on realism with live television and a news media increasingly sophisticated at creating a "truth stranger than fiction." The new production companies were like a collective hustler who forced the studios to bankroll films over which they had little control.

Other trailblazing "indies" were Kirk Douglas' Bryna Films (*Paths of Glory*, *Spartacus*) and the Woolfs' Romulus Films (*The Good Die Young*, *Cosh Boy*, *Room at the Top*). Here we see illustrated an indispensable component of the hustle: not only must there be a Star and a Maestro, sometimes combined in the same person (particularly in film), but fortune favours the hustler who, seeing the arts and entertainment business in transition and confusion, moves quickly to take advantage. Once the hustler's vision becomes box office, the supporting players follow the money and a new cycle begins with a freshly shuffled deck.

The success of Otto Preminger raised the ante considerably in the clash between the new Hollywood and the old. Films like *Carmen Jones*, *River of No Return*, and *The Man With the Golden Arm* brought old-fashioned star power to themes and attitudes that had never received big budget treatment before. Frank sexuality and drug addiction had been sensationalized often but never with such moral ambiguity and high production values. Otto's eye for a beauty with that something "extra" was not the least of his talents. Pace *American Idol*, he "discovered" the star of his adaptation of Shaw's *St. Joan*, the luminous Jean Seberg, from among 18,000 hopefuls who entered his much publicized contest for the leading role.

Paul Newman and Otto Preminger

When Dorothy Dandridge first auditioned for the lead in *Carmen Jones*, she was already a veteran of boffo appearances at the Cotton Club, the Mocambo, and the Waldorf-Astoria Empire Room. Dandridge's ultra-chic image hid insecurities stemming from the sexual and physical abuses visited upon her by her mother's lover, yet Preminger remained unconvinced she had the depth to portray a complex working-class character. Dandridge persisted and landed a second audition for the all-star all-black production. This time, the night club sophisticate was

...med by a tight skirt, tighter blouse, a Southern accent and a hair-do that would do Ronnie Spector proud.

She was so convincing that Preminger cast her for the female lead on the spot. Dorothy and Otto began an affair that ended in her having an abortion, while on the other hand her performance in *Carmen Jones* was nominated for a best actress Oscar, a first for an African American actress. They parted when Dorothy came to realize that Preminger would never obtain a divorce, and the rest of her life was marked by numerous financial and personal troubles. It seldom works in the star's favor when the hustler crosses the line from professional to personal.

At the top of his game, Preminger brought the alleged "communist" Dalton Trumbo back from blacklist exile to write *Exodus*, a huge-scale film guaranteed success by virtue of Leon Uris' best-selling novel and half a dozen well-known stars, including Paul Newman and Sal Mineo. Preminger rubbed a cowardly Hollywood's nose in Trumbo's triumphant return, giving him unusual prominence in the credits. Preminger's reward for his hustling bravery was free publicity from anti-Red pickets outside the theatre and a $22 million gross against a $4 million budget.

While the British film business had never been as "industrial" as Hollywood, it gave rise to Sir Alexander Korda, a producer/director who became Britain's Cecil B. DeMille with better taste. In the 1930s, having learned his craft at United Artists, the Hungarian-born Korda became a British citizen and transformed the making of films in his adopted land. A brilliant combination of super salesman and colossal dreamer, he would plan dozens of projects at the same time, as inspiration struck him. He preferred properties which resided in the public domain and therefore did not require him to purchase rights at extra expense.

Yet Korda's films were the first British talkies that had the air of class and quality heretofore associated with Irving Thalberg at MGM, with its unparalleled stable of stars and super-sized budgets. During the silent era, the percentage of British-made films shown in the United Kingdom had fallen so low that an act of Parliament was passed to establish a more equitable balance with the superior American products. Korda took advantage of the transition to sound, and his *The Private Life of Henry VIII* became the first British film to be nominated for a Best Picture Oscar. Charles Laughton as Henry won the Best Actor Academy Award in 1933. Thanks to Korda, British film was now globally recognized as financially and artistically successful.

One afternoon in 1954 when a ten-year-old's fancies were first taking flight, my mother and I caught a glimpse of Sir Alexander as we walked towards the Bayswater Road. This was before the days when a Bentley's rear windows would be tinted black and I can still remember his grey double-breasted suit as the stretch limo passed through the gates of Millionaire's Row, just off Hyde Park. I had just seen ambition on wheels and, as a young tycoon of teen, one of my first purchases would be a Rolls Royce of my own.

If Sir Alexander was the epitome of class for the masses, then the bare-knuckled hustle of Mike Todd meant the circus never left town as long as one of his epics was appearing in a theatre near you. His movie *Around the World in 80 Days* was a benchmark of self-promotion, the culmination of a career that had already elevated Todd's name beyond any of the many so-called stars he danced around his private play-stage. Todd lived his life as if it were a film, but his legacy lies in the technical innovations he brought to theatrical film presentation. At a time when a high-end TV measured but 14", Todd-AO took spectacle to new heights and gave one a reason to leave the house and go to the movies.

Though he was a flamboyant showman in the Barnum tradition, I did not hear of Todd until he had married Elizabeth Taylor and produced *Around the World In 80 Days*. Magazine photos of the couple were mesmerising. They appeared as iconic as Karsh portrait subjects even when photographed by lesser lensmen. Miss Taylor, at the time widely considered to be the most beautiful woman in the world, had a hustler's eye for situations that would further her agenda. Upon arriving in London to begin work on one of her lesser films, she resided on a boat in the Thames, rather than a luxury hotel, so that her dogs would not be subject to the quarantine laws.

* * *

When I was 12, in 1956, my mother moved us to a basement flat at 44 Belsize Park Gardens, a wide avenue parallel with Haverstock Hill in Hampstead. For whatever reason, the flat was far bigger than we needed, especially as I spent so much time in boarding schools. So Mother decided to take in a tenant, renting a large back room facing the garden to a Ms. Gladys Byrne, a stern lady given to wearing tweed trousers, no pearls and sensible walking shoes. Gladys worked at the BBC, as did Bob, a demure, passive little fellow who lived in the next block, and who seemed, albeit with one hand tied behind his back, to be stepping out with Gladys at the time.

Completing the mysterious trio was Gus, Gladys' brother, my own favourite of the three figures who apologized for the intrusion as they variously swished or marched through our basement hallway, en route to Gladys' self-contained garden suite. Chubby, cheerful, bright-eyed and enthusiastically Irish, thirty-something Gus always stopped by to see me on his way to visiting his sister. I looked forward to the moment when he'd look into my room, answer my questions about show business and relate the latest gossip from the Beeb.

My mother, whose sphere of social acceptability was circumscribed indeed, did not look forward to these visits in the slightest. Gus did not wear sensible walking shoes. He wore slip-ons and crossed his lower legs tightly, hips erect in Alexander technique position, perfectly poised as his hands conjured his stories out of thin air for an audience of one, who preferred him to any magician. You could serve tea on him.

The BBC in the mid-1950s was a near-mythical place, still ruled in spirit, if not person, by John Reith, the septuagenarian Scotsman who was appointed its first ever Director General in 1927. Vast, mysterious, all-knowing and all-seeing, the BBC was our lifeline to the manifold worlds that existed outside of Hampstead. It brought us our news, it brought us entertainment, it brought us music, comedy, drama. Eventually, it even gave us television, which immediately became the altar piece in every home that could afford one.

Gus' tales of everyday life in the corridors of Broadcasting House had an added piquancy in being informed by his extroverted gayness, though I was too young to notice much what my mother found to be outré. When homosexuality was still against the law in Britain, almost all gays out enough to be identified as such were entertaining, if not extremely talented, and the many who came to be affiliated with the government-supported BBC enjoyed a special status not extended to those firmly in the closet.

Alexander Korda

Gus gushed to the all-ears me because he and his sister were as close to the business of show as I had yet come and I suspect we both enjoyed making him feel more special than his professional circumstances would indicate. Gus knew of my mogul-crush on producer Mike Todd and noted my knowledge of Preminger and Korda. But, though he admired my interest, he was less enamored of my choice of subjects. Should I of tender years really be interested in knowing about the man who changed art in the 20th century, then he would introduce me to their own guv'nor—Sergei Pavlovich Diaghilev, maestro of the *Ballets Russes*, producer and *pimpresario extraordinaire*.

Though the ballet was as far off my radar screen as a Balinese shadow play, Gus deserved to set the agenda for our get-togethers every so often. So I listened. The gods were sending all kinds of subliminal data to my precocious mind while I slept, so perhaps they signalled, "Relax, it's only pop" (remember we had no rock 'n' roll at the time).

Diaghilev was born on March 19, 1872, in the barracks of a military estate in Novgorud, an Imperial Russian province that was a long way from Moscow, which was a long way from everywhere back then. As a youth, he flirted briefly with a career in law, even moving to St Petersburg for that purpose. But friendship with the composer Rimsky-Korsakov began drawing him away from his legal studies toward a circle of writers, artists and aesthetes led by the painters Léon Baskt and Alexandre Benois.

At 27, Diaghilev founded the progressive art journal *Mir Iskusstva* ("World of Art") and, for a while, his ambitions appeared to be satisfied. A respected publisher, he wished for no grander title than patron of the arts. But, as time passed, his interests evolved from the fine arts to the performing arts. So while 1904 found him in Paris organising an exhibition of Russian painting, by 1908 he was treating the art capital of the world to a full-blown production of *Boris Godunov*.

With each escalation of his developing skills as an impresario, Diaghilev faced more financial responsibility and risk. In a sense, bringing together the performers, musicians, and set designers was the easy part; Diaghilev's real talent lay in choosing (later commissioning) musical scores and scene sets that would excite both his artists and their audience, and in finding money to support his projects before the public voted with their ticket purchases.

And that, of course, is why we designate him a hustler supreme. He realized that without popular acceptance, as measured by income, his dreams would die stillborn. In fact, the *Ballets Russes* never performed in Russia. They couldn't afford to. And even in Paris he innovated to accommodate popular tastes. Programs seldom consisted of full-length ballets. Instead, Diaghilev offered individual acts produced as self-sufficient set pieces and commissioned shorter original works that would accentuate his flair for the visual. And still, the vast majority of Diaghilev's time was spent raising money. He perfectly illustrates that one can be selfishly devoted to one's vision without "profiting" from it.

The formula had wide implications. When enough record players had been installed in American living rooms (long before radio of course), Enrico Caruso, tenor with the Metropolitan Opera, became the world's first million selling recording artist, with a repertoire that spanned famous arias and Italian street songs. Indeed, Caruso's records were a reason to go out and get a record player, what Silicon Valley calls the "killer app" that every new hardware breakthrough needs to prevail. His business relationship with the Victor Talking-Machine Company spanned 17 years and 500 recordings, netting Caruso himself over $2 million, an inconceivable income from the arts in those days.

Let us note that technology gave the Victor Company and Caruso a considerable leg up financially over Diaghilev. Caruso could spend an afternoon in a recording studio ten minutes by cab from his Manhattan hotel room, attired in a smoking jacket if he so chose, and low-cost manufacturing and distribution took it from there. On one hand, the leading producer of the arts in the world was barely breaking even, and on the other, due to mass acceptance of a new technology, Victor was realizing astronomical profit margins. So, memo to would-be hustlers: Make sure your vision isn't on the wrong side of the next techno wave.

We might also point out that when "race music" became a goldmine for record companies in the 1920s, there was no business reason for depriving African American musicians of royalties. Racism was probably not the motivation; black artists were simply "handled" by the wrong kind of hustler. Many a lily-white yodeller was similarly "victimized."

In regarding Diaghilev's place on the hustler continuum, we find him firmly in the center, neither overly swayed by financial pressures nor too much in love with his performer partners to demand the best of them. Dancer Tamara Karsavina recalled, "Sometimes he could be quite ruthless and work his artists to the limits of their power. Diaghilev had a tremendous gift of persuasion, very great charm and wonderful tenacity. He could talk one into anything, even against one's better judgment." While Lydia Sokolova concedes in John Drummond's *Speaking of Diaghilev*, "He could be terrifying," she wouldn't have had it any other way. Once when she was in great difficulty the maestro took her aside to tell her, "'Now, I want you to remember that I can be as a father to you, and when you are at any time in trouble, real trouble, either in the day or in the night, and you send for me, I will come.' He was to keep his word, so how could I not love anybody like that? Of course I loved him."

He lived his genius, never letting his guard down, always dressing for drama. The man was crafted in a way that only the truly self-confident can ever pull off. Karsavina continues, "He was very good-looking with his famous white streak in his hair. He walked with a sort of rolling gait, rolling his head from side to side. He reminded me very much of a sea lion, who looks awkward, but manages to have perfect grace. He lived in a bachelor flat with his collection of icons, where he attended to details. In that way he was rather like Napoleon, who had a wonderful gift for detail."

So intensely did Diaghilev believe in his vision, and so single-mindedly did he pursue it, that even at his most successful, he was never what you'd call wealthy. Every franc he earned was ploughed back into the act. "He never thought of financial success," Karsavina concluded. "The first priority with Diaghilev was to produce good things."

Most importantly, Diaghilev remained a true fan throughout his career. And not simply a fan of the dance or dancers, painting or artists, music or musicians, but of the unique whole their contributions comprised when the production came together. Passion (or perhaps more correctly, *objective* passion) is an uneasy bedfellow to pragmatism, but it is the quality most required for the hustler to avoid becoming either a shark or a sap. He must be *taken up*, engaged, promised to, and blinded by the light but nevertheless painstakingly productive.

As a teenager, when chronic depression began to dog me, I grasped at every detail I could discover about Diaghilev to shore up my shaky sense of self, actively seeking out similarities between his way of life and my way of dreaming. No connection, no matter how tenuous, was overlooked—everything from the day upon which I was born and the numbers of the street where I lived, to the proximity of Monty Morris, an outrageously eccentric magpie whose collection of Diaghilev memorabilia was legendary even before he loaned it to posterity as a framework for Drummond's *Speaking Of Diaghilev*.

Creative visualisation was my spiritual practice: if I was walking from 44 Belsize Park Gardens to the Haverstock Hill or Swiss Cottage tube, I would pace the walk to the credits of an imaginary production that would end with "directed by" flashing across my screen as I entered whatever tube. As it happened, I was much better at daydreaming than more mundane adolescent pursuits, such as shoplifting or hooliganism; my life played better on the screen.

By this time, Cliff Richard and Eddie Cochran had supplanted my 'tween infatuation with Johnnie Ray and I gained a new appreciation for Diaghilev's finest and most controversial achievement: the 1913 production of Stravinsky's *The Rites of Spring* provoked a riot in Paris that was pure rock 'n' roll. *The Guardian* described that evening in a recent retrospective: "The fashionable audience at the Théatre des Champs-Elysées disintegrated into violently opposing factions. Amid jeers, whistles, jostling and fighting, one chic society woman slapped her neighbour, noisy wits screamed for doctors and dentists to aid the 'suffering' performers, and the composer Maurice Ravel (seen applauding in the audience) was called a 'dirty Jew.' The ballet's critics lost no time in re-titling it *Massacre du Printemps* ('Massacre of Spring')." Having proved his point, Diaghilev pulled the *Rites* from the company's repertoire after only a handful of performances. Although Diaghilev took pains to mollify his paying audience, one wonders if his equally passionate superstar, Nijinsky, was equally philosophical.

Diaghilev had cool, and he hustled cool. He produced "popular art" in the same way that the brazen '60s astounded, entertained and offended. And before we leave the maestro, it is instructive to consider the differences between pop, art, and pop art. We make no qualitative distinctions here, but simply point out that one's intentions are as important as one's product, *if* one is to sustain oneself as a successful hustler, be it producer or performer.

The long-running Broadway musical *Mamma Mia*, based on the songs of ABBA, is an excellent example. The high-grossing, award-winning show is nothing more or less than "pop," a slick and fast-moving recycling of tunes attractive to the audience because they are so familiar. The bar for quality is set much lower because the producers had no intention of creating something original or innovative. One needs a different vehicle for a quick trip to the market and the Indi 500.

The collective oeuvre of Bjorn and Benny, on the other hand, amply fills the bill as "pop art" of the highest calibre. Inspired by the Beatles, Phil Spector, and the Archies, ABBA intended to produce something entirely new, yet compellingly entertaining, and as a result, the template established with "Waterloo" stood up over time, even as the arrangements veered toward disco and the foursome strained to put on a happy face once the girls began to chafe under the guys' firm hand.

In a similar way, Elvis and the Colonel were on the same page in the beginning for very different reasons and were so successful with the original concept that it survived years of horrid movies before Elvis came back full circle with his triumphant '68 "Comeback" Special. Although there is no record I know of to confirm that Elvis and Sam Phillips ever discussed Sam's dream of discovering a white singer who sounded black and made the public like it, it's safe to assume that

Elvis bought into the hustle completely, and it brought music out of him that his appreciation of Dean Martin never could.

But Elvis needed a higher order of hustler in the form of Tom Parker if he were to become *all* that he could be (apologies to the US Army). By the time Elvis moved from Sun Records to RCA, it was clear that he was much more than a new and distinctive singing voice. The frenzied response Elvis got on the road hadn't been seen since a skinny Frank Sinatra took the stage with the Dorsey band. No wonder Leiber and Stoller, Doc Pomus and Otis Blackwell eagerly provided material on a completely different level than that which they had provided Big Mama Thornton. One imagines that at this point, there was so much money to spread around that everybody was hustling everybody, an ideal situation as long as everyone keeps moving.

And to be somewhat controversial, I would contend that Elvis' career was never of the highest degree of pop art, because after a while the Colonel stopped getting what Elvis was all about: a white guy who loved black music, black musicians and black food (my more severe critics have levelled the same charge against me as regards the Stones). Of course, Elvis succumbed to the overwhelming pressures of unprecedented stardom and let mediocrity happen to him. All praise to Keith Richards who never used drug addiction to excuse bad music. But just imagine if Elvis had been a rockin' Nijinsky to a rollin' Diaghilev.

We may say in closing that there is nothing wrong with pop musicians attempting "art," as long as they choose lifestyles and business partners appropriately realistic. While nothing is more beside the point than a pop artist who wishes to be taken "seriously," an arty popster who remains true to his vision might yet attract the kind of financial success that comes with luck, timing, and yes, integrity. At its best, the contemporary indie music scene is the music business' only alternative to devouring its young and killing the golden goose altogether. Seemingly modest products hustled prodigiously with an eye on the far horizon can provide happy surprises we should all look forward to.

LARRY PARNES

IT IS HARD to exaggerate the bleakness of the Britain in which I grew into a teenager. If our national culture lent itself to grey resignation and emotional constipation, the War calcified many of our worst traits while it stole the stoic nobility that all our various castes upheld. Those of our parents who survived were distressingly mum about the details of their six-year 9/11. Many, like my mother, felt that God had failed them. There was no wearing of hearts on sleeves or weeping on national television as is the way today; no impromptu shrines of flowers and teddy-bears marked the spot of Britannia's last stand. But somewhere between the end of Lend Lease and the humiliation of Suez, it became bruisingly obvious that our kingdom was done for, and there was not much to be done about it except to get on with the lot we'd got.

Britain's economic shambles following 1945 shaped the cultural awakening of the 1950s. The frustration of living under economic privation whilst watching America re-build Germany into George Lucas splendour was the catalyst for John Osborne's rumbling *Look Back In Anger*. Those of us punters not yet a part of the new intelligentsia nurtured the hope that someday soon our lives would resemble the American movies we loved; we'd trade places with a miserable young James Dean in a flash.

We had no perspective on Britain's glorious and unrecoverable past, so we lived in a make-believe present time inspired by Hollywood and rock 'n' roll. In a Britain as removed from the Blackboard Jungle as the Congo, rebellion remained implied for most, yet no less powerful for being latent. Let the teddies emulate American greasers by trashing cinemas, the rest of us had a secret love no less dear for being held close to the vest.

Dreams were important because our elders had run out of them and therefore aspiration belonged to the young. Rock 'n' roll was ours because it was American and our parents didn't want it. They had Liberace, Mantovani and Nat "King" Cole. Besides, there was an unspoken resentment amongst our elders about how and when America had entered World War II, two years after the rest of the planet, then stage-managed the end of it, four years later.

Where was Uncle Sam when the tanks rolled over Europe? they asked. Where was Lady Liberty when the Germans were blitzing the heart out of London? Those of us who played in the underground as toddlers while bombs dropped over us had no such feelings. We had rock 'n' roll. We had this important, explosive, evocative rhythm, accompanied by a totally new approach to how English was spoken or sung, a combination that lifted us out of our own emotional slums, and put us in touch with heaven; which, in turn, gave us additional hope and energy, so that we might rail even harder against the place that had been set for us with no future . . . because that's how bleak our lot was supposed to be.

And we had Johnnie Ray. He was the first witness preceding the overweight avuncular Bill Haley, the first to sing the blues and take his cues from outright need, from angst and pure, undiluted physical emotion, fortified by a shot of rhythm 'n blues. And only after we'd accepted him into our hearts were we ready for the rest of the deluge, helter-skelter via vinyl and the silver screen: Elvis Presley, Marlon Brando, Gene Vincent, James Dean, Little Richard, "Fats" Domino, Eddie Cochran, Buddy Holly.

Suddenly, life had vision, attitude, leaders and a plot. And they were all-American, all Americans. Elvis Presley ruled our world from the moment his "Heartbreak Hotel" crashed onto the UK charts in the spring of 1956 and introduced us to an "aw-shucks" sexual belligerence that could not help but microwave the coldly stoic British soul. The song itself was alchemical, its lyrics transforming base instinct into emotional gold, emboldening images, fuel that inspired us.

Previously, a "hotel" was a place in Torquay where rich people spent two weeks every year. Its conjugation with the word "heartbreak," another unspoken British emotion, brought a cognitive dissonance worthy of Brecht that was pure genius. If Presley had disappeared after that song, like so many of his mid-'50s peers, it wouldn't have mattered. Look how iconic the completely naff "Rock Around the Clock" has remained despite its being the best big Bill could hope for.

Elvis didn't disappear. Instead he came back with more. A September '56 follow-up, "I Want You, I Need You, I Love You" was just as disturbing and brilliant as its predecessor. Its title was enough to cause British hormones to o'er-run the levees.

Where did I gain this premature insight, this ability to see past the façade and into the heart of whichever depths of darkness were working behind the scenes? Brando in *The Young Lions* helped; so did James Dean in white tee and denim. But if I had one lesson that I never forgot, it took place over the course of an hour-and-a-half-or-so, that cloudy afternoon in 1957, when I first saw *Sweet Smell of Success*, a movie that made such an impression upon me for the mad and the good. I was thirteen at the time and if there was ever a movie that deserved a PG rating it was *Sweet Smell*. Although I doubt many of our parents would have been able or willing to discuss the film's bottomless pit of amorality and evil.

Author Ernest Lehman was a lower-league press agent in post-war New York, one of the bitter bottom-feeding brigade whose entire career revolved around snatching snippets of gossip to feed to the big syndicated columnists of the day, a coterie headed by the legendary Walter Winchell, the Crown Prince of Gossip for 60 million Americans. It was not a job that Lehman relished; when he'd first stepped out into the world as a writer, he saw great novels and movie scripts in his future. Instead, he toiled among the lowest of the low; and, as time passed, his resentment of his demeaning role in life, and of the high rollers he served, grew to demonic proportions.

Finally he cracked, dashing out a short story for *Colliers* in April 1948, titled "Hunsecker Fights the World," thus placing Winchell—scarcely disguised as the unscrupulous, vindictive and vitriolic JJ Hunsecker—firmly in his sights. In an age when people devoured magazines, as opposed to scanning the edited highlights on the CNN ticker, Lehman's piece caused a serious stir. Many silently applauded Lehman's vivisection of the abusive Winchell, while maintaining a diplomatic and judicious silence themselves. *Cosmopolitan* was impressed enough to commission a novella-length successor and in 1950, *Sweet Smell of Success* debuted under *Cosmo's* own choice of title, *Tell Me About It Tomorrow*. Apparently editor Herbert Mayes objected to the word "smell" appearing within his decidedly fragrant pages.

No matter, the story kicked up a stink regardless, not only among Winchell's own apologists, but also among his subservient press agents, all of whom saw a little of themselves reflected in the second of Lehman's great media anti-heroes, the wonderfully loathsome Sidney Falco—a flashy little runt whose fawning devotion to Hunsecker knew no limits whatsoever. Among the tribe of friends and associates winged by Lehman's no-holds-barred assault on their way of life, one Irving Hoffman was especially incensed. Himself one of Winchell's most "reliable" sources (Lehman's own material was routinely funnelled through Hoffman, before it ever reached Winchell's desk), he was convinced that the world would now see him as the Falco character, just as they recognised Winchell in JJ.

While Lehman and Hoffman had once been fairly close, they would not speak again for several years, until they were reunited by a mutual friend. Hoffman proffered the greatest olive branch at his disposal: an invitation for Lehman alone to write Hoffman's next column for the *Hollywood Reporter*. Lehman accepted, and transformed the page into an advertisement for the story that had started the dispute, targeted directly at a film industry which had long tired of rejecting his insistence that *Sweet Smell of Success* would make a great movie.

"The world I want to see on film," Lehman-as-Hoffman wrote, "is . . . the world of Winchell and [Earl] Wilson, [Ed] Sullivan (the future TV host was himself a former gossip monger) and [Louis] Sobol . . . of columnists on the prowl for items, press agents on the prowl for columnists." And the only person who could write such a world, and make it believable on the cinema screen, was Ernest Lehman. A fortnight later, Lehman's telephone started ringing. *Sweet Smell of Success* would be made by the production company of Harold Hecht and James Hill, vouchsafed by the already established stardom of Burt Lancaster. For a time, Lehman believed he would be directing the film; for almost as long, all concerned believed that Orson Welles would be playing the role of Hunsecker. By the time the film finally went before the cameras, however, Lehman had been side-lined for Alexander Mackendrick, the Boston-born, Glasgow-raised director of the Ealing classic *The Ladykillers*. Welles was forgotten the moment Burt Lancaster committed to portraying Hunsecker with unparalleled relish and mustard. In the role of the snivelling Sidney Falco, Tony Curtis risked his future as a conventionally handsome is as handsome does leading man. The performances of Susan Harrison, as Hunsecker's cosseted yet abused sister, and Marty Milner, as her hapless jazz musician lover, were all the more powerful for the cluelessness of their characters.

I fell in love with it all. I can never forget the black and white wonder of Manhattan's Broadway after a rain, gleaming with a surreal sheen from countless neon signs and thousands of Cadillac headlamps, as Falco began his "work" day at an hour when decent folk were on their way home. It wasn't Falco's profession that attracted me so much as his outrageously seedy lifestyle, taking him from beatnik haunted Greenwich Village jazz clubs to the Stork, where Hunsecker/Winchell literally held court with the help of a portable phone brought to his table on demand. It was Falco's unapologetic zest for the hustle that I loved, all the more so as I inhabited a country that simply didn't hustle at all, where the professions of advertising and public relations were considered one made-to-measure suit above being a pimp. Our hustle, such as it was, hid behind an RAF blazer, drinkies at the club, old chap, and an accent acquired with the wife's country seat.

Sidney Falco made no bones about being desperate, an emotion I could relate to. It seemed to me that Falco's take no prisoners approach to survival was just what the old sod needed. At 13, I already felt my life drifting away, being pulled not so much by birth right as birth lot. Despite even the most charming pretensions my mother had to middle-class respectability, in truth we were *lower* middle-class and expected to live in service to the system and the man. My mother was scheming and saving desperately to get me a place in our nation's public school system, under the naïve assumption that if I schooled with the "right sort," I'd become the right sort. Of course the second and third-rate schools that would take me were full of chaps who would never be any sort at all. I already knew that he with the most money or land wins. They'd taught me that in school, without giving me the wherewithal to obtain them. But I also understood that those rules did not apply to this wonderful world called entertainment, show business, life amongst the shills.

Neither were these thoughts a passing adolescent fancy. The ruthlessly unscrupulous events depicted in the movie were not necessarily to my temperament. But the manner in which wheels spun within wheels, webs were woven and then laced with tasty flies, seemed an apt enough prototype for my escape plan: the whole relationship between Falco and Hunsecker stood me in good stead when I set out on my own to hustle the pubs and newspaper offices of Fleet Street and Shaftesbury Avenue.

When I landed those first column inches for the Rolling Stones in the UK press, justifying my existence to the band, the papers, and myself, it was Sidney Falco sitting on my shoulder like a dark angel, making it happen. There were other lessons of more immediate value. Chief among them was that no one who wished more than one audience spoke truth to power before power had something to gain in the conversation. Those who remember the brash Andrew of my early years with the Stones can have no idea for how many years I kept my powder dry, as I gauged how much of myself to reveal to those whose good opinion of me was absolutely essential to whatever hustle had led them to engage me.

My first opportunity to put these new skills into action arrived within weeks, maybe even days, of my first heady inhalation of the *Sweet Smell*. So deftly had I absorbed them, however, that it was decades before I realised I'd even employed them. In 1990-something, browsing through an English film guide that had miraculously appeared in a Bogotá bookstore, I read of the death of Harold Lang.

Harold Lang. I hadn't heard that name in so long that several lifetimes had passed since I'd even thought of him. He'd passed away in 1970, before he even reached the half-century mark. But there was a moment in time, somewhere between my ages of 12 and 13, when much of my world revolved around him. He was already into his mid-30s at the time, and had been acting for most of his life. With the exception of *The Quatermass Xperiment*, you probably won't remember the majority of the films he made, scrappy little Anglo-Amalgamated B-movies that came and went in the time it took to buy your popcorn and settle down in your seat. When I found his address in the phone book, I was stunned to discover he lived just round the corner, so without so much as a visiting card, let alone a legitimate excuse to intrude, I went a-calling.

To me at the time, Lang was an impressive looking gent, his noble peroxided quiff surmounting a frame that rendered his every motion a vastly exaggerated image of grace. Even pouring a cup of tea for his young visitor, something that he found himself doing a lot of as my visits became more regular, was a thing of beauty. It came as no surprise, a few years later (I think 1961), when I switched on the BBC one evening, to discover an hour-long instalment of the Monitor arts show was dedicated to his career as a drama coach at the Central School of Speech and Drama, down the road in Swiss Cottage. There he spoke of secrets that he and I had never shared—of how a teacher should be willing to learn from his pupils; how his own work as a tutor benefited from his students' knowledge that, outside of the classroom, he too was an actor and, as such, was as susceptible to failure as he was capable of brilliance. Which was vital, because it allowed the class to regard him as a colleague, not a Colonel.

"I can go to them and say 'I gave a lousy performance last night. Help me to try and get it better'," he once said. When I knew him, of course, my interests were those of any 13-year-old fan, desperate to discover as much as possible about a world that existed only in pictures. "Have you met . . . ?" "What's he like . . . ?" "Who's the best director . . . ?" "How do you do that?" Harold answered my queries graciously as he refreshed my cuppa, and as gravely as my own serious expression demanded. Like Gus before him, he knew how much his stories meant to me, how I would store them away for a future sunny day. His willingness to learn as well as to teach was not what I'd come to expect from an adult and was all the more charming for his failing to take obvious notice of my very tender years. Sometimes he would suddenly invert my questions, in order to help me refine my young opinion of something or other, and at others, he seemed to take my opinions on board and employ them as a springboard to further conversations.

Which, God bless Sidney Falco, was something I'd never given much thought to. I fell so hard in love with the rapid fire one liners that zapped back and forth between Sidney and JJ, that I completely overlooked the occasional advantages of an open-ended chat. You can blind folks with science when the moment demands it. But sometimes, if you just shut your mouth, you might learn something to your greater advantage. Harold Lang taught me how to be interested and interesting and, for a few years, that held me in good stead. But then Sidney Falco took over again, and most of the ensuing years are a blur of often useless verbiage. In the mid-'90s, as I commenced the slow rehabilitation of the skills I'd once taken for granted, so I found Harold, with his kindly tutelage, sitting on my other shoulder as a kind of good angel. And today, I promise, I will listen to everything you tell me. Then I may do what I was intending to in the first place.

* * *

Johnny Jackson, *Expresso Bongo*: "The picture in the fan mag showed this gangly kid in jeans and a sweatshirt, his face contorted, mouth wide open, beating with both hands on a bongo set round his shoulder, over it the headline 'BONGO SCORES AT TOM TOM.' The same terrible stuff but this time it was good cos it was me who dropped the deadbeat drunk columnist a fiver to run it. Because this new boy Bongo Herbert, playing nightly for the past week at the Tom Tom Express back of Frith Street, he's under contract to nobody but me. Half of the ten pounds he picks up this Friday comes to me. Half of everything he beats out of those little bongos for the next three years comes to me.

"I had wet-nursed this kid along, bought him cigarettes, coffee and sandwiches, a couple of sweatshirts with bongos painted on them, a pair of tailored black jeans, and a fancy haircut. Turned him from Bert Rudge, snotty-nosed nobody, to Bongo Herbert, Britain's latest answer to America's latest solution of how to keep discs selling by the million."

Through reading about Tommy Steele, I understood that the new British rock 'n' roll scene was all happening in the coffee bars of Soho. Here, young hopefuls sang, sneered and swiveled their hips. Managers plucked them from obscurity and launched them to fame in the charts. Business was conducted in Tin Pan Alley, where agents, publishers, managers, producers and songwriters all worked their magic.

Soho's Tin Pan Alley was not what I had pictured in my imagination. I expected a glitzy Mecca for fantastic-looking rock 'n' rollers, and what I (and everybody else) got was short, shabby Denmark Street, just off Charing Cross Road. Tin Pan Alley was an inhospitable place, full of brutish men with none of the grace of those I felt I had come to know from the world of film and television.

Nevertheless, I returned to Soho as often as I could—its neon hustling crassness was like a drug before drugs. I was lying to my mother, of course, telling her I was visiting a friend in the evenings, then rushing off to Soho to the coffee bar on Old Compton street where British rock 'n' roll was being put on the map. "The world famous 2i's coffee bar, home of the stars," the neon sign above the door proclaimed. The 2i's had started playing host to "live" rock 'n' roll and skiffle acts in early 1956, when Australian wrestlers Ray Hunter and Paul Lincoln took over the lease. Downstairs, in the tiny basement that had been decorated by the soon to be successful songwriter Lionel Bart, a regular crowd of two hundred teenage hipsters danced the night away.

The most unforeseen mutation of the atomic age—teenagers with disposable income—called the 2i's "coffee bar" home. This is where Cliff Richard, Ian "Sammy" Samwell, Lionel Bart, Jet Harris, Hank B. Marvin, Tony Meehan, Bruce Welch, Mickie Most, Adam Faith and all of the charter members of the British rock 'n' roll hall of fame played the game and found their musical legs.

I was only twelve and hadn't a farthing, but I stood for hours outside the 2i's, watching the customers slide downstairs to the 'skiffle' bar. I was on the outside looking in, checking the names on the shining jukebox placed strategically in the window and chatting to the female doorkeeper, Nora. After many such evenings window shopping, the kindhearted Nora took pity on me and let me downstairs without paying the usual one-shilling cover charge. Here I saw my first live rock 'n' roll shows, courtesy of Vince Taylor & The Playboys and Paul Raven (Gary Glitter in the making). Eventually, I started lugging cases of Coke downstairs at the 2i's for a few pence a night.

The coffee bar was a haven for managers and agents on the hunt for fresh talent, eager to cash in quick on the current teenage thirst for rock 'n' roll. Eventually, the thriving scene came to the attention of Larry Parnes, who became Britain's most successful and notorious pop music manager.

If even so prolific and seminal a hustler as Diaghilev begins with what he likes, then Larry Parnes' rise from rather dubious aesthetic origins should prove instructive.

British, Jewish and entrepreneurial, Parnes was also decidedly gay, as evidenced perhaps by his production of other 8-year-olds in a theatrical while growing up in Kent.

Billy Fury and Larry Parnes

His bent found its first professional outlet when at 18 he started a chain of three women's clothing shops in Essex, of which two lost money. That Parnes was gambling with his family's money may give some indication of both his front and his ethics.

A fist fight in the West End between two bar owners led to his partnership in La Caverne, frequented by the London equivalent of Damon Runyon types. Theatrical. Footloose. Fond of a drink.

So much did Parnes appreciate his new sideline that while in his cups he signed on to invest in a play entitled *The House of Shame*. Doubtless the performance and players were enchanting in their way, yet Parnes' losing streak continued. Evidently great personal enjoyment of one's occupation is not quite enough to sustain a profit.

When Parnes met publicist John Kennedy they apparently decided that the problem was that the play's title was too subtle. Presto chango, *The House of Shame* re-opened as *Women of the Streets*. Looking at Parnes' career as "svengali" some years later, one might be tempted to conclude, "It's *all* in a name."

Not content with half a loaf in the makeover department, Parnes and Kennedy persuaded two of the cast's more presumably shameful members to stroll the sidewalk in their costumes before the theatre opened. Smoking cigarettes and chatting with passersby as they must have, it was not surprising that the local constabulary considered their idling to be solicitation and picked them up, so to speak.

Shocked at this unforeseen turn of events, Parnes' new partner recovered his professional poise overnight. Kennedy suggested to the more sensational national dailies that an outrage had been perpetrated on the arts and if only the theatre-loving public would see *Women of the Streets* for themselves, all would be set right. The play eventually broke even.

While some years later it was quite possible to be a rabid fan of the Beatles or Stones in, say, Chicago and have no idea whatsoever what Brian Epstein and I looked like, in Britain, Larry Parnes was a media figure as close to parity with his stars as possible. Billy Fury, Marty Wilde, Dickie Pride etc. etc. went from complete obscurity to national prominence in almost the time it took for Parnes to change their name and turn them out on his non-stop packaged tours. I will leave it to you to decide if pop music today is better for Simon Cowell being even more famous than his "artists."

Larry Parnes was the perfect manager for what seemed at that moment in the late '50s, a near perfect time. Parnes was eminently equipped to nurse a new breed of pop star, not the least because like all gentlemen sportsmen, he bred litter after litter. Yet he was of the showbiz old guard and his "secret" was not wrapped up so much in the vision thing. It was just that he so terribly enjoyed gambling and winning that he couldn't stop himself, and in the casino of hustle, as in Monte Carlo, everybody loves a winner. How satisfying it must have been for him to know that thousands of Britain's most nubile teens considered his taste in men to be *ne plus ultra*. One wonders if Mrs. Bertram of Romford, Essex, coming upon a photo of Larry with HRH Princess Anne at a charity affair remembered with fondness the gingham day dress he had sold her some years before.

British pop was a stunted little beast in those days. The British music industry had long grown accustomed to playing second fiddle to whatever the Americans sent "over there," from ragtime to swing, banjo-playing minstrels in black face and boaters to bobbysoxers. This new fad, rock 'n' roll, was no exception, and Parnes, whose taste ran to singers rather than songs, had no reason to believe it might be. But he lived, breathed and slept the objects of his professional desire, from the moment he "discovered them" to the moment the public discovered someone else.

So many of us dreamed of winning a trip to Hollywood and never coming back, it never occurred to Parnes that any of his boys wouldn't want a new name to go along with their new life. Reg Smith became Marty Wilde, Ronald Wycherley became Billy Fury. Only one, Joe Brown, resisted Parnes' show dog name; "Elmer Twitch" wouldn't do for the "Picture of You" boy. Other young scruffs whose birth names are not worth remembering became Duffy Power, Johnny Gentle, Dickie Pride and Vince Eager, and it all seemed so exciting at the time. Who wouldn't want to wake up in the morning and discover that, while they slept, they'd been renamed Rocky Thighs, and there were girls screaming their name in the garden?

But Parnes had no magic formula, just a good brain for names, an appreciation for tight jeans and pretty faces, and a dress salesman's gift for schmoozing in the showroom. Larry walked a broad, comfortable lane as he set about rebranding his band of fresh-faced angels; the "establishment" was eager for his next find after the first couple scored. Where he stepped off that path was in the lengths he went to find them in the first place. Joe Brown was plucked from the boardwalk at Butlin's while Billy Fury risked his already weak heart laboring as a longshoreman.

It was if Parnes was waging a one-man crusade to reduce the United Kingdom's population of potential rent boys to those too fat or ugly to mount a stage. The strangest part of the Parnes saga is that he is almost always portrayed as the all-knowing savvy pimpresario when the truth is that, before he got used to winning and opted for it as a way of life, he was poles apart from the entrepreneur or hustler. In fact he was the mark. And all because of Tommy Steele, coffee-bars, and an evolutionary off-shoot of Sidney Falco by the name of John Kennedy, who fancied himself a "publicist" before street-walkers would blow him on the cuff.

In fact, Kennedy was almost equal parts Sidney Falco and JJ Hunsecker, who from beginnings as an under-employed paparazzi at Heathrow created a new profession for himself from whole cloth. His soon-to-be partner Larry Parnes was all too happy to shop his artists to the music business establishment while Kennedy gave the powers that were a run for their money worthy of the fictional Johnny Jackson.

As it happened, John Kennedy hung out at the 2i's between hustles and when an opportunistic blond merchant seaman called Tommy Hicks strapped on his guitar, he saw his next move and a few beyond that. Kennedy knew that no matter how much potential he himself might have seen in Hicks, his friend Larry Parnes would be aroused to the core. Kennedy took Parnes to see Tommy Hicks perform at the Stork Room on Regent Street. Parnes' recollection of the evening reveals a seamstress' eye for fit: "The first time I saw Tommy, the moment he hit the stage in his jeans, it was electrifying." As was *Le Sacre Du Printemps* in its day, Tommy's first hit, "Rock With the Caveman," was met with equal derision and just as little appreciation for its place in history.

John Edwards profiled the kinetic Mr. Kennedy in a panegyric in the *Daily Mail* as "The First Man to Rock the Nation."

"The Two I's came out as one of the best places on earth," Edwards modestly averred. "Write it down, September 14, 1956. It was the day when rock 'n' roll began in England. Kennedy had no more of an ear for music than a tree. What he knew about, and knew a lot, was style and promotion and a teenage kid they could look on as a hero. . . . Kennedy spent a lot of time thinking about a switch from newspapers to show business. At least show business was more fun. This boy on stage at the Two I's would be the push he needed.

"There hadn't been a man like Kennedy before. Show business was part of the Establishment. Now there was this tall, slim, handsome guy strutting around cutting deals in the offices of people who wouldn't take a phone call from him before. He was the first one of that kind of agent/manager and afterwards they came along like rain. . . .

"Kennedy prospered. He bought Jaguars and had his suits cut in Savile Row. The newspapers put the rise of rock down to him. Tommy was out front pushing it. John Kennedy was the magician in the wings. Life became a roar. He liked the jewelry of the good times. So it was out of a bed-sit into Dorothy Foxon's great and fabled drinking club next to Harrods and into a penthouse on Half Moon Street, Mayfair. Nothing in between.

"He gambled, sat there at four in the morning opposite Sammy Davis Jr. in Dorothy's betting three queens against two pairs. There wasn't a second of the day which wasn't touched by fun and glamour. Rock 'n' roll was down to him and Tommy. History has to rate the two of them as the people who brought it from America."

Without Parnes, however, who served to make an investment in rock 'n' roll safe for record companies and theatre owners, it's doubtful that Kennedy would ever have gotten a look in. Billy Fury's wife Lee Everett suggests that "Larry Parnes was the first British impresario to be examined by the media and made famous. In his own way, he embodied the music biz concept, 'Artists may come and go, but Larry Parnes is forever.' . . . I was in cabaret at the Bag O 'Tel in Bond Street. When Larry came in, all of the girls used to put the make on him. They thought he was fabulous. The hostesses and cigarette girls were all over him, Larry was a particularly handsome man, he had great charisma, he was wealthy, and he wore it well. He was also a gambler, and later on, when he was in Gamblers Anonymous, in a low-profile way, he'd help people out that had gambling problems."

However infantile his taste in material, Parnes did help to move the British music scene in a more contemporary direction. His network of highly placed contacts included

A&R managers Hugh Mendl, Dick Rowe, and Jack Baverstock, whom he presumably played off against each other under the assumption that all the boys were fungible and any one of them could become the next Tommy Steele. The television producer Jack Good was also keen to benefit from the flow of new teenage talent, featuring them prominently on his much watched BBC variety show, *6.5 Special*.

BBC's 6.5 Special

When in the late '50s Parnes began to sign new artists on an almost monthly basis, counting on television exposure to sell their records and concerts, it was easy to dismiss him merely as a lover of youth rather than a calculating star maker. Biographer Johnny Rogan, however, credits Parnes with an Olympian vision that transcended rock 'n' roll and even mainstream showbiz, which Parnes considered to be his true mistress.

"With their exotic titles, these boys sounded less like pop stars than allegorical figures from a medieval moral pageant," Rogan suggests. "The struggles between the Proud and the Eager, the Power and the Fury and the Wilde and the Gentle were no longer restricted to Miracle plays, French romances or Spenserian epics.... Parnes had virtually transformed pop into his own Technicolor epic where moral conceits and aspects of personality took on human form.... This was more than rock management; this was almost a new form of art.... Parnes had become a god, and in the microcosm of pop had unwittingly fulfilled (a) dream—the transmogrification of art into life.... (Parnes') real importance lay in his commitment to youth." Heady praise for a fan who became the angel investor of early British rock.

However, Parnes' failure to anticipate the next wave of guitar-driven groups meant he fumbled opportunities to manage the Silver Beetles and Joe Meek's Tornados, and in 1967 Parnes announced that he had outgrown the world of pop and would be devoting himself to the theatre. "I wasn't interested in signing groups," he would later say. "Groups, as far as I was concerned, didn't exist then. It would have been a question of signing four or five people, which I didn't want." In reality, his peculiar talents had become redundant some years earlier. It would take more than a quiff and a clever name for British rock 'n' roll to come into its own.

ALBERT GROSSMAN

"You are an artist; you can do anything you want."

— *Albert Grossman to Terence Stamp*

IN THE INFAMOUS *Panorama* documentary on Larry Parnes' "stable," Johnny Gentle, Billy Fury, Duffy Power and Vince Eager loll around on a couch in "the Great Provider's" London flat while interviewed by the BBC. Behind them, a toothsome portrait of Tommy Steele, Crown Prince of Parnesdom, beams toothily at his offspring from a gilt-edged place of honor as the first, but certainly not the last, of Larry's boys. When asked if they felt manipulated by name changes and Larry's special sauce that allowed for pot-smoking but not marriage, young Mr. Eager sneers, "It's all up to having faith in your manipulators, in'it?"

At roughly the same time, John Hammond went back to work at Columbia as talent scout, producer and publicist for acts that reigning A&R queen Mitch Miller wouldn't touch. Already in his 50s, Hammond's inherited Vanderbilt wealth provided him with both a sense of entitlement and financial independence. With a combination of exceptional musical taste and a unique idealism, Hammond had launched the careers of Billie Holiday, Count Basie, and Charlie Christian, while encouraging his brother-in-law, Benny Goodman, The King of Swing, to become the first white bandleader to feature black musicians in performance.

Miller, on the other hand, had A and okayed the worst of Tony Bennett, the birth of Johnny Mathis and the ickyness of so much more. Only toffee apples stuck with more retentive glue. Hammond was brought in by the ineffable Goddard Lieberson, something of a corporate Diaghilev greets Gore Vidal. Lieberson was executive in charge of the Columbia Broadcasting Systems' considerable investment in music software and its rivalry with the Radio Corporation of America, cross-town in Manhattan. Always in the forefront of racial integration in public performances, his Carnegie Hall concerts the gold standard in high pop and cultural legitimization, Hammond took to the late '50s folk music scene. He had signed Pete Seeger and rejected Joan Baez (too much money for too few original songs) when he came upon Bob Dylan while A&R stalking Mimi Farina.

Soon enough Hammond and Dylan had a conversation about contracts. Hammond recalls in his autobiography, *John Hammond on Record*:

"I asked him how old he was.

'Twenty.'

'That means you have to have your mother and father sign the contract, too. The New York State laws won't allow a minor to sign a legal agreement without his parents' approval.'

'I don't have a mother or father,' Dylan said.

Did he have any relative who could sign for him?

'I've got an uncle who's a dealer in Las Vegas.'

'You're trying to tell me you don't want anyone to sign for you, aren't you?'

"John,' Dylan said, 'you can trust me.'

And I did."

Bob Dylan and Albert Grossman

It's a lucky young artist who has one commercially astute older pro interested in him. Dylan had at least two: John Hammond who signed him and stuck with him through poor record sales and unprecedented exposure as the "voice of a generation." And Albert Grossman, a manager whose fingerprint on Dylan's art would remain invisible but whose hand on his way of life was for a great run steady and stimulating. Hammond took him to the river; Grossman parted the waters and created the loaves, fishes and platinum copyrights.

Silent and powerful, with one of the greatest talents of the 20th century under his wing and an industry of crooks both at arm's length and at his fingertips, Grossman's position was enviable. Though he often dressed as if he were an accountant undergoing an especially wrenching mid-life crisis, he was in fact one of the boys, a founding member of the American club, revered, respected and enjoyed by the next gang that could, the likes of Shep Gordon, David Geffen and Elliot Roberts. Grossman was the godfather of a new denim-clad, well-dollared pop royalty that would fill the halls of culture with rebel sounds, more controversial for conveying political soundtrites. Grossman was the gatekeeper to a world of talent he had personally cultivated out of a belief in genius and profitability, both his own and that of his clients.

To many, Grossman was an opportunist whose vision of uniting the commercial and artist worlds was at odds with the puritanical folk community. To others, he was a tough son of a bitch whose refusal to compromise his ideals or those of his clients made him a hated, yet respected, man. In the words of Stones and Dylan collaborator Al Kooper, "(He gave his artists) a mighty steel wall façade along with demands that record companies and concert promoters had never encountered before." And what did he get back from his artists? Muses Kooper, "Much more money than I assume they knew about at the time."

At worst, Grossman was a rich bean-counting Hamletic eccentric, who ended his career secluded in Bearsville, New York, the once idyllic world that he had created and ruled — his own Xanadu. At his best, he made his money only with artists of the highest quality and was fiercely loyal to them. While we might thank him or damn him for it, Grossman's coupling of art and commerce, bohemia and business, enabled those who had enough gall and talent to make it out of the cafés and onto the street, with some pit stops at the concert hall, the television studio and the bank. Not to mention Martin Luther King's March on Washington. But the ultimate haven his hard-nosed business practices created for his protégés was a place where one could speak poetry or nonsense and be amongst their own. He might have been a devil to the record companies and the other cogs, but Albert helped a vast new audience to experience a revelation every time one of his artists would enter the chart, and just as importantly in his secondary role as cultural matchmaker, to find each other.

Grossman's view of the world was sharply divided between fakers and poets; having assigned one to either camp, he would cradle or dismiss you without a second thought. But as a freelancing teenager desperate to avoid a day job, I had the fortune to experience another side of Albert Grossman over a few days in 1962 when he and Bob Dylan were re-writing management gospel on the fly. Between the classy commerciality of Peter, Paul and Mary and the train-wreck of Janis Joplin's solo years, Bob and Albert forged an ordination platform of impeccable legitimacy that profoundly empowered each to do his own thing on a scale of historic proportions.

I first met Albert when he was accompanying the then-unknown folk singer to London where Bob was to appear in a BBC drama. I was eighteen and trying to convince myself, my mother, and my clients that I had a career in independent PR. I was having the time of my life. I had clothes, friends, and attitude as I wormed my way into the lives of UK popsters and visiting US stars slogging through a six-week tour, in the course of which my colleagues found me variously amusing, bemusing and, frankly, annoying.

My PR clients Chris Montez, Brian Hyland, and Johnny Tillotson, along with their slick'n nice three button roll collared managers, all helped me to understand how the slightest of opportunities required prodigious effort to extract some payoff from a momentary sighting on the charts. In between his rehearsals for *Madhouse On Castle Street*, my job was to take Dylan around Fleet Street where the soon-to-be youth spokesman plied his rap on coffee-stained lunch-drunk journos. I got the gig by bumping into Albert at the Cumberland Hotel. He took me upstairs to meet his Bobness: they shrugged their shoulders and slightly smiled at one another, and Albert agreed to give me a fiver for the week.

Even then, when "success" was hardly assured, there was never the slightest suggestion that the artist conduct himself in a manner deemed appropriate by his manager. Albert was challenging but his attitudes once assumed proceeded evenly along a predictable track; Dylan's mercurial intelligence, humor, and latent anger were vexing to anyone who did not completely accept him as the star he was in his own mind. And to Dylan the benefits of stardom did not so much reside in fame or money as in his apparently complete confidence that he was playing the role of a lifetime.

New York folkie Mark Spoelstra met Bob the year before and noted, "The first time I met him, he was always acting . . . You can go anywhere you want when you're somebody else." Looking back on a relationship as personal as Dylan had with anyone in his formative years, Joan Baez says, "He has to change . . . and it's a pain in the ass if you're trying to work with him. Or it's a pain in the ass if you were expecting something different from him." Dylan puts it even more succinctly: "I was a musical expeditionary. I had no past."

During that week in London, Dylan and Grossman were inseparable and conspiratorial, a rare occurrence back in the days when management was a marriage of convenience between a pimp and his tart. Grossman's devotion to Dylan was total. He was not there to serve; he was there to deliver. The two of them had something figured out that the rest of the unsuspecting world didn't. Dylan himself has said of the artists that most influenced him, "(There was) something in their eyes. 'I know something you don't know.' I wanted to be that kind of performer." Even then, Grossman's relationship with Dylan had a strong foundation of paternalism underlying its fast moving waters. It was a far cry from my own innings with the Stones, where I was one of the boys, both literally and liberally. Looking back on that day at the Cumberland, I'm surprised I got the gig.

Dylan was wiry and wired, well-heeled and icepick thin, given to deciding without asking. The gray in Bob's face reflected the infinitude of monochromatic shades he discerned in the world about him, while Grossman's Shetland sweater brought out the premature touch of grey in his still business-like coiffure. I was Sidney Falco meets Priscilla, Queen of the Desert in a wasp-waisted, vested suit and Chelsea boots. My life has always been blessed by encounters with incredible ladies and gentlemen who with Zen-like mastery of the present moment knew about me that which I did yet not know about myself.

Fast forward four years that might as well have been four decades, and Grossman would shed his neat sweaters and suits, grow his hair out to a leonine mane he wore in a ponytail, and become the squire of Woodstock where he provided the managerial backdrop against which Dylan would rewrite the possibilities of popular song. Dylan's rise was meteoric but his rocketing career was launched from the *terra firma* of Grossman's careful husbandry.

While many would have to stretch their minds to picture "the Bear" as a round little boy playing with his trains, Albert Grossman was born to two Russian immigrants in Chicago in 1926. The self-described "Jewish businessman" attended Lane Technical High School and graduated from Roosevelt College with a degree in Economics. During his brief stint as a public housing administrator at the Dearborn Homes on Chicago's rough South Side, Grossman was a regular at a club called the Offbeat Room, where he would hang out and take in the breadth of the scene.

It's important to note that Grossman wasn't just a suit amongst the denim denizens. He was a true lover of the music and, as such, the bongo tappers and the sawdust folkies respected him. This land was his land, too, if you follow. But for all their talk of collective action, the folk singers and git pickers of the pre-Fabs, pre-prefab folk scene were a very elitist lot who didn't take to outsiders, especially managers. Managers were devils, capitalists who practiced economic repression of the worker and for whom Marx was a comedian. Still, Grossman was not regarded as an intruder (because he wasn't), but simply someone who was different (which he was.) In many ways, he was an outsider and a bounder, an outcast same as them.

Along with his business sense, it was this ability to see a universe of possibility through a keyhole that propelled Grossman to find and nurture the most influential pop artists of the decade. Together they delivered "capital A" Art and turned it into "capital C" Capital while demanding previously unheard of artistic control from Grossman's strategic business partners. Grossman was determined that the medium of commercial music would never obscure his artists' message. A new generation demanded diversity and integrity in its entertainment; Albert fostered a wide-open psychic space in which artist and audience could promiscuously explore their bonds to each other and their differences from the establishment they both wished to overturn.

Grossman became a fixture on New York's Greenwich Village scene, holding court at various coffeehouses in silent contemplation, smoking his cigarettes in that odd way that he had. Al Kooper remembers it vividly: "He'd place a lit cigarette between his 4th and 5th fingers, then close his fist, and draw the air out from the hole created by his thumb and second finger. He'd smoke the entire cigarette like that. Never saw anybody else do that in my entire life."

Dave Van Ronk was one Village fixture who found Grossman's naked ambition both powerful and somewhat off-putting. Although he and Grossman flirted with the idea of his joining the "supergroup" that would become Peter, Paul and Mary, Van Ronk was never comfortable taking Albert at his word. Speaking to Dylan biographer Bob Spitz, Van Ronk recounted a time when Grossman caught him in the headlights. "I ran into Albert at a party and before long we were off in a corner together, ruminating about the business. 'Dave,' he said, 'I know how I can make a fortune for you. If this doesn't work, I just don't know the business, and to show you how sure I am of it I will personally guarantee you a three hundred thousand dollars gross for your first year.' As Albert saw it, I didn't have to change my style of singing or my repertoire, I just had to change my name—to Olaf the Blues Singer—and I had to wear a helmet with horns growing out of it and pretend to be blind. I laughed, thinking the scheme was a marvelous joke, but he wasn't kidding. He wanted to turn me into a novelty act, not out of avarice or marketability, but because it would prove that I was corruptible. Integrity bothered Albert; he used to say that there was no such thing as an honest man, and it was merely a question of finding out what my price was, even if it cost him three hundred thousand dollars of his own money. That was the kind of guy Albert really was."

Oh well, Van Ronk never really had the look Albert was seeking. It was at the Café Wha? on MacDougal Street that Grossman saw him standing there. Him being one Mr. Peter Yarrow, the first "P" in Peter, Paul and Mary, whom Grossman would assemble from the ground up to the top of the charts via a cover of Dylan's "Blowin' In The Wind." Equally inspired by the beat writers and the French new wave cinema, New York produced whilst London lounged. Small wonder that one scene birthed a Picasso from one born Zimmerman and the other spawned Donovan, the ultimate Starbucks artist.

"Grossman walked out in the middle of my show the first time he saw me," remembers Yarrow. "He later told me he had some place to go and had seen all he needed to see." Grossman's instincts were both of the minute and in for the long haul; like Sam Phillips forced by his secretary to audition a recording Elvis made for his mother as a birthday gift, Albert was decisive when his needs came into unexpected alignment with his wants.

Grossman and Yarrow found Mary hung up on a wall. Well, at least her picture, which they came across at the Folklore Center, run by Izzy Young, which Travers described as "a little store where Izzy put up pictures of everybody who's ever uttered a note of a folk song," including, of course, Mary Travers.

"I saw a picture of Mary, and I said, 'Who's that?'" Yarrow recollected, "because she was just bursting with energy and very beautiful and all that, and Albert said, 'Oh, she's terrific, if you could get her to work.'" And they did, which left the trinity only one short. Then Albert found his Paul, Noel Stookey at birth, and the furthest thing from a folk singer. Never mind that the only song he could sing that Mary and Peter knew was "Mary Had A Little Lamb"; the register was perfect, the unity of elements complete.

Mary might have been a serendipitous missing link, but she was the key to Albert's plan. An interview with John Cohen of the New Lost City Ramblers in the documentary *No Direction Home* reveals a telling anecdote. Mary Travers had been working with the group in Florida and had just returned to wintery Manhattan when Cohen bumped into her in the Village. He's amazed to find her as fair as if she'd spent the past few months in her apartment. She explains that "Albert wants me to be the pale, blonde, indoor type." Commenting in the *Boston Phoenix*, Jon Garelick concludes: "There you have it—folk authenticity packaged as pop commodity. Yet has there ever been a folk group more committed to their ideals, sticking through one leftist cause after another through decades?" Note that at the time, Cohen was offended by Mary's willingness to follow the script.

It's not much different from me entering a party off Baker Street in the early spring of 1964, seeing Marianne Faithfull sitting on a radiator by the window and knowing another ship had just come in. She breathed and her breasts strained heavenwards, she talked and I knew I could hear her singing. I left the party with strains of Grace Kelly's duet with Bing Crosby on "True Love" from 1957's *High Society* caroling me home on a note of hopeful ambition.

Or wandering the streets of Soho in a desperate funk to find the Rolling Stones a hit song that would complement the rising hysteria of their live performances and running into Lennon and McCartney. Resplendent and slightly drunk in their four-button bespoke Dougie Millings suits, John and Paul gave the Stones much more than a silly song guaranteed to chart. By pretending the song was "unfinished" and proceeding to work it out on the spot in the Stones' rehearsal space, Mick and Keith were treated to an unforgettable example of the Beatles' creativity in action, an experience that appealed to their competitive natures and drew them closer together, even as it served to push Brian Jones, who didn't quite get it, farther away. To Brian, what was important was that through the Beatles he might become successful; to Mick and Keith, success became writing so many good songs, you could give them away.

Stookey tipped off Grossman to go see this kid named Bob Dylan, who, like Grossman, was accepted by the folkies, but was also recognized by them as being different. Grossman was interested in Dylan, but was committed to seeing his vision of a popular three-piece folk group through. After shopping the group around (this would be the last time Grossman would need to do such a thing), Albert decided that Atlantic Records would be their home. A contract for the release of their single, Pete Seeger's "Where Have All The Flowers Gone?", was drafted with Atlantic Records Vice President Jerry Wexler.

The deal was sealed, but not signed and delivered. The day the session was supposed to take place, Wexler got a call from Grossman: "Mary has laryngitis." Even with the passing of time, this move still strikes you for what it was—not dishonest, but coldly calculated and shrewd. Grossman would repeat this "Manhattan purchase"-style deal when he bought out Dylan's publishing contract with Leeds Music. Hammond tells the story in a way reminiscent of my sending Brian Jones off with £90 to purchase the

Stones' earliest masters from Glyn Johns and IBC Studios. IBC had obtained a six-month option on the group in return for letting them record five songs with Johns. So Brian was coached into a pathetic story about "needing his freedom to pursue different aspects of his career" and a gentlemanly set of studio owners bought the jive and set Jones free.

Back on slightly higher ground, John Hammond recalls that "(Dylan) sang 'Blowin' in the Wind' one night in a Greenwich Village joint before his record was out. Peter, Paul and Mary happened to hear it, liked it, and took it to their manager, Albert Grossman, to arrange for recording it on their next album for Warner Brothers Records. Their songs were being published by Artie Mogull of Warner Brothers and when he heard 'Wind' he wanted it. Of course, Dylan told him that Lou Levy had already signed him for all his songs. Mogull said he thought he could take care of that. 'How much advance did they give you?' he asked. "Five hundred," Dylan said. Mogull handed him $1,000. "Why don't you go find out if you can buy your contract back?"

Grossman renegotiated Dylan's first contract with Columbia on the grounds that Dylan was a minor when he signed it, much to Hammond's chagrin, of course. The too-trusting John Hammond and Columbia's newest legal ace, Clive Davis, managed to extend Dylan's original three-year contract long enough to enjoy the sales that eluded them on the first two albums, but Grossman remained a stone in Columbia's shoe for the remainder of their profitable relationship.

Apparently his protean capacity for deal-making couldn't be confined to taking major labels on a ride. Grossman began to show an interest in Bennett Glotzer's small business when he learned Glotzer had received a lucrative settlement from his stint as co-manager of Blood Sweat & Tears. Knowing of Glotzer's admiration for him, Albert offered him a partnership in his management firm for the exact amount of the settlement. If Bennett had hair, it would have been flying back at that time as he rushed to Albert's office to close the deal. Once ensconced, Albert let Bennett bring Glotzer's management roster in and Bennett was only allowed to deal with the same artists he was already managing. Albert slyly pocketed Glotzer's BS&T settlement and that as they say, was THAT.

Sharp-shooting aside, Grossman's most precious contribution to the game was undying belief in the magic of his artists—their innate abilities to create their visions and give them over to the people. Grossman's magic was to provide the circumstances that would let them do this unconstrained by the tentacles of the business. Before Grossman, record companies told performers what to record and when. In an interview for his study of the music business, then and now, *The Mansion on the Hill*, Fred Goodman suggests, "Albert Grossman is a guy who has always been portrayed as the evil manager of Bob Dylan. And that just doesn't do the guy justice. He's the guy who said, 'Bob Dylan's a real artist. He should do whatever the hell he wants—and who the hell are you? You are just the goddamn record company.' . . . Everybody talks about Brian Epstein, the Beatles' manager—the Beatles had bad deals. They got half a penny a record. Or Col. Tom Parker, the legendary manager of Elvis. What did he do for Elvis? He helped him make a lot of bad B movies."

Fifty-two years after Diaghilev sparked a riot with his premiere of *Le Sacre Du Printemps*, the Newport Folk Festival of 1965 found Grossman literally coming to blows with the purists over Mike Bloomfield's right to plug in his guitar, while the next day Dylan's electric debut brought tears of grief to mentor Pete Seeger's eyes. Jac Holzman, founder of Elektra Records, depicts the scene vividly in his memoir, *Follow the Music*: ". . . On the Saturday afternoon of the 1965 festival there was a blues workshop. Alan Lomax was hosting the black traditionalists. Alan was the son of John Lomax, two great white collectors, for whom traditional music seemed to freeze-frame about the time of the Tennessee Valley Authority. Alan was the last protector and refuge of the lone voice from Mutton Hollow.

"The second segment of the workshop was slated to be white urban blues, featuring the Butterfield Band. Due to the amazing sales of 'Born In Chicago' on the Elektra sampler, and the buzz that went with it, I had arranged for them to perform at Newport. Albert Grossman, the manager of Bob Dylan and Peter, Paul and Mary, was in full hover over them as future clients."

Lomax couldn't resist slighting the very young and very white boys up next by taunting the crowd of a thousand folkies, "Let's see if they can play this hardware at all." Paul Rothchild picks up the story: "Grossman took it the worst way. Lomax comes down from this little stage and Grossman coldcocks him. And for about the next five minutes these two leviathans, monsters, both kings in their own right . . . (are) groveling in the dusty dirt of Newport over the Paul Butterfield Blues Band. It was wonderful. Holzman was laughing his ass off."

For Grossman "freedom" wasn't just another word for nothing left to lose; it was the keystone of all his business dealings. Warner Bros. executive Stan Cornyn remembers of Peter, Paul and Mary, "they would take as long as they wanted to record their album. Deliver it when it was finished and mastered to their satisfaction. Ignoring entirely any schedules we had set for its manufacture. And they would deliver the artwork for the front and back. This was unheard of. Unheard of!" Speaking of the *Highway 61 Revisited* sessions of '65, producer Bob Johnston says, "There were no clocks (in that studio). I took them all down. It wasn't like four songs a session and out."

Dylan had noted with financial satisfaction and aesthetic disdain the chart success "rock" artists such as the Byrds, Sonny and Cher, and the Turtles had been having with covers of his songs like "Mr. Tambourine Man" and "All I Really Want to Do." His competitive response was the first US radio hit to ever run over five minutes. Remember that the length of a single had been determined decades earlier by the number of grooves that could be squeezed onto a 78-RPM lacquer disc. Despite advances in phonograph technology which allowed for up to 20 minutes per side of a long-player, radio was happy to squeeze more hits into every hour, leaving room for more commercials. The Rolling Stones' debut single, "Come On," released just two years previously, ran to one minute and forty-nine seconds, which seemed quite enough time to get the point across. Slugging it out for the biggest hit of the summer of 1965 with the Stones' "Satisfaction" and the Beatles' "Help" was Dylan's six minute masterwork, "Like A Rolling Stone."

It was at that moment that the new, exciting, dangerous, sexy, improbable and offensively hip world shot its way into the collective consciousness and into living rooms from Ohio to Manchester. It was a rock and roll poem—a blast of pure youth fired with the precision of a marksman. To the folk claque that had long been harboring resentment of Dylan and Grossman for defiling the holy order by being ambitious and daring enough to break free from their constraints, it was sacrilege set to a backbeat. To Columbia Records, it was black gold. But to Grossman, it was proof that his undying belief in the abilities of his prodigal son had paid off. Dylan was an Artist—and the streets shook with his new sound.

The sound was the ultimate hustle, a direct connection between the madcap world of Napoleon in rags and the bums and their dimes and the finest schools and the mystery tramps and the millions of people who, whether they knew or it not, needed to be shown that world. It was also, as many hustles go, a necessary act of rebellion—a call to war and a dividing line. This was the golden child of the folk movement, the Jewish Woody Guthrie, the male Joan Baez, turning his back on tattered workman's shirts and conventional protest music. Now Dylan was simply himself and the one who was dressing so fine.

The turns that Dylan took between his first album and *Highway 61 Revisited* occurred so rapidly within such a short amount of time that one can easily forget that between each new album, there was a progression that was far more orderly and organic than any imagined directive from Grossman to "go electric" or "stop being folk." Each record was a new statement, a new set of questions. After you heard "A Hard Rain's A-Gonna Fall" from the second album, "Pretty Peggy-O" from the first seemed as archaic as Blind Lemon Jefferson.

During these years, Dylan played many roles: the vagabond acolyte of Woody Guthrie, Joan Baez's lover and rival, the love-sick man-child, the stoned visionary hipster, the absurdist pop star, the hated sell-out and finally, the motorcycle martyr. You can hear all of these characters on his early records. Sometimes they carry over from one to the next, but more often than not, they morph into someone new, someone who Dylan wanted to become and who Grossman wanted to see him become. After all, following each release, Dylan was playing bigger venues and selling more records.

After cutting his teeth on dead blues singers and Victorian ballads, who was better equipped to lead the movement than the stern denim-clad protest singer on the cover of *The Times They Are A Changin'*? Yet six months later a seemingly confused romantic brought us "To Ramona" and "Spanish Harlem Incident." Only to return to his rock 'n' roll roots with *Bringing All Back Home*, almost certainly inspired as much by the Beatles as they would then be inspired by him. By now it was clear to all what Dylan himself had always known: he belonged to no one but himself. Albert Grossman had made sure of that.

Unlike Brian Epstein, who could have continued running his father's record shop instead of managing the group responsible for keeping those shops in business, Albert lived out his bohemian dreams with his clients and not through them. Pennebaker recalls of the 1965 tour that provided all of the footage for *Don't Look Back*, "When we went to England and were hanging out with the Beatles, we never saw Epstein. They had nothing to do with him. He was like some outsider, and they always made slighting references to him. But Albert hung out with us all the time. Dylan really liked that. He was kind of a father."

Al Kooper's take is Brooklyn rye with seeds: "Dylan's relationship with Grossman was the Jewish equivalent of Elvis to the Colonel; Albert painted Dylan into the Savior of All Things Worthwhile in the '60s and kept him secluded as much as possible." This was the tip that Tony DeFries was to adapt maladroitly in the early '70s as he sheltered Bowie from the press and showered him on the street. The true evolutionary step was Shep Gordon and Alice Cooper who raised taking the piss to a new high and profited from it, while controlling the press like political operatives shepherding Bill Clinton.

It shows Albert's preference for the singular, however. After Peter, Paul and Mary, he seemed to accept groups as reluctantly as Larry Parnes. He waxed wrathful when Paul Butterfield sought to share his new deal with the band, and threatened to cancel it. It is rumored that Albert selected Robbie Robertson as the brains behind the Band and cut a clandestine deal with him. Years later, after Grossman's demise, all royalties went to Robbie and the others were cut off. Details regarding your financial legacy were not questions Albert encouraged, evidently.

But by the dawn of the '70s, Albert had fostered Bearsville Records and his few employees were dedicated, talented, and productive. The artistic centerpiece of the fledgling label, Todd Rundgren, is not so often these days closely associated with Albert. But taking Todd from under-appreciated solo debuts on the short-lived Ampex (makers of studio recording tape) label, Albert also employed Todd's friend and associate, Paul Fishkin. A former apothecary who had begun to dabble in band management until he found his calling as a radio promotion man, Fishkin mentored a 17-year-old under assistant in Marc Nathan willing to call 200 stations a week if necessary.

Albert had encouraged Todd to spend time at his then new and very artful Bearsville Studios. The result was that the self-taught wunderkind engineered the Band's understated pop success, *Stage Fright*. Todd went on to his own Top 40 hit with "I Saw the Light" on Bearsville while producing even bigger hits for the likes of Grand Funk, on Capitol (who also had The Band). Later, Grossman gave Fishkin enough rope to develop

Foghat into one of the most successful "album oriented radio" acts of the mid-'70s. All of this is to say that Albert was a fine record man in his own way, as well as a producer of magic shows. As to his passing the largesse forward, young Marc soon enough was able to pay for a nice one bedroom in Chelsea.

Mike Friedman, who worked with Rundgren between his Ampex and Bearsville deals, told Goodman in *Mansion* that, "It was essentially a business of children and outcasts. It was such a primitive business that no one really knew how to do it. The rules were being created, and he was just making it up as he went along." Today, benefactors of rock's own civil rights movement, like Jack White of the White Stripes, control their publishing, recording, management and touring, accepting such creative freedom as a birthright as natural as Diddy's right to vote.

Nowhere was this made more clear than in Grossman's protection of the media-weary Dylan. If the first job of the hustler is to convince the artist and later the world of their greatness, the second is protecting that greatness from coming under damaging scrutiny. While the Fabs would smile and take their medals and crack jokes about those not with it, Dylan would taunt them with cryptic and often nonsensical remarks. But this was nothing compared to lashings they would receive from Grossman.

Peter Yarrow recalled to Robert Shelton in 1970, "(Grossman) kept us insulated from the flesh-peddling aspect of show business. Next to Albert, Dylan was an amateur at cutting people down. Albert is an expert at destroying other peoples' sense of self." This was true—one need only look at the famous scene in *Don't Look Back* when Grossman answers to charges of loud noise coming from Dylan's room and the question of who was in charge of Bob Dylan with a torrent of curse words and the now legendary demand,

"I'm not in charge of Bob Dylan . . . but I want you to leave this room at once. We've got valuables in here [camera on Dylan] and I need you to leave." Yarrow further explained the bonds between Dylan and Grossman. "(Albert) is very shy and very cynical because he has seen friends corrupted. He is also an idealist. (Dylan) was imitating everyone at one stage and he naturally began to imitate and learn a lot of Albert's tricks. I think that Albert stimulated Bobby a great deal."

By 1966, the sheer number of opportunities (and obligations) that Grossman was creating for Dylan was proving to be detrimental to both his artist and their relationship. Between performing with Robbie Robertson and the Hawks to a soundtrack of insults and boos on a grueling world tour, Dylan began a second tour film, "Eat The Document," which would be rejected by ABC-TV as far too impressionistic for would-be advertisers. Stretched to his limits, the boy genius was starting to crack. In this dawn of mass communication, Dylan was everywhere and yet, nowhere. His work was very much accessible to the public and his presence in the cultural marketplace was felt everywhere, yet he was becoming increasingly removed from even the chosen few who had always been satellites in his universe. Grossman's attention to Dylan was becoming his domination of him.

While it is a caretaker's job to provide all he can for his star, he must also recognize that complete satiation does not an artist make. There must always be something missing, that the artist intuitively relies on the manager to provide. Once a growing boy has had his fill of milk, the need for someone to hold the bottle disappears. It is a sad fact of the hustle that the best hustlers ultimately eliminate themselves from the picture. In the case of Grossman and Dylan, the famous July 1966 motorcycle accident that took Bob out of sight and out of commission expedited this process and perhaps saved both of them from a great deal more pain down the road. With Grossman reported to have asked the question, "How could he do this to me? Does he have any idea how much it takes to set up forty concerts?" while Dylan was still in his hospital gown, it was becoming apparent that things were coming to an end between the two.

Dylan, laid up in Grossman's Woodstock in the months after his accident and following his recovery, used his newly rediscovered legs to walk out on Albert, just as he had walked out of Minnesota and the coffeehouses on West Fourth Street and all those people he said goodbye to in "It's All Over Now, Baby Blue".

Surely Dylan was concerned about how much of his bread was feeding Grossman, but to chalk their fall out up to money is as simplistic as saying that "Like A Rolling Stone" is a great song because it earned both of them considerable sums. Fred Goodman observes, ". . . I can't find a moment in Dylan's career when he makes a record for money. He gets as much money as he can from the record company, but show me the record he made to be a hit. There's no moment in his career like that moment in Springsteen's career when Landau's going, 'God damn it, let's have that hit already.'"

Personally, I don't believe it was merely a fortunate meeting of the times and a song that sent "Like A Rolling Stone" to the top. I think it was Bob's intention to take back some of the glory that the Beatles and Stones were reaping by stretching themselves to live up to his example. But while pride and ego may have played a role in the single's creation, it was certainly not a commercial calculation. Dylan risked the large audience of folkies he already had without any certainty that the younger fans besotted by the British Invasion would include him in their fave raves.

Simply, Dylan had fallen out of love with being the prodigal son and thus had to remove himself from his provider and father figure. The hustler finds peace through his work and in moments of loss and confusion, can only hope to have his passion reignited by another set of jewels to polish. Grossman was blessed to find two more in Janis Joplin and Robbie Robertson and the Band, but by this time the environment for making music had become so filled with booze and drugs and so toxic that Grossman could do no more as a manager and a friend than to keep his artists afloat. No longer able to impart his vision to them, Grossman was instead faced with the task of propping them up and getting them to see straight. He was still hustling, but his artists failed to hustle back. Goodman suggests, "Grossman is a guy who's not really interested in being a big business mogul. He likes money, he gets it, and then he goes off and he grows pot in upstate N.Y. and sits around and eats a lot. That's what he wanted to do, God love him."

The Eden that Grossman had created in Bearsville that birthed phenomenal work from Dylan, the Band and Van Morrison was short-lived. The once safe haven for Grossman and his "people" and for Dylan and his art had now become a zoo filled with sycophantic hippies prowling its grassy knolls hoping to catch a glimpse of someone famous writing a song, getting high or fucking. Al Kooper dryly puts in his oar on paradise in the Catskills: "Albert, for all intents and purposes, founded Woodstock as The Hamptons of the '60s. He had a nice spread up there and Dylan would spend a great deal of time hiding from the world at Albert's estate. After a while, Albert steered Bob to a place of his own in the immediate area where Grossman could still keep his eye on his client.

"Musicians and know-it-alls flocked to Woodstock along with real estate agents to move as close as they could to The Savior of All Things Worthwhile. Soon, what was good about Woodstock was instantly destroyed by all these invaders. Woodstock, the Festival, completed the destruction. Today, it bears no resemblance whatsoever to the sleepy little innocent hamlet it was before Albert came along residents-wise."

I was in Bearsville in 1978. I had married in London in 1977, travelling with my wife Esther to honeymoon in New York. Studio 54 opened and we decided to stay awhile. I was looking for a project and found the Werewolves, a Texas band that had come to Manhattan to make it big. I took on their management and produced two records for them on RCA. My breakup with the Stones was by now nearly a decade in the past, but it had taken me that long to commit to a long-term rock 'n' roll hustle. I recorded up in Bearsville at Albert's studio, because not only was it a state of the art facility, but I needed the time to bond with the band away from the distractions of Manhattan.

I took a break one day to visit one of the gourmet restaurants Albert had opened for his own enjoyment. At one point he'd whisked an up and coming Chinese food maven from his job as a maître d' into one of the many homes he owned in Bearsville on a day's notice. He wanted "The Bear" to serve only the finest, most authentic and rare regional cuisine in a beautiful Victorian house that also came to include an ice cream parlor stocked by direct deliveries from the plant in Philadelphia. His manager, young Ed Schoenfeld, was charged with hiring the Chinese chef and kitchen help, who Albert put up in a former motel he owned. The Chinese loved having exclusive access to the motel pool on sunny days. And what he was paying them to live in upstate New York, one can only guess.

You couldn't spend any time in Bearsville without eventually running into the burg's lord and master, so when I spied an anorak'd grizzly Albert, I re-introduced myself. He remembered me; we asked each other after time. He was knowing in the wind with a sadness that was overcoming. My own consciousness was certainly altered by one of the various "serial addictions" with which I constantly flirted and I'm sure a wave of "Where have all the good times gone?" swept over me. I will never forget the upward tilt of his chin, his all-seeing eyes peering at me through his granny glasses as if I were asking Ben Franklin to bail me out of a gambling debt. It was almost goodbye Mr. Chips-ish; the headmaster had spotted a long ago student whom by now should have settled down.

Yet Albert seemed heavy for reasons of his own; the Chinese restaurants and ice cream parlors, even a classy boutique imprint at Warners, couldn't possibly occupy the man who had once dedicated his life to letting Bob be Bob. Discomfited by what I felt was his unspoken criticism of my wayward career and lifestyle, it seemed somehow we had come full circle together, though years apart in age. He was already wondering what would become of both of us. I felt him miss the Cumberland Hotel.

BRIAN EPSTEIN

"He was very good. He started like we did. He didn't know the game, neither did we, really. We knew how to play, and he tidied us up and moved us on."

— *Ringo Starr*

Young Brian Epstein

BY THE MID-1960s, the whole world appeared to have become successful. Anyone who could master three chords, squeeze into tight pants and manage a falsetto yeah-yeah-yeah was inciting riots among screaming dolly birds. God had evidently looked down into the bowels of post-World War Britain and worked out which wee bairns would emerge from the nursery as pop singers in embryo. Because God is Good he gave them all great hair.

Food and the little luxuries of life were not the only things that had been rationed during the years of privation; the overwhelming cost of "victory" had tended to make the stiff upper lip even stiffer. Now, an entire generation had passed since the ruinous peace was declared, and emotions that had been kept in check were suddenly unleashed at the first signs of returning prosperity. The kids were determined to have their day and their way.

And just as determined to relieve them of their shillings and pence was an army of would-be Johnny Jacksons. Skuzzy Odeons from Liverpool to Brighton, which had scarcely recovered from the damage done by *Blackboard Jungle*, now hosted one package tour after another. The motorways were jammed with the bright sparks of the moment hustling their way from London to the industrial midlands in order to make a hasty back-stage appearance before speeding off back down the B-road.

Brian Epstein and the Beatles started a disease.

Hordes of misfits used fashion to scoff at the hard-earned toe-hold on middle class respectability their elders had struggled to bequeath them. Shopping became the favorite past-time of young males as well as young girls: basics from Burton's and Hepworth's were accessorized by a little Daks or Simpson's with an assist from Austin Reed. If for whatever reason one was reluctant to pick up a guitar, a smart appearance and a freshly printed "business" card were all the more de rigueur. Poor dental cosmetics were no barrier to a smile that said to the latest "undiscovered" beat group, "I think I might be able to help you."

If one were reasonably well spoken and well-dressed one might find oneself enjoying the right sort of bar with the man himself. But Brian would have been better dressed than you and probably glancing at his gold wristwatch because he had other places to visit that night. Once he left the exclusive night spots we managerial types frequented on our rare evenings off—the Ad Lib, the Cromwellian, and the Scotch of St. James—he sauntered off into the night to even darker venues where neither his money nor his success were likely to impede the rough treatment he was after.

Love and companionship were likely not his goals. A product of his unenlightened times, Brian sought in his most private moments a validation of his shame. In public the luminous Alma Cogan provided Brian with an image polite society could not help but admire and approve. It was even rumored that Alma and Brian contemplated a sort of marriage to each other. The highest paid female performer in Britain, Alma was equally famous for the fabulous all-night parties she threw in her Kensington flat. Likely to meet the Beatles, as Paul ran through the yet to be titled "Yesterday," were Cary Grant, Lionel Bart, Noel Coward, Sammy Davis Jr. or Princess Margaret. One wonders if Cynthia Lennon had occasion to draw Brian aside to ask discreetly if he would interrupt the lively flirtation her husband was conducting with the older star he nicknamed "Sara Sequin."

Perhaps it was the rejection of his true personality Brian carried with him throughout his life which prepared him for the challenge of the Beatles, who were certainly nobody's darlings until they were everybody's. Brian's unwavering belief in his

Boys, if not himself, gave him a will of steel. Like innovators in any field, the Beatles were considered to be impossible before they became unavoidable.

Before the Beatles, rock 'n' roll in Britain was merely a Yank wannabe, a road to nowhere traveled by coquettish, gypsy eyebrowed, greasily quiffed rockeroos who were successful to the extent that their curled lips and fake American accents excited equally the Evening Standard's pop writer Nik Cohn and the legions of hot-to-trot dizzy miss lizzies newly liberated by the Pill.

As an eighteen-year-old freelance publicist, my first exposure to the Beatles set my heart racing, and the affair took wing once I'd met them. I'd prided myself on knowing the difference between the real American deal in pop music and its pale British imitation—"Love Me Do," the Beatles' first Parlophone single, sounded remarkably more like the former than the latter. The mood was more like sex than skiffle and yet the overall effect was as British as bangers and mash. In those days, records spoke to me with intimacy and impact and I looked forward to sharing more pillow talk with the Liverpudlian foursome.

We met a couple of months later at a rehearsal for television's Thank Your Lucky Stars. I was with my client Mark Wynter, who was promoting his cover version of "Venus in Blue Jeans," which might fairly have been said to represent pop's past rather than its future. As I watched the Beatles run through their second single, "Please Please Me," their sound became three dimensional. Love was in the air and I was certainly not alone in my infatuation. There was a rough readiness about the Beatles that their Epstein-coordinated togs could not altogether camouflage.

I went up to John Lennon and told him he was good. He agreed. When I asked who handled their business, John pointed over his shoulder to an elegantly dressed somewhat older gent who indeed looked all-business, despite his jaunty paisley silk scarf. Brian was chatting with Ringo though his attention seemed elsewhere. It's often easier to talk to the drummer when you're distracted and you've got nothing to say—they don't mind, they are elsewhere as well.

I button-holed Brian and talked him into letting me represent the Beatles in London. By that time I'd racked up a bit of a track record with the press and radio and heaven knows, at 19 and self-employed, I was cheap enough. Besides, it appeared no one else had asked, proving once more Woody Allen's maxim: "Eighty percent of success is showing up."

Liverpool was a long way away from London in those days, and people didn't like to make long distance phone calls, except to report a death or a marriage. I would eventually make extensive use of one of the first car phones to be found in the UK, but at this stage of the Beatles' career toll calls were out and a personal touch was what was needed. Tony Barrow had been sending out press releases, moonlighting from his day job at Parlophone's rival Decca, but Brian was too busy to be the boys' minder and could use a loyal pair of eyes and ears when they were far from home.

A month later, the Beatles were on tour with Helen Shapiro and Chris Montez at the Granada Bedford when I succumbed to one of the most truly surreal, drug-free epiphanies it's ever been my good fortune to experience. The Beatles had started the tour at the bottom of the bill and were moving up it in increments as "Please, Please Me" climbed the charts.

By Bedford, they were closing the first half of the show but there was no doubt whom the noisiest and most hysterical fans in the audience had come to see. The pandemonium was reaching Johnnie Ray levels with a mere 300 or so punters raising a din more worthy of 3000. Paul, in particular, grew a whiter shade of pale as one by one the kids broke the backstage windows and shards of glass exploded a few feet from where the boys were smoking fags and drinking Coke. For as long as it lasted their lives would never be the same; as it happened the screams never stopped for a long seven years and beyond. The impact that being with the Beatles in the beginning had on my own ambitions was incalculable.

In their very early twenties, the Beatles were both worldly from their sojourns to Hamburg and naïve in that no one could have predicted how dramatically things would change for them and the world at large in the next few years. They were completely "Alternative" without any real thought of being so. And it all started with those guitars, stunning as Bren guns, and those songs they wrote themselves.

For all the windows he opened upon rock 'n' roll's future, however, Brian Epstein was a false alarm, a slightly more cultured, or coddled, version of Larry Parnes, without the veneer of seamy experience. He was skittish, hysterical, arrogant and insecure—which shouldn't have barred him from his chosen career as an actor had he possessed talent in addition. Upon leaving school and an unsuccessful stint at RADA, he resigned himself to his lot in life and threw himself into his parents' business, a Liverpool furniture store, with a sideline in sheet music, instruments and phonograph records (The North End Music Stores). In fact, the Beatles were customers before they were clients.

Born in Liverpool on September 19th, 1934, he was a Virgo born to Lithuanian Jews. Virgos are fastidious, Jews often are. "Fastidious" is not the first adjective that comes to mind when one is describing Liverpool. So as much as he might have been taken by the Beatles' cheek, they were not as he found them perhaps the right sort in Brian's eyes. He takes the four rowdy but adorable lads, scrubs them up and makes history. A bit later, I encouraged some rather better kempt youth to muck about and get dirty.

Whatever Brian's personal and professional liabilities and shortcomings may have been, we are all his legacy. He is the cake that got left out in the rain, the yellow brick toad we walked over on our way to the top, the mantelpiece that was leaned against in such awful TV programs as the BBC Arena deathfest that "celebrated" Brian's life some half dozen Christmases ago.

His former organization trolled across the TV screen; the Miss Moneypennys, who seemed to lack a bit of a life after Brian, drove past his Belgravia house describing tearfully the last harrowing months. A couple of males leaned against the mantelpiece and confirmed how well meaning, disorganized and dizzy he was, vexed after all these years that damned few knew how damned good they were at doing his job. (He wrote to his secretary in the year of his death, "be a bit tolerant of me at my worst.") Gerry Marsden of the Pacemakers implied that he was one of the few true friends Brian had. God bless you Gerry, were that Brian's life had been that simple.

Of course, despite the pretensions of those interviewed for *Arena*, Brian did not "make" the Beatles single-handedly. George Martin, Norman Smith, and Ron Richards were joined later by such luminaries as director Richard Lester and PR hustling saint extraordinaire, Derek Taylor. Of all those who shared Brian's unwavering belief, it is perhaps our greatest loss that Derek was no longer available to set the record straight.

Taylor was a Liverpool lad, twenty years the Beatles' senior, and a jaundiced veteran journalist by the time he saw the Beatles for the first time, at the Manchester Odeon in May 1963. In his review the next day he wrote: "The Liverpool Sound came to Manchester last night, and I thought it was magnificent . . . The spectacle of these fresh, cheeky, sharp, young entertainers in opposition to the shiny-eyed teenage idolaters is as good as a rejuvenating drug for the jaded adult."

On that we all agreed.

Derek interviewed Brian Epstein, who gave the go-ahead for him to ghost a "column" by George Harrison, with whom he grew to be especially close. After penning Epstein's "autobiography," *A Cellarful of Noise*, in 1964, Taylor became Epstein's personal assistant, scriptwriter and Beatles press agent, travelling the world with the band. He moved to LA to helm his own public relations company, where Paul Revere and the Raiders, the Byrds and the Beach Boys were touched by his magic. And when the love boat launched in 1967 at the Monterey Pop Festival, Derek Taylor was there to help explain it to a mainstream press still catching their breath from the "British Invasion." Only Derek could have placed a garland of hippie beads around the neck of the Monterey Chief of Police and made him like it. He set a very high standard, an example that we entrepreneurial types such as myself and Kit Lambert did well to emulate.

When Derek returned to England and the Beatles' newly-formed Apple Corps in 1968, he would become a jovial Albert Speer to the frustrated band, orphaned by Brian Epstein's sudden death and now all marching to a different drum. It was Derek who could give voice to the lads' inchoate aspirations, taking their occasional tantrums in stride, with strokes of attitude and wordism that define the time today. He was truly the man who told the world.

After we were both super-successes and ostensible rivals for the lucrative affections of beat crazed teens around the world, Brian and I had our own awkward television moment. His super soft Pringle-tailored suits notwithstanding, Brian was uncomfortable in his role as sometime British host of the leading American pop show Hullabaloo! By September 1964, we had closed the gap somewhat with the Beatles and television was proving to be much better to the Stones than radio. Brian's second-tier was by then well populated by the likes of the Pacemakers and Billy J. Kramer, but I myself was very well pleased to be promoting our own first extra-Stones release, all the more so since Marianne's "As Tears Go By" was a Jagger-Richard-Oldham composition.

Up to my eyeballs in speed, I'd have denied my name was Andrew had Brian asked the question directly. Gracious as ever, he let me flop around on his line while he informed the American audience that I had once worked for him, no doubt wondering to himself if he could have had the Stones had he kept me.

I was jolted back to real time when Epstein pitched me an innocent softball question that was actually anything but. "How did the Stones and I enjoy recording in Los Angeles?" He might as well have asked when we were letting Marianne out of the dungeon—by no stretch of the American musicians' union rules or the interests of the Internal Revenue Service were we permitted to be doing any such thing, albeit the fruit of our surreptitious labors was "Satisfaction." Brian seemed satisfied with my non-answer and I got a glimpse of how it felt to be one of his acts, in a word, "nice." I'm lucky there was no YouTube back then to permanently archive the gaffe.

As for whether Brian might have had the Stones, it's true. He might have. Back when I first saw the Stones, I knew I would need an experienced partner. The band needed work above all else, and I was not a booking agent, nor at 19 could I have been legally licensed as such. I had terrible doubts about partnering up with my landlord, Eric Easton, who was a booking agent. Besides, it was my duty, based either on the ethic my mother had taught me or that I had picked up in the cinema, to call my present employer, Brian Epstein, and let him know what I was up to, and at least sort of offer him an interest in the Rolling Stones. I did, but I hoped he was not listening; he was not, so I made my bed with agent Eric Easton and the Stones jumped in with me. As Dino might have put it, "Memories are made of this . . . ."

On the face of it, we would have been better off with Brian, begging the question of whether the Stones would have been content to be second bananas for long. Although in the beginning the Stones were most properly respectful of the Beatles for all the right reasons, Brian Jones being of course the most sickeningly sycophantic, once they began to write their own material and realized it was good, the game changed for the much bigger and the much better.

Brian Epstein mightn't have minded the "competition" with his first loves so very much, I suspect, as long as the boys all got along, which as it happens we did. Moving in the highest circles apart, the Beatles and the Stones got a great kick out of each other, so had I not been as egocentric as Marianne might have me, things might have been different. Brian did have "good ears" for his generation, certainly better than most of the

A&R reps his age at the record labels. Though if we're honest, we both gambled and drugged in our own way, and that might have been uneasy, especially once Robert Stigwood poked his nose into the tent.

Like me, Brian actually enjoyed the youthful high spirits of his somewhat younger charges, and it was more than his attraction to their earthy masculinity. His sense of refined propriety may have dictated the lads wear matching suits and politely bow to their audiences but it was only because like any good Jewish mother he was so awfully proud of them. There was never anything "second best" about the Beatles in his mind and heart. It's doubtful on the other hand that Eric Easton could have tolerated a road trip with Mick and Keith, and he did little to disguise his loathing.

Brian Epstein had all the right slights in life to become a manager, an impresario. His own father had told him, "I just don't know what we are going to do with you." What an awful thing to be told. My own mother only took it as far as "I just don't know what you are going to do." It's a shame Brian could not reach the simplicity of Diaghilev, wherein it would have been okay to be described as one who did nothing. But he was of unsettled ambition, and that was just not enough to sustain him when, later, the Beatles questioned their own existence and therefore his.

The accomplishments of the five of them remain amazing. As Paul McCartney finally said, "If anyone was, Brian was the fifth Beatle." Brian set things up so that all the act had to do was be good on stage; there should be no such thing as a bad night. He handled hotels, transportation, per diems, the lot. He had started off at the top . . . with the Beatles.

By the time Brian saw the Beatles at the Cavern at lunchtime in November 1961, the band were already at the top of their game, and even if Brian found the rebel yells and their loutish treatment of their audiences less than charming, he obviously got it. Before "Love Me Do" was released, the Beatles had already played half of the gigs that they would ever play, and it is this that provided the muscle that allowed John and Paul to say to Brian, after watching both Cliff Richard and Adam Faith limp home from lackluster stateside expeditions, "We don't want to do America until we're number 1."

The accomplishments that followed were an amazing force that tied up pop music from that moment until now. Whatever anyone else's accomplishments were, they pale by comparison because they were done when we already had a business to be in. Brian and his lads had no such thing. But George Martin opened the door and let them in. In the very next year, 1963, Brian Epstein and George Martin would own the # 1 position in the musical charts for thirty-two weeks.

Within three years, after having turned them down not once but three times, the head of EMI in America was complaining that the success of the band had reduced Capitol Records to "the Beatles' company." And although all pop stars made films, no one, including the kids who went to see them, took them seriously; they were just another piece of disposable merchandising fodder.

A Hard Day's Night was as different as the Beatles themselves. Alun Owen, a tough no-nonsense Liverpool playwright, eschewed the usual pop pap about early struggles and eventual triumph. In Owen's yarn, the Beatles, albeit in a slapstick way, were inmates of an asylum of their own devise. When A Hard Day's Night was premiered in Liverpool, the Beatles appeared on the balcony of the Town Hall to be cheered by 50, 000 fans. Do we really remember how huge the Beatles were?

Speaking of merchandising fodder, I personally believe it's time to revisit the Seltaeb deal for all those thousands of Beatle wigs and lunch boxes. It was Brian's most embarrassing failure as a businessman. But Brian never saw the merchandising as more than a sideline or, worse, a distraction. It's a pity that Tom Parker never shared with Brian the astonishing fact that Elvis made $20,000,000 from merchandising alone the year before he was inducted into the army.

Overwhelmed by licensing requests he could not evaluate, Brian kicked the ball over to his attorney, David Jacobs. Jacobs was no showbiz neophyte—he repped Marlene Dietrich, Diana Dors, Judy Garland, Liberace and Laurence Harvey—but the scale of the potential business eluded almost all of the principals. Except for well known "Kings Road Rat," playboy Nicky Byrne, who slyly offered Epstein 10% of the proceeds, thinking Brian would certainly want to negotiate the rate up. To Byrne's everlasting benefit, Brian and Jacobs were paying no attention and by the time the rate was renegotiated the resulting licenses were so complex an army of lawyers was required to make sense of them. By 1968, both Epstein and Jacobs were dead, Jacobs under sordid and suspicious circumstances, while Byrne had retired to the Bahamas. It was an instance where Brian's knowing what he did best, while at the same time relying on his "peers" to behave like gentlemen, backfired horribly. "Seltaeb," by the way, is "Beatles" spelled backward.

But their merchandising troubles notwithstanding, the Beatles revolutionized the music business as dramatically as they revolutionized music. They, not the Rolling

Stones nor Led Zeppelin, invented stadium rock and then they refused to tour at a time when they could have received any fee Brian Epstein might have demanded. They went from being the lovable lads to, as George Melly phrased it in his remarkable Revolt Into Style, the "arrogant leaders of the popocracy"—even more so than the Rolling Stones, at least as a group, because the Beatles were an equal opportunity experience, four quads with uniquely different talking heads. It was always John, Paul, George and Ringo. It was never Paul and the rest, as in Mick or Brian Jones and the rest, as it was with the Rolling Stones.

As much as the Beatles provided the Rolling Stones with a model of success, the Stones were also allowed to indulge in bad behavior that came much more naturally to the Liverpudlians. Perhaps after a while, the Beatles somewhat resented the Stones' relatively greater freedom to express themselves, a bit the way the first-born son is held to a different standard than his spoiled brat of a little brother. The party line has always promoted the friendly rivalry that existed between the two groups, but it was a rivalry nonetheless.

In 1965, Lennon and McCartney hosted a Granada TV special in which John slags "I Wanna Be Your Man," knowing full well we gratefully considered this gift from the Beatles a lifeline when the Stones had recorded it but two years earlier and released it as our second single. Not worthy of the Beatles, John sniffed. What that said about the Stones who in the earliest days couldn't write anything that good (or bad) themselves was pretty disrespectful. When success gave Mick and Keith permission to be Bohemian with a capital "B," they were perhaps too quick to scorn Paul's traditional bourgeois affectations. But there is no doubt that the Rolling Stones came in a poor second during the Flower Power period, before jumping back into the game a year later with "Jumping Jack Flash" and "Street Fighting Man." The Beatles, during this period, never joined the crowd, they created it.

Of course, it didn't help that Mick was never a believable spokesman when discussing anything beyond the activities of the Rolling Stones Ltd. Brian Jones, who was altogether too visible for his own good, was just too stoned to make any impact beyond that rather odd cadre who considered him their "favorite Stone." Keith Richards remained the quiet dedicated Nelson Riddle of the blues, letting the music speak for itself; only in the mid-Eighties, when it wasn't quite doing that anymore, did he step out and have his say. Oh, the Stones were still changing lives, but they were past changing direction.

The same could not be said of the Beatles. Mr. Melly put it nicely at just about the time the Beatles were to be no more, at least in the configuration we loved best: "They have been loved and have deliberately courted rejection. They seemed immune and have succeeded in provoking the authorities to harry them. They embraced philanthropy, but abruptly dropped it in favor of ruthless business maneuvering. They were inseparable, but are now more often apart. Yet none of this would matter except in so far as it has helped them preserve and develop their talent. While themselves admitting to being interested in only what they are up to at any given time, they have succeeded in producing a body of work which has illuminated and enlarged the horizons of a whole generation."

The bell started to toll for Brian Epstein by the end of 1965. I did not see him anymore; he did not seek me out and I was too busy to give our lapsed relationship much notice. His addictions enabled shamelessly by Harley Street's finest, Brian's self-medication was of an entirely different order than that of John or Paul, Mick or Keith. We might have had a lot more in common during his later years when drugs took front and center in both our lives, but we never had the occasion to discuss it. Brian was coming apart.

George Martin stated that, "after the Beatles, Gerry and the Pacemakers and Billy J. Kramer, Brian realized he had the makings of a kind of latter-day Diaghilev. He saw himself as an impresario with a stable of great stars, and certainly it was a great kick-off to a career like that. Later, I became increasingly worried that everything that Brian brought me was gradually getting not quite so good."

Alan Livingstone, the clueless head of Capitol Records, condescended to say, "With all due respect to Brian, I think his one major contribution was to pick up the phone and convince me to put out the album, and to insist that I spend $40,000 to promote the first single." Mr. Livingstone conveniently forgets that Brian had lined up the Ed Sullivan appearances before he picked up the phone to his hapless American label head. Fuck them and the boat they creeped in on, both George and Mr. Livingstone. There is such a thing as the law of diminishing returns and self-serving revisionism.

He had been the very best of managers for all of his acts, but too many of them, apart from Cilla Black in general, Gerry and the Pacemakers for a while, and Billy J Kramer with "Little Children" and "Trains and Boats and Planes," depended on the Lennon and McCartney song machine. There came the day when the most that John and Paul could do was service the Beatles and there was little Brian could do about that. For all his self-destructive foibles, Brian Epstein was no squeamish queen.

As the evening of the day came to collect him, and darkness squeezed out the last beat of his heart, it was that heart, so broken in some ways and so true in others, that really mattered. He made his way up and through the tough world of the Liverpool show business underground, taking on the most established local promoters if he saw the Beatles getting some advantage out of it, and if he was given an inch he'd demand a mile—such as the time he was offered a 50-50 share of promoter Sam Leach's lucrative gig at the Tower, and promptly demanded a two-thirds cut, as his brother would also be involved. He may have seemed green when he got to London, but in the 'pool, Epstein wore his own colors proudly.

He was not a hustler—he was a lover—and that was both his glory and his downfall. We are all better for his love because Brian Epstein hustled with his heart.

KIT LAMBERT AND CHRIS STAMP

Chris Stamp, Pete Townshend and Kit Lambert

I have known Pete Townshend just short of a golden half century, since my dear doomed friend Peter Meaden gave his all to transform four teenaged R&B fanatics into Mod icons, temporarily branding them as "The High Numbers." So I always look forward to seeing Pete and company, on or off stage, although their status as "The World's Third Greatest Rock and Roll Band" has never sat comfortably with their leader and lyricist. I know that every time the band performs, their collective neuroses will compete with their brilliance for my attention.

It seems that Pete Townshend the tortured adolescent was indeed father to Pete Townshend the fretful middle-aged legend. Many men settle into a groove in their thirties and forties until a mid-life crisis makes them aware of their own mortality and shakes up their lives. But Pete's life has been in many ways one self-induced crisis of conscience and creativity after another since he was one of those kids who were alright. No other "act" that has survived since the Sixties is so ripe with psycho-drama on those odd occasions when they regroup to entertain us.

And so it was when the Who celebrated their 25th anniversary together at Radio City Music Hall in New York, during Christmas week of 1989. No one is more nostalgic for the '60s version of the Who than Pete himself and his realization that the band can never compete successfully with its glorious past has led to some strange productions, most of which always involve "Tommy." The Radio City Show was a prototype of the Las Vegas gigs Elton John and Rod Stewart would be happy to get two decades later. Except, of course, the Who at their best are authentic in a way that Elton and Rod couldn't care less about as long as the paycheck is fat enough.

Giving it the benefit of a doubt, the show was viva Ann Margret entertaining yet always with a touch of the sadness Laurence Olivier captured so well in the role of Archie Rice, the aging vaudeville star of *The Entertainer*. Once again Roger Daltrey's perennial lack of self-reflection provided a cheerful if rather churlish balance to Pete's solemnity, ever the chav he portrayed in *McVicar*. Or perhaps it wasn't so much that Pete was solemn, although that is his baseline disposition, as so awfully . . . well behaved, as if the management had told him they refused to replace even one more smashed guitar. It seemed pretty clear he wasn't enjoying his silver anniversary.

John Entwistle, on the other hand, having never bought into or been bothered by the Who's pretentions and concerns, pulled the whole thing together. The Ox, true to his nickname, made no effort to fit into what his band-mates were playing. They could bloody well follow him.

Fluid, driven, revolutionary, firmly grounded on his wedged Beatle boot heels, Entwistle's snow frozen beak pointed the way, his mane of lacquered black, grey and white hair, the coif of a grown man rather than a boy, both contrasting with and complementing the iconic Union Jacketed drag he'd worn so well for so many years.

The background chorus was also rather good, if a bit enthused with itself à la Steve Perry and Journey. It was nice to see Billy Nicholls, who'd recorded for my Immediate Records so many years before, getting his Hullabaloo groove on. It was all rather soft-sell, substituting a Motown middle of the road giddy-up for Townshend's lashing, slashing six string razor. And truth be told, the audience, which had paid a premium to attend this "special event," wouldn't have wanted to take on any amount of aggro. No wonder Pete seemed ill at ease. When *Life* magazine proclaimed Woodstock to be the dawning of a new age, Townshend spat angrily that he'd never been so poorly treated by a promoter in his life and the thousands in attendance were useless stoned hippies who would have been beaten to a bloody pulp had they shown up at the Marquee in 1965.

Yet four years later after Radio City, Pete was back for more at the Broadway premier of *Tommy*, which in its first incarnation had rocked the Metropolitan Opera House. Des McAnuff, who would perfect this shtick with his 21st Century direction of "Jersey Boys," was at the helm and Tim Rice, by this time one of Broadway's majority shareholders, was on hand to for moral support.

While all this was going on, I was ensconced a few blocks away at the Un Deux Trois café on West 44th Street. In the company of my boon companion, filmmaker Rafi Ameer, my nostrils were still flaring from having just seen Al Pacino in *Scent of a Woman* when who should bustle into my favorite haunt but Pete, Sir Tim and an entourage of seemingly satisfied hangers-on. I was aware of Tommy's impending Broadway run but had made no plans to see it, so it was nice that fate had brought Pete to me and allowed me so conveniently to offer my congratulations.

I have never particularly enjoyed the Broadway theater, Christopher Walken aside and David Mamet excepted, and my ambivalence crested when Allen Klein forced me to sit through an August Wilson production. Despite Mr. Wilson's multiple Pulitzer prizes for drama and Allen's determination to have him write The Sam Cooke Story, I didn't last past intermission. In fact that evening, as I often found it to be on my nights on Broadway, the audience was far more entertaining than the play. This particular outing was brightened by a glimpse of Craig "Peter Gunn" Stevens and the beautiful actress Alexis Smith, who happened to be Mrs. Stevens. It is typical of my selective (but very good) memory that what I remembered of the show was that Gunn's Rolls had but one headlight.

The play itself was a dreary exploration of African America's struggle to find its place in the sun, and the almost exclusively white limousine liberal audience was eating it up. Frankly I thought *West Side Story* a more realistic depiction of the American Dream just out of reach and wasn't able to encourage Allen much in his seduction of the playwright.

Even the most self-aware rock stars get bored with uncritical acclaim and the business of music, and Pete Townshend is nothing if not self-aware. Pete, at least, was wise enough not to fancy himself a movie star, although he was presumably quite alright with *Tommy* and *Quadrophenia* being translated into celluloid. Even David Bowie, who must have made more films than any of his contemporaries, is hit or miss as an actor, his limitations as a thespian often compounded by a dubious taste in material. *Into the Night* and his rather charming video for *Blue Jean* don't really make up for the aridness of *The Man Who Fell to Earth* and the shallowness of his one-note Andy Warhol in *Basquiat*. Not to mention his decided lack of chemistry when paired with such divas as Marlene Dietrich and Catherine Deneuve.

Jagger one supposes will keep trying until the box office, the critics and Keith all agree he got it "right." Keith of the Johnny Depp Pirates franchise. Good luck with that. Mick's taste in projects is at least interesting although the result is usually less than satisfying. Playing himself in *Performance* the sheer malevolence of his self-interpretation saved the film from its overbearing pretentiousness. *Ned Kelly* isn't even worth a Netflix rental. *Bent* was rather daring if not massively appealing in its odd conflation of homosexuality and the Holocaust. *The Man from Elysian Fields* pretty much succeeds all round so credit where it's due. There are frequent rumors that Mick and his admirer Martin Scorsese have a development deal with HBO so we'll have him to kick around as a movie mogul for a while yet.

Elvis, of course, was terrific in all the films he made before he went into the army, because each of them had a character all its own and Elvis had to challenge himself to create an appropriate persona. When he returned to Hollywood the films never rose above the B-level with the exception of *Viva Las Vegas!* Although a lot of pretty girls got their start in them.

However, Pete Townshend's astute assessment that he was no Elvis did not prevent him from devaluing and losing control of his greatest achievements once they took on lives of their own on stage and screen. He should have known better but the ambition to go above and beyond rock and roll is a powerful drug. At the core of rock is tension and tension is an emotion that most commercial "art" seeks to eliminate, especially as regards Broadway. How many Arthur Millers, Edward Albees or David Mamets have been launched from the Great White Way lately?

So, remembering the Las Vegas revue I'd seen at Radio City, my expectations for Tommy On Broadway were not high. At Un Deux Trois that evening Pete seemed immersed in his party of eight but I couldn't leave the restaurant without acknowledging him and his big night. I wondered if Tim Rice and I had previously met. I was not unduly impressed by his having acquired the stature of a latter day Cole Porter for Secondary Modern-level lyrics. Although one could not fail to acknowledge the torrent of cash they had generated.

I was not actually surprised when he told me I had turned down his cover of "Get Off of My Cloud" in 1966, though amused the Great Man still remembered it as one of his early failures. I'm sure it was fairly dire given what was to follow. Even more amusing was his habit of addressing letters to his future writing partner Andrew Lloyd Webber as "Andrew Loog Webber." Why, I haven't the faintest idea but I guess in their very beginnings they aspired to the kind of success they believed I had already achieved.

It is truly amazing how many people have an Andrew Loog Oldham anecdote in their repertoire whether I've ever met them or not.

Pete and I shared an awkward if sincere rock 'n' roll hug that to the café patrons looking on must have resembled two made men kissing each other on both cheeks. I wondered to myself if Pete was recalling one of our more memorable meetings back in 1965, though it was probably more significant for me than him. Allen Klein had flown the always restlessly seeking Pete to New York sub rosa to meet with us regarding management. How serious Pete was about abandoning his long-time managers Kit Lambert and Chris Stamp is a question. But knowing of Klein's reputation and what he had promised to do for the Stones, he was probably trying to get the highest possible appraisal of his potential worth.

Allen, who always liked to think he was looking out for me, was offering the Who as a consolation prize, since I had recently ceded my management role with the Stones to him. Financial, personal and professional pressures were threatening to drown me, so Allen had very graciously offered to save me from myself for a not very nominal percentage of my deal with the Stones. Just 21 myself, I admired the way the up and coming Who had kept their connection with the street, and say what you will about Allen he was certainly far more capable of bullying record companies out of serious cash than Kit and Chris.

The trip had its perks for Pete who had yet to win the rock 'n' roll lottery: he got driven to his first class flight from Heathrow in my Rolls Phantom V, which came with a cannabis bar he surely sampled.

Allen put him up in a five-star hotel in Manhattan, which he most assuredly did not destroy during his stay. Perhaps I'm giving him a little too much credit for wanting to check out alternative business arrangements; he might just have been a kid happy to enjoy an all-expenses-paid trip. In any case, nothing came of it; I doubt Pete had ever intended otherwise.

Later, of course, Allen Klein would get his dibs into Townshend's songs as a result of Allen finally finding Essex Music London boss David Platz's Achilles heel, the usual greed and money ankle, and David turned on his boss Howie Richmond, the founder of Essex Music, now unhappy with his lot. I remember Allen telling me with glee how David Platz had joined him in the Mediterranean on the yacht Allen was using whilst producing the Anthony Quinn big screen soap, *The Greek Tycoon*, more than loosely based on the romance between Aristotle Onassis and Jackie O. David wanted in on the tycoon tag shortly thereafter.

Soon Allen was calling me in Bogotá asking me to remember his way the songs I had intended to be with Essex Music, as opposed to administered by them. I was still quite legless and adrift at sea but I do recall wondering what the songs of Jerry Ragavoy, songs I had written with Jimmy Page and songs of the Rolling Stones had to do with each other. Around the same time Kit & Chris's minder of their storm, Pete Kameron, threw in the towel and a big hunk of Pete Townshend's songs became part of the new tower of song built by Allen and David Platz.

At Un Deux Trois I was a bit self-conscious about my own straitened circumstances when compared to Pete's potential turn at Broadway's Tony awards ceremony. But I was very pleased to see him and briefly share his vibe of pure love and demonic possession. Seemingly apropos of nothing at all, he pulled me close and whispered in my ear, "51 million, Andrew, 51 million." What on earth was he talking about? 51 million records sold? Tommy's box office receipts? Or even a gargantuan loss? It would have killed our intimate moment to ask for an explanation, but Pete seemed to be impressed with a very large number he wished to confide in me.

Back in 1965 Townshend might have done well to heed to Allen Klein's mantra, as opposed to his proposal, a little more seriously, at least so far as immediate financial security was concerned. With the possible exception of the Dave Clark Five and the Beatles, almost every successful group of the Swinging Sixties' first wave was a business disaster, a ticking time bomb of tax debt, bank overdrafts, paternity suits and past due bills for tailoring, sports cars, band gear and recreational gear; i.e., drugs. The Dave Clark Five stayed afloat because the band was one, and the one was Dave Clark. He produced himself, managed himself and reported to no one, and he ran it like a corner shop, not as if he lived in Harrods. The Beatles, of course, made so very much money that not even the very legal screwing they received from both foreign song publishers and their own record company did anything to dent their Rolls Royce fenders or manor house doors.

The Who, in particular, aggravated their strained circumstances by behaving like four teenage gangs vying for control of the same turf.

Though visionary and creative, managers Lambert and Stamp indulged their own alternative lifestyles and when they did come back to planet earth they found reality all too real. Between Pete's endless demands for disposable guitars and Keith Moon's bottomless appetite for plunder, Allen Klein was probably the only manager in the business that could have reined the Who in, just as he attempted to do with Apple Records some years later. But then the Who wouldn't have been the Who.

Chris Stamp and Madame Keith Moon

To make matters worse, the band and their managers were in over their heads with experienced music biz hands Shel Talmy, their producer, and Robert Stigwood, who had become the Who's booking agent for a mere £500 advance. (Ironically, Stigwood got his foot in the door by subletting office space to Kit and Chris, which was the exact same arrangement that would come back to bite me with Eric Easton.)

The Who came to resent the five-year production contract they had signed with Shel Talmy but, objectively, his contribution to their early success was undeniable.

Perhaps because he wasn't as accomplished at self-promotion as certain other Sixties pimpressarios, Talmy has been somewhat underestimated as a seminal figure of the "invasion" era. He was a Yankee in King Arthur's Court at a time when the Who's generation saw themselves taking their place alongside the Beach Boys, the Four Seasons and Motown, if not surpassing them. And he famously did not hang out, interacting with artists in the studio rather than the pub.

His legendary hits for the Who and the Kinks came as early as 1964, which was early indeed. Less well known is his work with David Bowie (1965) who was not quite ready for prime-time, Manfred Mann, Amen Corner, the Easybeats, and Creation. It didn't hurt that he had a touch of the con man that helped so many of us on our way in the early days. An engineer in Los Angeles' Conway Studios, but not yet a producer, he arrived in London with tapes of the Beach Boys and Lou Rawls his friend at Capitol Records, Nik Venet, told him he could claim as his own work. He had started on his own version of "The Grand Tour" of Europe but wasn't averse to working if it came his way.

Talmy found his way to the office of Dick Rowe at Decca, who long before his star was tarnished by turning down the Beatles was considered one of England's premier A&R executives. In those days, decisions were made quickly and easily (in the case of the Beatles and Decca perhaps too quickly and easily) so impressed by Talmy's Capitol "bootlegs," Rowe had Talmy in the studio with the Bachelors before the ink was dry on the contract. Their first record together went to number six, the second was a number one. It was looking like the European continent would have to wait a while for Shel Talmy to get around to resuming his vacation.

But Dick Rowe was beginning to show the signs of short-sightedness that would permit the Beatles to get away ("Guitar groups are over," Dick pontificated, so claimed a disappointed Brian Epstein). When Decca passed on Georgie Fame and Manfred Mann, Talmy decided to go independent, a nervy move I could very much relate to since at the same time I was making my way as one of the only "independent" publicists in London. He might not have spent much time hanging around in clubs but Shel was a fixture on Denmark Street, which was to London's music publishing industry what Fleet Street is to newspapers and Harley Street is to physicians.

His loitering paid off when the manager of a young group called the Ravens played him a demo he successfully shopped to Pye . . . on very bad terms as it happened, which would come back to haunt him. Now renamed the Kinks, Talmy and the Davies brothers would soon have huge hits with "You Really Got Me" and "All Day and All of the Night," establishing a sound that was as emblematic of the times as George Martin's "I Want to Hold Your Hand" or my own "The Last Time."

Talmy's relationship with the Kinks would produce some really great records, Ray Davies, however, never stopped resenting the meager contract they'd received from Pye. For all their excesses most rock stars, particularly lead singers for some reason, are typically as cheap as they come. As Talmy put it, "Ray Davies makes Rod Stewart look like a philanthropist." But while the hits kept coming everybody just got on with it, and frankly the Kinks had so much trouble with touring and their relationship with their American label, their studio work with Shel was a bright spot in a management nightmare.

The tension made Talmy more determined not to let personal friendships with his artists sway him. His youth was an advantage because the bands could relate to him, but it also made the temptation to cross the line more important to resist. As an independent, Shel was spending his own money in the studio which ultimately made his decision to keep things only business an easy one.

So even before he met the Who, Shel Talmy had created a successful and somewhat unique formula that would reach its ultimate fulfillment with a quartet of unruly Faces from Shepherd's Bush. Talmy recalls being invited by Kit Lambert to a rehearsal: "It took me thirty seconds to realize they were the best rock 'n' roll band I'd ever heard. So I signed them to my company, spent my own hard earned money to record them, and went back to America to sell the first record, the Townshend penned 'I Can't Explain'." It hardly mattered to the composer that Talmy applied the Kinks' template without constraint. To Talmy's credit (and Dick Rowe's regret), if guitars were king again in 1964, they rang loudest and proudest in the first records by the Kinks and the Who. It might even be said that they were the acorn from which Heavy Metal would grow into a monumental oak.

The Who's management were apparently less appreciative and the lack of a unified vision would come to hinder the band. Talmy found Chris Stamp utterly confounding: "I doubt whether I said more than ten words to him during all the time I was working with the Who. He'd turn up every now and then to a session, stay for about twenty minutes at the back of the room, and then piss off. As far as I'm concerned he was a complete nonentity. Chris Stamp, as far as I'm concerned, was the invisible man."

Since Stamp is a man of no few strong opinions himself, one is led to conclude that Stamp had nothing to say to Talmy either.

Shel's dislike of Kit Lambert was more pronounced and judgmental. Kit's very British form of homosexuality struck the rather unworldly Yank as merely "nasty." "He was the kind of fag that really disgusted me. I didn't like him at all. He was all over young boys, he just pissed me off. All he cared about were young boys; he was doing that with the band." They were soon enough drawn into a battle royal for the soul of the Who. However much Kit may have disliked the financial terms of the production deal with Talmy, it was the influence Kit felt the producer was having behind his back that really pushed his buttons. Lambert pressured the band to break their contract with Talmy.

The timing was unfortunate. The next single scheduled for release was "Substitute," a pop masterpiece that raised the bar on the style they'd perfected with "Anyway Anyhow Anywhere" and "My Generation." Their booking agent, Robert Stigwood, had started his own independent label, Reaction Records, and the Who were looking to get out of their contract with the more establishment Brunswick Records. Stigwood would also seek to release "Substitute" in the U.S. through his arrangement with Atco Records, bypassing U.S. Decca, otherwise the Who's label for almost their entire career.

Talmy refused to surrender. After all it was his money that had financed the recordings, not Lambert and Stamp's. For six months he held up release of the single via pending litigation, a lifetime in the fast moving pop scene of the Sixties. As he should have, he won that battle, but he lost the war. He would never record the Who again.

Objectively speaking the Who were ill-served by their management and business partners by this period of tension and uncertainty, which might have been avoided but for Kit and Chris' intransigence. One can imagine Townshend feeling a bit like Marlon Brando in his famous scene with Rod Steiger in *On the Waterfront*. Broken-hearted and broken down the ex-prize fighter confronts his ruthless brother: "You was my brother, Charley, you shoulda looked out for me a little bit. . . I coulda been a contender." Fortunately for them and for us, Pete Townshend would persevere through the hard times to outlast most of his contemporaries in the "first wave."

Chris and Kit were not the only managers at the time to match their artists' excesses drink for drink and hit for hit, but they were even more financially naïve than most. The business people they brought in to "help," Stigwood and Pete Kameron, weren't close enough to the band as people (not that a meaningful relationship with Keith Moon would have been easy for anyone) to offer much more than complex deals their younger partners were expected to deliver on.

Lambert and Stamp, like so many of their management contemporaries in the early Sixties, started out in life with no intention of becoming tycoons of teen. Film was their bag and their ambition was to independently produce a documentary on the burgeoning beat scene of 1964. They had already landed some assistant director gigs when Kit on his own happened upon "the High Numbers" at the Railway Hotel in the Wealdstone suburb of London.

Peter Meaden, with whom I'd worked on an ill-fated publicity venture, had persuaded the Who to become the High Numbers as part of his campaign to make them the Mod-est Mods. As the High Numbers they'd just released their first recording ever on

Fontana, "I'm the Face," which was nothing more or less than an arrangement of an old blues chestnut. Lambert was immediately converted and took Stamp to see them the very next weekend at the Trade Union Hall in Watford. Whether or not Lambert had management in mind at this early stage, time was of the essence, as nobody knew better than I from my first encounter with the Stones. I have often said that had I met the band two weeks later all of our lives would have been different.

Though we hadn't seen much of each other since our publicity debacle, Peter Meaden and I always had a friendly competition going so he was particularly eager I see "his" band and presumably share in his good fortune. Despite an erratic and sometimes irresponsible personality, Peter had influenced me to venture from my mother's comfortable Hampstead enclave into the dangerous and exciting world of Soho. Now that success with the Stones seemed imminent I felt a little guilty for having lost patience with Peter, who tended to lose focus when it was needed the most. I went along to see his band.

Of course, the band were very good, particularly when they veered away from the "R&B" the Stones were in the process of blowing up and toward the Motown groove they excelled at. As Peter tried out his most outrageous hype on me I noticed an attractive couple in the audience who divided their watchful attention between the group and Meaden.

When I asked Meaden if he knew the pair with the hungry eyes, he dismissed them as a couple of "film ponces." When Chris and Kit decided to manage the Who rather than film them, who can say, but Meaden was clearly out-matched because very soon he found himself odd man out. Was my developing bond with the Stones so very much stronger than Peter Meaden's with the High Numbers? Or was it more a matter of luck than talent and affinity? I went on to produce "Satisfaction" while Peter . . . never recovered from the blow, an old lad who had sped away his time way too soon.

You might even stretch a point and speculate that in many ways the Who had more in common with Peter Meaden than they did their newly adopted minders. But it was no matter. Peter could never have managed to complete a marathon and spent the rest of his short life butterflying from project to project, fueled by pills, and never totally in touch with reality.

Turning our attention to the couple who would take the Who from the Marquee to Woodstock, we begin with the earthier of the two, Chris Stamp, brother of another Sixties icon, Terence. Less theatrical than his partner Kit, Chris Stamp's contribution to the Who is sometimes underestimated. At a time when it wasn't quite legal to be so, Lambert was flamingly out of the closet. Stamp's persona was ambiguous but he had a kind of street suss about the sexual politics of the day. He is said to have been told that when Jimi Hendrix and Jim Morrison first met, they "made out together," and to have blandly replied, "you've got to realize they are both sex symbols. What else could they have done?"

For those of us a bit put off by Lambert's often self-destructive eccentricity, Chris provided a buffer. Each of them was capable of completely outrageous brainstorms that the other would often modulate into a winning idea. But it was true enough that the day-to-day execution often fell to Stamp. Chris was self-possessed even while still in his early 20s. And while he possessed the kind of working-class good looks so in vogue at the time he seemed indifferent to his reflection in the mirror, a regular guy for all that.

Terry O'Neill posed Terence Stamp and Chris Stamp as gangsters.

Terence Stamp remains one of his brother's biggest fans and, since Chris and I somewhat avoided each other in the Sixties, being friendly rivals, he graciously agreed to help make our portrait of his younger sibling here more three dimensional. Terence takes up the story.

"Late in 1960 my mother called me and said she was a bit worried about Chris because he was in a gang and hadn't got a proper job and she wanted me to talk to him. So I invited him up to this basement in Harley St. which I was sharing with two other actors, unbeknownst to my parents. They didn't know I was trying to be an actor. They just knew that I had left home as it were. Chris came up and he was very sort of sullen and detached. And didn't really want to be there.

"I made it as nice as I could. I started asking him about what he was really interested in and he was really nihilistic. He didn't seem to be interested in anything. And then finally he confessed that the only thing he was really interested in was girls. I said, 'What kind of girls do you like?' What he really liked were slightly muscley dancer girls. And I said to him, 'Wow, man, I've got a great idea for you. I've got a NATKE union ticket that allows me to work backstage and I could lend you my ticket and you could go along to Sadler's Wells. You might be able to get a gig, you know. 'Cause most of the guys are gay and these girls are all super fit and very horny. You'd be in your element!' So that kind of caught his interest. I gave him my NATKE ticket and off he went.

"In truth, I didn't hear from him until a couple of months later when he called me from Glasgow. And he said, 'I've just shagged all the corps de ballet. The last one's here. She wants to say 'hello' to you.'"

Chris' way with the ladies was to prove useful to him professionally as well. "Later on when Chris became well known, Maureen Cleave wrote an article about him in the *Evening Standard*. And I always assumed that when he opened the door to her he just kind of shoved her up against the wall of the passage and gave her one. Because her first paragraph was, 'I've just been to meet Chris Stamp, the more handsome, less photogenic brother of actor Terence.' And I heard that from quite a few chicks. He was considered more handsome by women (than I)."

Eighteen-year-old Chris Stamp was on his way, but it wasn't easy for either of the brothers, raised in the ambition stifling East End of London, to escape their background. "It was a miracle we both got to grammar school," says Terence. "We could hardly read so it was a real helping hand from the universe. We both left school at sixteen and we both had street smarts. Chris was much more street smart than I. Mine was embedded but Chris saw how to use his. He saw how a working class spiv had an edge on middle class guys just trying to make a living.

"If you were born and raised in the East End there was no possibility of you getting into the theater, film or show business. Even though there were theaters there it would never have occurred to any East End guy to try and get a job in one. It was another world. After I left home I daren't tell anyone in my family, even Chris, that I was trying to make it as an actor."

Without his older brother's timely intervention, Chris Stamp's life might well have taken a very different turn. "The Krays were always on the lookout for young likely lads," Terence told me, "and Chris' gang were already getting free entry into dance halls in Stepney where they offered to 'keep the peace.' Billy Curbishley (who came to manage the Who many years later) was the strong man of Chris' gang. But so far as I know, except for Curbishley they weren't committing crimes. Curbishley was a 'tea leaf,' thief, you know."

Chris, however, was something else, although at the time he hadn't much of a clue as to what that might be. Over fifty years later, Terence's tone is admiring: "You have to understand this guy has a lot of front. He had more front than Harrods even at 18. He talked his way into a job at Her Majesty's Theater and what happened to him was that he saw and heard *West Side Story* and it changed his life. Many years later he told me he'd never seen or heard anything like it. And from that moment he knew that he was destined for show business in some way." So even though when they entered the pop business Chris and Kit were looked upon as "film ponces," Chris had paid some dues that no one in the music business really knew about.

Chris was opportunistic but often opportunity found him. "Early in 1961 I was in a play called *Why the Chicken* which was being directed by Lionel Bart, even though it wasn't primarily a musical and he hadn't written it," Terence recalled. "It was about the soulless life of kids on the new estates. The playwright John McGrath was the first to see anything special in me at all and he wrote the part I played with me in mind. And when we were at the end of our tour, Chris just showed up for a matinee and came backstage. And as I was leaving with him to have a cup of tea between shows, Lionel Bart set eyes on Chris and I thought he was going to pass out.

"Lionel came to me and said, 'Your brother is like the perfect man.' I told him, 'You know my brother is young but he's an alpha male.'

Lionel said, 'Yeah, but I'd just like to talk to him. He just seems so amazing. Would that be OK?' I said, 'Of course, I'll have him call you.'

"I told Chris, 'Look, Lionel's completely gay but he's a very interesting guy. And I'm sure you've got a lot to say to him.' And Chris said, 'Oh don't worry about that. I know about queers. Of course, I'll give him a ring.' "The next thing I knew he was working at Lionel's publishing company and then very quickly he was running Lionel's publishing company."

Chris Stamp and Kit Lambert

All of us understood the gay world and felt very comfortable in it, but none of us wanted to end up married to an old geezer. The attention the gay show-biz establishment showed us and our charges was both flattering and useful. Like the old queens who fed off our youthful energy and hoped for the low-lying fruit that might fall off our tree, we aimed to live in an unreal world while earning real money. Not for the first time, the East

End wide boy and the public school ponce rubbed elbows or other body parts in the cellars of Soho, but this time the global success of Britain's pop music made queer gear. A little later, David Bowie's is-he-or-isn't-he image would top the charts, and later still Morrissey and George Michael could claim, "I most certainly am" and be more successful still.

The wunderbar Lionel Bart was a shamanic songwriting hustler who blessed and anointed so many of our young lives in the early '60s. A Leo, born Lionel Begleiter in the East End in 1930, he was almost or just over a decade older than most of us '60s new kids on the block and an inspiration to us all. Like us, Lionel could neither write nor read a note of music, but, boy, could he hum it into a hit tune. Keith Richards and I used to like hanging with Lionel as long as he didn't start playing us any of his awful and awfully successful tunes. We loved it when we went for a spin in his one-off Facel Vega. Lionel was a mystic from Stepney who knew how he had done it and enjoyed letting you in on the game; I don't recall Mick enjoying the Lionel routine—another Leo in the room syndrome.

Lionel had started out on the washboard in skiffle group's at the 21's. Soon he was co-writing hits for the U.K's first naff Elvis, Tommy Steele, and later wrote alone the song, "Living Doll" that catapulted the slightly less naff second U.K. Elvis, Cliff Richard, to #1 in the charts and into the hearts of English mumhood in the space previously occupied in safe sainthood by Liberace and Johnnie Ray. He went on to write the music for "Fings Ain't Wot They Used To Be" with my Hampstead days upstairs neighbor Frank Norman and the music, book and lyrics for the bigaroonie on stage and screen, *Oliver!* We liked Lionel because he had done it our way. He had not taken the safe route

John Osborne had seemed to take by sticking to the velvet underground mafia that controlled the London theatre scene and moved him from the earthy *Look Back In Anger* to the crossover but formulaic *The Entertainer*.

Frank Norman

Lionel, and most of that which flew into the West End from Joan Littlewood's Stratford East Theatre, remained rebellious, left-wing and cranky. It did not stop him from writing the James Bond theme for 1963's *From Russia with Love* and by the time

Oliver! hit the big screen, Lionel was out of our lives and reputed to be earning 16 quid a minute. *Oliver!* had been created in true zen hustler form; Lionel wanted the big White Way, the Yellow Brick road as the pop troll route via Cliff and Tommy Steele failed to satisfy his Broadway and cinemascopic yearnings. Lionel sat down with pen and pad and ran the David Lean 1948 version of *Oliver Twist*, he wrote down the best bits and had his book. Next he hummed his magical ditties to a transcriber and the score to his *Oliver!* was born.

    We loved him then, and he loved us. He lived in Reece Mews off of South Kensington next door to the painter Francis Bacon. Then it all went to his head and nose. He moved into a grand mausoleum of which I cannot remember the address because I was never invited there, somewhere nearer the grand museums further up the road. Now he fawned over Nureyev, Princess Margaret, Alan Jay Lerner and Noel Coward. By the time he crashed in '72, most of the young dudes had moved on. Jimi Hendrix, Brian Jones, Jim Morrison . . . all gone.

    The rest of us busy trying to hang on, for in the '70s the '60s meant hardly anything near to what it conjures up today. Terence asked me recently why I had not included more on Lionel in a book devoted to hustlers. I replied to the effect that I could not because all too soon Lionel had hustled himself out of the shop window. He did indeed finance my recording of Marianne Faithfull's "As Tears Go By." He was so encouraging to so many of us, but pretty soon he had himself believing that he had signed my management contract with the Rolling Stones because I was under age; that he had written "Satisfaction"; that he had discovered Jimi Hendrix and written "Purple Haze." I am sure all of this played well with his new friends but they in turn played Lionel well and soon they were gone.

In a word, you always allow yourself to be screwed, it always takes two or three. Lionel allowed himself to screw himself. I recently saw a photo of Lionel and John Lennon at an Ivor Novello awards dinner in London in 1963. Lionel is the master and John is the pupil. It's a shame he could not have stayed that way. Not many of us did but we are lucky that the detour did not kill us. We are all able to alter the whole aspect of what is into a confused conundrum of wants and needs and, dangerously, what should be. The "isms" at work as the mind, ego and many so-called friends including ourselves attempt to topple that which we have received.

For that wonderful while Lionel was home to the '60s. Some of the Beatles, some of the Stones, the Stamps, Jimi, Donovan. You'd get out at South Ken station or park your car and walk onto the cobblestones to 6 Reece Mews. You'd holler up to the second floor and he'd appear.

"Hallo, Ang," he'd smile, day or night "Come round for a cup of tea?"

We all did . . . .

After he had worked for Lionel for a while, Chris Stamp his NATKE ticket from the stage division to the film division. He started working as a prop man on movies like the Laurence Harvey remake of *Of Human Bondage* and then joined the directors' union. He went off to Norway to work on Anthony Mann's *The Heroes of Telemark* with Kirk Douglas and Richard Harris and was quickly promoted to second assistant director.

In a very short time, Chris Stamp went from an aimless discontented hormonally driven boy to a man with a mission. "When Chris was an assistant director he came across Kit Lambert at the Shepperton film studio and they got on very well," Terence explains. "By this time they both wanted to direct movies. And the idea that came up from their meeting was that they would find a group, make the group famous, and then direct a film about them. That was their initial impetus.

"They met the Who when they were briefly named the High Numbers and managed by Peter Meaden. It must have been very hard for the Who to resist two young guys like Kit and Chris. They really had it covered. Chris was like the new working class hero and Kit was the son of a genius father who knew everything about music."

In a phone conversation that supposedly took place between Kit in London and Chris on an Irish film set minding the likes of Laurence Harvey versus Kim Novak, the following exchange took place:

Kit: "I think we should not just make a film with this band, I think we should manage them."

Chris: "Manage a band? We're filmmakers. We don't know anything about managing bands!"

Kit: "Chris, I've had a good look at the managers out there. They don't seem to know much about it either . . ."

Kit Lambert was most decidedly not a "regular" guy. An aristocratic flamboyance was hard-wired into his DNA. His Oxford education and pedigree as the son of Constant Lambert, Diaghilev collaborator and lover of diva Margot Fonteyn, permitted him a certain louche griminess. He reminded me of the teddy bear Sebastian carries everywhere in *Brideshead Revisited*. And like Sebastian he took advantage of his background to justify the most outrageous behavior, fueled by homosexual lust and various chemical dependencies. And like Sebastian he could be most persuasive when he felt like being charming.

Terence Stamp was as close to his brother's partner as he was to Chris and understood that a dramatic and terrifying close encounter with death had marked Lambert forever very early in his life. Shortly after graduating from Oxford, Lambert set out for the Amazon with his closest friend in an attempt to trace one of the great river's tributaries to its source and make a film about the expedition. Everything was to go horribly wrong.

"He was madly in love with the guy who went with him on the Amazon expedition. And the fellow was ambushed and beheaded by tribesmen before Kit's very eyes. Kit himself only just escaped with his life. You can only have an inkling as to how that would affect the rest of your life. He was just out of university, seeing himself as an explorer, going with his great friend, and then barely escaping with his life. Watching his mate have his head chopped off."

To make matters worse, Lambert was arrested on suspicion of murdering his friend by Brazilian officials. Only after the *Daily Express* newspaper, who had financed the adventure, came to Kit's defense was he released. Already complex, moody, and different, Lambert would never be the same again.

His friend Terence believes that "the Kit Lambert that I met, the recklessness, the unfathomability of him, the lack of regard he had for the world's opinion, I put it down to that event. He became cynical and very introverted. It was very very hard to get Kit to talk about any of his deeper feelings."

Kit was a very distinctive looking gentleman. Distinctive, but not necessarily distinguished. He always put me in mind of a naughty sulking schoolboy, who had either been deprived of his food or his first crush. He was not tall, but he spoke big with a voice that for sure could reach the back of the circle. He had a formative influence on the young Pete Townshend, who unlike my Mick and Keith, needed little prompting to write his own material. Kit exposed Townshend to new musical and literary influences, advising him to steer clear of the love songs that came easily to the Beatles and hard to the Stones.

"He educated me by encouraging me," Townshend remembers. "It's what made him a great mentor. He could see that I was at my best when I was dealing with my conscience. He'd never sneer at me for saying things that were pretentious, or which had been said before. In fact, he'd align me with things that had been said before. I'd play him my tapes and it'd be one of the great joys I had to play him something and hear his comments. I'd produce four or five songs a week, and he'd come and listen to them . . . and that's when the conversations would begin. He'd talk about his father, he'd recommend books to read, music to listen to—great think tank sessions."

For someone with little prior exposure to the pop music business, Lambert was surprisingly suss, as Terence points out. "Pete Townshend's dad had to sign for him because he was not of age. Cliff Townshend was a working professional saxophonist in the Royal Air Force Dance Orchestra, popularly known as the Squadronaires. While he encouraged Pete's musical ambitions, Cliff understood that managers always fucked their artists on publishing. What impressed Townshend's dad is that from the get go Chris and Kit made it very clear that if Pete composed, he would get the bigger part of the publishing."

Chris, too, did everything he could to educate Townshend, and Terence made his own indirect contribution. "The first thing I bought when I started making money was a Zenith radio which at the time was the be all and end all of portable radios. You could get stations from all over the world, America especially. It was a fantastic object to have. And Chris asked me if he could borrow it because they were encouraging Townshend to write and they wanted him to hear things that were happening in America before they ever got to England. I always knew that it was them that encouraged him to write."

I, too, thought Kit was brilliant—"mad as a snake" but God knows he came from a notorious line of genius/lunatics. He could be so cherubically sweet, gentle, and generous "with a wonderful kind of lugubrious grin"—and a minute later morph into a two-year-old having a major meltdown. Other times, he might present a philosophical point, debate it with himself for fifteen minutes, then segue into a monologue on the TV soap *Coronation Street* with equal interest and import. 'Tis strange how the hustler saints need their time off, and often on the most mundane level.

He realized that those lower on the social scale often envied the freedom he took for granted as one to the manor born. Surely Kit took a greater satisfaction from styling Tommy as a rock "opera" than John Entwistle or Keith Moon, for whom the double album at last provided an opportunity to share songwriting income with Pete Townshend. He confided to Arthur Brown one evening that with Tommy, he "was going to appeal to their snobbery."

"I'm going to call it an 'opera,'" he explained, "and get those people out there, the punters, hooked." But "the rock opera" was a concept about which both Kit and Chris were equally enthusiastic. Chris told Terence, "It's very difficult to do something new because the Stones and the Beatles have done everything. But Kit and I have an idea: Kit's gonna try to get Pete to write an opera. And what we are going to do, is we're going to rent opera houses around the world. That will give us a real edge because that's something the Beatles haven't done."

Pete was not convinced at first. Terence asked Kit how he was going to get Townshend to write an opera. Kit said, "Oh, no worries, I've had a long talk with Pete. Pete said, 'Look Kit, I've only just started writing songs. I can write a few songs, you know, but I can't write an opera.' And I said, 'Look Pete, you write me twelve songs and I'll make it into an opera.'" The result was "A Quick One" from the album of the same name.

After Tommy had sold millions of albums and earned the Who hundreds of thousands on the road, a movie version was announced with a whole new flood of merchandising tie-ins. The New Musical Express would comment drily, "Tommy—it'll tear your wallet apart." And the financial success was met with equal adulation from the mainstream press which had rushed to anoint Sgt. Pepper among the finest artistic works of the latter 20th Century.

It is a credit to the Who's integrity that *Tommy* survived the tasteless treatment it received at the hands of the late Ken Russell, who has made more dreadful films than one can count on both hands. Kit might have enjoyed the idea of promoting *Tommy* as a rock opera but there was nothing cynical in his hype. He was too close to Pete for that and Pete, the cynic who condemned Woodstock, was anything but cynical about *Tommy*. One supposes Russell conceived of the film *Tommy* as a dark comedy but it is a joke without a punch line.

As a matter of fact, Terence "begged his brother not to allow Russell to direct the film. I thought Chris and Kit were much better suited to produce and direct it themselves. Chris later told me he wished he had taken a stronger stand with the studio."

Chris had at least one other disappointment as regards *Tommy* the movie. He had always wanted Elvis Presley to play Tommy's father and he actually got a meeting with Colonel Tom Parker to pitch it. The Colonel was surprisingly accommodating and told Chris, "You pay my boy what I'm asking and he'll show up anywhere you want." The figure named was of course astronomical but Chris regretted not fighting to get it into the budget.

Before *Tommy's* success threatened to overshadow the Who themselves, in 1966 Lambert and Stamp had embarked on their own version of Immediate Records, Track. Quirky yet appealing artists like Thunderclap Newman and the Crazy World of Arthur Brown kept the doors open, but signing Jimi Hendrix for the UK mere weeks after his manager Chas Chandler brought him to London from New York made Chris and Kit look positively brilliant. Once again, Terence Stamp had a glimpse of pop history in the making.

"If Chris was doing anything big or sexy he would invite me. He called and said, 'You know the old Saville Theater?' I knew the Saville well. I dressed Paul Scofield in a show there called *Expresso Bongo* as an evening job when I was at drama school. Because it was a straight theater it was dark on Sunday night, so Chris and Brian Epstein had rented it and they were using it to promote new acts. He said, 'We're launching this new guy so I want you to come. Dress up, bring a chick and whomever else you want, I really want you there, it's gonna be a happening.' And that was the first time any of us had ever seen Hendrix.

"What happened was a girlfriend of Chas Chandler had called him from New York and said, 'You've got to come over and see this guy.' Chas was blown away and brought Hendrix to London, straight to Chris and Kit. Chris took Hendrix to see the Who and the next thing you knew Hendrix was ripping up his guitar and stuff. Townshend said, 'Oh yeah that's the great idea of my fucking managers.' I heard from a friend of Mitch Mitchell just recently that Chris was at every Experience recording session.

I should mention here that the girlfriend mentioned in the above was Linda Keith, who was Keith Richard's girlfriend at the time. She had invited me in New York to witness Jimi Hendrix whilst Keith was with the Stones somewhere outside of the apple. I did indeed witness Hendrix but could not entertain the idea of taking on Jimi as, one, I had my hands full with the Stones, and two, Jimi seemed to have his hands full of Linda.

Terence continues, "After the Saville show, Epstein had a party at his penthouse apartment in Knightsbridge. Chris said, 'Let's get off to Eppy's, there's always a lot of action there.' The door to the apartment was open when we arrived and at the other end of the drawing room there was a group of people that included Eric Clapton, Ginger Baker and, I believe, Jack Bruce, who were whispering to each other in a huddle. And from across the room Chris says in a very loud voice, "Don't worry boys, there will always be work for good white guitarists!"

By the mid-Seventies, Chris and Kit's inconsistent attention to the Who's business affairs would be their undoing. Author Chris Charlesworth described the demise of Lambert and Stamp this way, "The style of management provided by Kit and Chris, the stretching of checks, the snappy ideas, the full tilt promotional thrust that characterized the workings of their New Action Ltd. were ideal for the '60s, but in the climate of the '70s, when the Who no longer needed promoting through outrage, when logistical professionalism and sound financial advice was required, the management team was largely redundant."

What happened next is like one of Terence Stamp's more recent movies. "After my brother left the East End in order to make his way in the business he had to cut off virtually all ties with it because it would have been too much of a pull. In the same way it was very very difficult for me to become an actor. It took every fiber in me to make that change of octave that was needed, to go from East End spiv to performing artist. So Chris saw hardly anything of his old gang once he'd gotten to the West End.

"Shortly after Chris got into show business, Billy Curbishley got nicked. He was framed, incidentally, for the thing he got put away for, unlucky enough not to have an alibi. The police had been waiting to do him and they got him put away for a long time. So he was out of the equation.

"Track Records had just started up and they'd moved into offices in Old Compton Street. The parole board contacted Chris because Billy Curbishley had given them Chris' name and they wanted to come and interview Chris. 'I was so naïve,' Chris told me, 'I actually went out and got my hair cut.' He thought there was something the police wanted from him. But they were simply verifying that Chris would be prepared to give Curbishley a job if they paroled him.

"Chris put Billy Curbishley to work and Billy started learning the business. They took him out on American tours where he was in charge of picking up the money from the promoters. He became an integral part of Track. He befriended Roger and when Chris and Kit were obviously under the weather that's when Curbishley moved."

A final blow was dealt to the Kit & Chris management team by a number of events and people. David Platz, Allen Klein, Bill Curbishley, Pete Rudge, Pete Kameron, whomever, even the guy who cleaned the cars. And, of course, Kit and Chris themselves. Kit and Chris were by now considered totally blottered and unmanageable by the act they managed. A different version of this always plays itself out for the same reasons. Albert and Bob; Brian and the Beatles, myself and the Stones.

The average are never let go. The bottom line is that once the act is there, wherever that there is, they have to continue on their own. It's part of the life and death consequence of making it. The act, rightly or wrongly, must now summon up and execute their own visions and demons. Your services are no longer required, we no longer require inspiring, we just need our money collected, and collected. And the moment you slip you will be told.

Kit took on an ungodly, reptilian sadness that haunted him the rest of his short life. His equally mercurial father had left his mother soon after Kit was born and had died in 1951 of acute alcoholism and undiagnosed diabetes just two days before his 46th birthday. His tortured son was to fall down the stairs of his mother's home to his death . . . days before his 46th birthday.

Chris Stamp eventually found his way into rehab and became an established drug counselor who specialized in, appropriately enough, psychodramatic therapy.

Terence's perspective is that "Chris and Kit really didn't need the fame. It's not like today where everybody wants to be famous for half an hour. What they wanted was to make this group and to make a film.

"Bill's done very very well by them financially. He's made them very rich boys. We can't take that away from him. But I don't see a lot of classics after "Quadrophenia." I believe that now Pete Townshend is finally acknowledging that the Who were six not four. Musically I don't think Curbishley's done anything for them at all. I'm glad to hear that Pete is circling back to writing another opera. Kit would be pleased. At a certain point Chris and Kit agreed that operas should be what the Who did exclusively."

Together, Chris Stamp and Kit Lambert were the gang that could not shoot straight, but they probably deserved a better fate than to have been abandoned by the band they loved and to be robbed by men they did not trust. Among my contemporaries it is hard to think of a management partnership that had the successes, thrills and spills that Kit and Chris had. It is said you make your own luck. Good luck is someone needing you. That is what happened between Lambert & Stamp and the Who.

As I mentioned in the above Chris and I were far too busy to socialize in the '60s. I saw a slight bit more of Kit. I remember inviting Kit around to dinner at a flat I had with my first wife Sheila on Kensington High Street. One of the other guests was Peter Noone. This apparent apparition more than put Kit off his food and he later threw up all that he had drunk. In the morning a large bouquet of flowers arrived for Sheila from Kit with profuse apologies over the previous evening's chuckfest. That was Kit.

Chris and I bonded in the '80s in New York in our ongoing aftermath to our '60s. For that while we licked and prescribed to our perceived war wounds. Kit had passed in the spring of '81 and, although we never mentioned it, Chris and I both knew we were, with Epstein also gone, the last of the first crew still manning the oars. Perhaps we did not speak of it because we both knew how far adrift we both really were. Chris came to first and started a remarkable second life as a psychodrama therapist and healer able to celebrate and enjoy his family, his wife and partner Calixte, and his many friends. The grey wolf was enjoying his turn at lapping up "the gravy"; he had become the song .... the seeker.

Then he became what we used to call "poorly." Poorly these days is a nearer threat than it used to be when the neighbor who used to bid us good day disappeared and we were told that he or she had got "poorly." I was in New York this past autumn and Calixte invited me to have supper with them both at what was Chris's first outing following a bad bout. I will forever be grateful to Calixte for that last opportunity to be with Chris. We slagged off the waiters, we dissed the adjoining tables, we laughed the laugh that had lighted up our lives as we chatted about our lives and the life to come. We were on the Upper East Side of Manhattan but we were on the Upper East Side of our East End-West End world.

His spirit was true and strong, his body was not. His heart was brilliant as he let me hold his arm and walk him home. It may have looked as if I was supporting him but I can assure you it was the other way around. He was giving me a lesson. His mind had merged with his heart and they were one and they were friend.

Chris Stamp

JERRY BRANDT

THE ABILITY TO discern quality in an artist may be helpful to the hustler but it's not a requirement. Likewise a fetish for "authenticity." Discernment and integrity served Diaghilev and Grossman well since their vision demanded that their own definition of quality be affirmed by popular commercial acceptance. But aesthetic taste simply didn't come into it with Larry Parnes, and his hustle was no less valid for his valuing his performers more than their performances. The important thing is self-knowledge and a willingness to make choices that mate opportunity with the creative material at hand, be that product a hit song or an individual that gets the hustler's juices flowing.

It is knowingness that makes Choice possible and a conscious decision rather than an impulse. You have to know what fits and what you can live with. It's fine if belief in oneself supersedes the quality of one's product, but cynicism does not an enduring hustler make. Without belief, one's run is apt to be short, brutish and nasty, removing any chance of immortality. There is a profound difference therefore between a hustle and a scam. A scam may pay the rent in the present, but denies the future. The ideal hustler—and his hustle—lives simultaneously in the past, present and future, informed by a calm, Zen-like wisdom.

And, with that in mind, I give you Jerry Brandt, a confrere of Sidney Falco, with grace, heart and wings. Let me say right off that there are many questionable stories about Jerry Brandt, and some of them may be true. But the naysayers got what they paid for, a front row seat to where the action was, at a price who can say was excessively exorbitant. Jerry's biggest financial successes came about when he created showplaces such as the Electric Circus and the Ritz, in the same way P.T. Barnum evolved from a simple shopkeeper into the maestro of the big tent and its three-ring circus. But, like Barnum and Mike Todd, Brandt hustled the idea of glamour and excitement as much as he did the experiences for which he charged admission. Considering Jobriath, Brandt's most outrageous foray into artist management, one is reminded that Barnum's earliest hustle was to promote a blind, paralyzed slave woman he actually owned as the 160-year-old nurse of George Washington.

Jerry is so damned imaginative I sometimes think he has spent the better part of his life avoiding his own ideas in case they killed him. From the moment I met him in 1965, he struck me as the embodiment of those hustlers I had idolized on the screen, Sidney Falco and Johnny Jackson. Our mutual Aquarian fascination with mankind in general along with a certain disdain for it in the particular served to infuse our friendship with an almost psychic rapport. For forty years, we have defended each other to our detractors with fraternal loyalty while supporting each other when certain times in our lives proved our detractors to be all too correct.

Born in Brooklyn on the same day as I in London, save on a maturer year, at the age of 15 he walked out the door of his home on the day he realized that there was no point in running from a threatening step-father anymore. Jerry was now bigger and could whoop step-dad, something he would not do in front of his mother, so he left. Years later in 1979, riding the tsunami stirred by the Brothers Gibb and John Travolta, Jerry mounted a Broadway flop that lasted eight performances called "Got Tu (sic) Go Disco," based loosely on Studio 54 and starring the doorman of the actual club, who by today's standards would be a celubutant in his own right. Jerry and I hugged at the elbows and both sighed. We drew up our shoulders and he said, "Well, at least I opened and my mom got to see me on Broadway." I'm not sure the backers of the show were as sentimental, though it was rumored that they were family men, as in one of the five families. And who else but Neil Bogart would release the title track as a 12" dance record by Pattie Brooks?

Credit Jerry with resilience and the insight that comes from a driving need for a new hustle: a scant three years later, he opened a ballroom cum nightclub called the Ritz that became the most important venue in New York for showcasing the new rock acts MTV was making into stars overnight. Billy Idol, Prince, Bow Wow Wow, Echo and the Bunnymen, Iggy Pop and Flock of Seagulls competed for the audience's attention with overheated lavatories that made Studio 54's seem quaintly for the senior set.

Perhaps most importantly, the Ritz became the venue from which Tina Turner launched her Ike-less rise to superstardom. Her new manager, Roger Davies, was looking to develop her as a rock artist, and several nights at the Ritz were booked in 1981 to showcase her new material and band. Rod Stewart happened to catch one of the Ritz shows and asked Tina to appear with him on television.

Despite her reunion with the Stones on tour and some record success in England, by 1983, Capitol was cooling toward Tina and about to drop her. At the time, David Bowie was coming off his biggest selling album ever with *Let's Dance*, and the EMI brass invited him to a celebratory dinner. David declined the invitation since he had already decided to go see Tina at yet another appearance at the Ritz. The label execs tagged along and the show they saw that night changed everything for her. Jerry would own the Ritz for close on to a decade, making the venue one of his most lasting achievements, which to this day repeats his formula in the same space in the form of Webster Hall.

Jerry was not to the showbiz manor born, however. "I didn't want to be in show business," he says. "I wanted to be a baseball player. I wanted to be Pee Wee Reece." But his parents were made of less ambitious stuff. "It all started because I didn't want to work, so my parents kept saying 'you gotta get a job, you gotta pay rent, or we're gonna throw you out.' So I read in the paper that there was a talent agency looking for an agent or something like that, so I went to this employment agency and they sent me to this talent agency. I was with a friend of mine and he gave me some speed, or something that made me crazy, and I went up to the interview and he waited downstairs . . . I remember his name was Happy.

"Anyway, I went to see this guy who stuttered, and I couldn't get a word in because he couldn't get a word out, and during the interview I realized that every time I touched his knee he was able to speak, so every time he got caught with a d-d-d-d, I'd slap his knee, and he finished the sentence. So I got the job. And I didn't have to start till 11 o'clock, so I went home and told my parents I'd got the job and they were so happy, and my dad was, 'what time do you go to work, maybe we could go together' and I was 'no, I don't have to start till 11. . .' 'Ah, that's why you took the job,' he said. And I said 'Well, that's part of the job.' And that's how I became a mailroom boy."

By the early 1960s, Jerry was working at the William Morris Agency, handling the likes of Sam Cooke, the Beach Boys and Sonny & Cher, although some seismic changes needed to rattle through the agency, "a throwback to the showbiz fifties" as he puts it, before it would ever figure on the rock 'n' roll scene the way it did in legit theatre and television. Brandt recalls, "When I got there, the biggest pop star they had was Connie Francis. There were just three people at the William Morris Agency who were forward thinking, and when they saw the first pictures of the Rolling Stones, basically they didn't wanna know anything about it. They were frightened to death."

They took them on, however, around the time of "Satisfaction," and that first tour with the Stones set Jerry up big time. The Stones left General Artists Corporation (GAC) when Allen Klein started representing us in '65; he had already worked with Jerry on Sam Cooke. "Prior to the Stones, there were no promoters in America," Jerry notes. "We had to take wrestling promoters and make them into rock 'n' roll promoters. There were no rock 'n' roll promoters except for maybe one in NY and one in Philadelphia; Bill Graham had the West Coast pretty much to himself. But it wasn't the way it is today; now every town has its guy. Back then, we had to buy out of town newspapers to find out who was booking rock 'n' roll and where they were working. We had to invent the game."

"At that time," Brandt continues, "there was, I wouldn't say a revolution, but an evolution going on. All of us, anything we said, everybody stopped to listen. It was one of those 'you couldn't do no wrong' times. It was quite easy, actually. Nobody would deny us and nobody would challenge us. We set up a 38 date tour, sometimes two shows in a day, and the Stones grossed pretty close to a $1 million. I'm sure they were in debt after previous tours."

It should be clear by now that what we are dealing with here in this primer/memoir is not really a business, it's an exploitation. And we exploit whenever we can, and once in a lifetime is usually as good as it gets; for those who are born to it, nothing less will do. It's not a matter of breeding; we are bled. We do not teach; we are observed and discarded at living will. Those who are born to it . . . our stars, our mavens, our glim reapers have a natural, intuitive need to work out something external in order to understand themselves. It's called performance, whether in front of or behind the lights.

Young Jerry Brandt

On other occasions we have all made do, and made well, from less than gods, settling for competent disciples of the real deal. And as one befriends the comedy of getting older and parlays the past into present time reality by writing memoirs, each gradient reveals new peels of actuality that refused to be called to the surface in memories past. With time, it all becomes very simple, and what may remain extraordinary to those who were not there, is seen to be as simple as having picked a pink toothbrush rather than blue. And the heroes and villains in your life get sorted out like a deck of cards face up. They cannot lie to you anymore and neither can you lie to yourself about them and if one is lucky, the heroes become friends.

    Jerry is a dark angel. He was an agent with a heart, and a *provocateur*. We'd fly from New York to reggae in Paris, first stop breakfast, second stop shoes. Jerry loved Carvil and liked Cardin. I loved both. There is a cool 1966 song by Jacques Dutronc and Jacques Lanzmann called "Les Playboys." It goes, "Il y a les playboys de profession/Habillés par Cardin et chaussures par Carvil." I have a Polaroid of Jerry I took at L'Hotel in 1974. He's tugging at his hair, using his eyes, *de rigueur* jean and blazer clad, and at his predator best. We were in Paris on a hustle. We had a deal going with a German record company which got blown because we said we could do it for four million when what the Germans wanted to hear was that we could do it for twelve. Animated or laid back he's a Francis Bacon, statesman and spy; relaxed, he takes you to where you think you should be or are. Something about him is from a better time in Europe and the rest is pure New York hot to trot. He fills up the room with his presence, often without words, and then starts leasing space.

    I think you bond with a person you have had the possibility of dying with. In Dublin in 1974, I shared a bomb blast with Tony Boland, an old mate who had been the Henry Kissinger of late night TV at RTE. The bomb only killed three people, and I say "only" given the state of the world today. The terror and mayhem that three dead causes makes today's headlines more than ungodly. I know it's part of the join with Tony Boland I share.

Jerry Brandt and I had a *Day of the Locusts* moment on the fourth Stones tour of North America when the stage collapsed on us in Montreal. We were both five bodies deep in a quicksand of panic and people and had to bash our way to the top. We were both suffocating under hysterics. You always remember such moments and those that you shared them with. Jerry recollects it this way: "I saw Andrew punching and kicking his way above the sea of bodies, finally we seemed to all crawl and gnaw our way off stage to the rotunda and into one of the limousines. The limo driver has to be sixty-five years old, the guy is fucking petrified."

Brandt stayed with William Morris until 1967, then he struck out on his own. In a small-world meeting of culture and commerce, Jerry bought the lease to a club Albert Grossman owned on St. Mark's Place in Manhattan called The Balloon Farm and renamed it The Electric Circus. Both Grossman and Brandt knew a good thing when they saw it. Previously known as The Dom, the space was a former Polish dance hall Andy Warhol rented during April of 1966 to showcase the Velvet Underground, several of his "Superstars," and some crude but cutting edge multimedia he was experimenting with. The entire concept was dubbed the Exploding Plastic Inevitable and despite a relatively high $6 admission, it was a financial success, said to have pulled in $18,000 in its first week. Note that at this time all the downtown action was in the West Village. St. Mark's place continued to be a run-down sort of high street for the still ethnic and lower class Lower East Side.

According to Sterling Morrison of the Velvets, the Factory crowd were shocked to find the Dom wasn't waiting for them when the band returned from a tour in mid-'66. "The Velvets were supposed to have a three-year lease on the Dom . . . and when we came back we discovered it was now called the Balloon Farm. Actually, our lease had been torn up and the director of the Polish home had been bribed and bought off and so our building had been taken away from us." However, neither Grossman nor the Velvets objected to their taking up residency once again in the space Warhol had established and business went on as usual, albeit with a new cashier.

Sometime in mid-1967, Grossman sold The Balloon Farm to Brandt, who quickly announced, "When you're finished with reality, come up here." *Life* magazine described the scene: "Magnified images of children in a park, a giant armadillo or Lyndon Johnson disport themselves on the white plastic sculptured expanse of the tent-like ceiling. Gigantic light-amoeba rove among the images, pulsating and contracting with the relentless beat of a rock band . . . A young man with the moon and stars painted on his back soars overhead on a silver trapeze, and a ring juggler manipulates colored hoops and shaggy hippies unconcernedly perform a pagan tribal dance . . . Stroboscopic lights flicker over the dancers, breaking up their movements into a jerky parody of an old-time Chaplin movie. But then loud, loud, the hippies' national anthem, the Beatles' 'A Day in the Life,' begins, and there is stillness, reverie." True to form, Jerry included a boutique within: "Clothes, Furbelows, Feathers, and Astonishments" were all purveyed.

Brandt managed to build on what the Exploding Plastic Inevitable had begun and by taking the concept even farther over the top anticipated by a decade the "decadence" epitomized by Studio 54 in an era that now seems far more than merely ten years separated from the '60s. The Electric Circus was conspicuously "dry." Jerry hustled the Coffee Growers' Association into investing $250,000 into the club with the provision that coffee would be his patrons' beverage of choice. Booze was hardly missed; partiers turned on and tuned in under a giant Bedouin tent created by Ivan Chermayeff who had designed the America Pavilion at the World's Fair. Jerry's sense of humor is displayed in the club's sobriquet as "the ultimate legal experience." As to the legacy of the Exploding Plastic Inevitable, "Eric's Fuck Room," a small alcove with old mattresses on the floor that had served as a casting couch for Superstar Eric Emerson, was replaced by the "Meditation Room" with carpeted platforms, Astroturf and a health food bar.

In the best Billy Rose tradition, Jerry took the Electric Circus on the road and opened a branch in Toronto, Canada. "We would like everyone to GROK!" Brandt told a journalist he was hyping before the club opened, invoking the popular science fiction novel *Stranger In a Strange Land*. Elaine Mitchell described several of the rooms being readied for groking: "Great Expectations (is) a large room composed entirely of foam rubber. Then there's the Kaleidoscope Room made of mirrors. Go in and you can see yourself for miles . . . and miles . . . and miles.

"The Graffiti Room is stark white. In here you can write and draw whatever you want. The Meditation Room is on two of the Circus' three levels and is perfect for meditating or talking to friends (two people can sit in each booth). There is a beverage area (serving cold drinks) and upstairs is a restaurant serving light snacks.

"Biggest of all the rooms is the arena which really isn't a room at all! This is where the groups perform, completely surrounded by a totally computerized environment."

Jerry Brandt, Ashford and Simpson, and Tina Turner, the Ritz, 1981

Never at a loss for an angle, Jerry announced, "Regular admission is $4.00. It's $3.50 if you're barefoot, $3.00 if you're wearing a bathing suit, and if you come naked you get in free."

Mitchell noted, "Each week, 200 free passes will be handed out and during each night the Circus is open, a clown will walk around its many rooms giving away money. It will cost you $4.00 (with regular clothing) to get in, but if you're one of the lucky ones, you'll get it back by the end of the night!

"I would like to turn Toronto on," the big-hearted Brandt effused.

Alas, Jerry's luck ran out in 1970 when, according to Greenwich Village historian Terry Miller, "a small bomb exploded on the dance floor, injuring seventeen people, and the Electric Circus never recovered from the adverse publicity that followed."

Nevertheless, before the Circus folded its tent, it was the subject of a scholarly thesis by James N. Lapsley, Associate Professor of Pastoral Theology, Princeton

Theological Seminary entitled "A Psycho-Theological Appraisal of the New Left." In an attempt to understand the youthquake of the late '60s, Prof. Lapsley suggested, "My starting point is 'The Electric Circus' and what can be learned from the perspective it affords about what is happening and what the implications of this are for theology, the church, and pastoral care." One can imagine the howls of roguish laughter such a premise would evoke from the maestro himself.

Not one given to understatement, Lapsley finds that "'The Electric Circus' is both concrete evidence for, and a powerful symbol of, something of great importance going on in our culture today. It is the place, as it were, where Marshall McLuhan meets Sigmund Freud, where fruits of the emerging culture can be seen, and an attempt made to understand what is happening . . . If you are over 35, don't stay in 'The Electric Circus' too long, or you may blow your mind."

Given his attraction to Freud, it's too bad the good professor never turned his academic powers of analysis on Jerry Brandt's hustle of a lifetime, Jobriath. Somehow Jerry managed to get Jack Holzman and David Geffen to fall in love with an artist he discovered as Clive Davis was passing on him. Brandt told Andy Warhol's *Interview*, "I was walking down the hallway at Columbia Records when I heard this sound coming out of a room. I walked in and said who is that? Three days later I was in California, where we met at the Bitter End . . . I went to an apartment that was unfurnished—a completely empty white room—in walked this beautiful creature dressed in white. We sat on the floor and he offered me a beer. I had no idea why I was there or what I was doing there. I said, 'why don't you come to Malibu and hang out' and that's where we fell in love because he showed me some tricks I didn't know."

Being openly, genuinely gay was only part of Jobriath's shtick: "Schizophrenia is my lifestyle," he told *Interview* without a trace of irony. "I think everybody is schizophrenic, but they're all fighting it. Music was never enough to keep me off the street. I added theatre, sets, costumes, my physical presence. I'm going to change my show every year. I love Aretha Franklin. I like the Doobie Brothers. I like Dr. John's arranger. David Bowie is a good lad. I become a true fairy on stage."

Jerry was more succinct if no less lofty when he told *Rolling Stone*, "Presenting Jobriath in the way he must be presented means you have to break all the rules. That requires the greatest promoter in the world. And I'm it."

Writer Stu Werbin observed, "It is a much easier task to get an interview from the world's greatest promoter than from a 'true fairy.' The promoter has something to say about everything. The future of the music business. 'The industry must turn to New York. California is putting us to sleep. It's time California either goes to sleep or comes here.' The public morale: 'The public needs somebody to admire and they need it desperately. Mick Jagger has had his chance and he blew it. Now he's old. The drug culture is dead. Broadway is dead. The only thing that's keeping us alive is sex. I'm selling sex. Sex and professionalism.'

"Which brings him, quickly, to Jobriath. 'The kids,' he says, 'will emulate Jobriath because he cares about his body, his mind, his responsibility to the public as a leader, as a force, as a manipulator of beauty and art.'

"To prove they're serious about their new frontiers, Brandt and Jobriath have booked passage on Pan American's first passenger flight to the moon."

But first Jerry planned to debut Jobriath's act at the Paris Opera House over three nights in December of 1973. Jerry's reasoning had a logic of its own: "I think if you're planning on coming to New York, Paris is the best place to come from." *Newsweek* was treated to some of Brandt's choicer *bons mots*: "The energy force today comes from homosexuals and Puerto Ricans. I see Jobriath as a combination Wagner, Tchaikovsky, Nureyev, Dietrich, Marceau and astronaut. To me, the '70s began yesterday. For the first three years they've just been repackaging dead people. We are the future."

Billboard took Jerry at his word as to what the show would look like: "One of the scenic effects in preparation is Jobriath's first entrance is a clown head floating from a box. The box then expands into a 36-foot-tower which becomes first a Kama Sutra altar and then the Empire State Building, where Jobriath is to re-enact the death scene of *King Kong*."

While Elektra seemed reticent to discuss the terms of Jobriath's deal, Brandt claimed he'd bagged a combined total of $500,000 divided between the American company and Barclay music who had the rights in all French-speaking nations. Meantime, full-page ads were placed in *Vogue*, *Penthouse*, *Rolling Stone* and the *New York Times*, all reproducing the sleeve image of Jobriath as a discreetly nude statue creeping on smashed legs, and proclaiming "Jerry Brandt presents . . ." above the artist's name. The image dominated Times Square on a 41-ft. by 47-ft. billboard over the festive period and was also plastered across 250 New York buses.

When the album was ignored by radio and made an object of fun in the skeptical rock press, Elektra put the Paris shows back to February and then scrapped them on the grounds of expense. A *Mojo* retrospective noted that "Jobriath's live debut came in the summer of 1974 with two sold-out shows at New York's Bottom Line, capacity 400. One reviewer shrewdly observed Jobriath was more like 'a slightly decadent Tab Hunter playing a Beverly Hills niterie than a rock 'n' roll phenomenon,' and that his 'melodramatic tone seemed out of proportion to his surroundings, like a grand opera staged on a flat-bed trailer.'

Interviewed long after the debacle, Jac Holzman was remorseful. After selling the Electric Circus, Jerry had brought him Carly Simon, who became one of Jac's favorite artists and emblematic of Elektra as they moved from bands like the Doors and the Stooges to the singer-songwriters that would define the label in the '70s. Jobriath had been his last major signing before turning over the reins of the label he founded to David Geffen.

Jerry Brandt and Ray Charles, the Ritz, 1982

"It was more as a favor to Jerry for letting us have Carly Simon than any real feeling I had for the music," Holzman told *Mojo*. "We never signed anyone for more than an album at a time. It was more like $50,000 for the record and perhaps $30,000 for promotion. However, I made two errors of judgment in my days at Elektra, and Jobriath was one of them. It was an awful album. The music seemed secondary to everything else. It was all too much too soon and didn't suit the label. Not because of the gay angle, it was just lacking in any sense of reality. It's an embarrassment, something that's come back to haunt me."

By the time Jobriath filmed a *Midnight Special* segment that would be the only evidence of the live show for some time to come, the true fairy was fed up. "After the filming of our segment there was a surprise birthday party for Jerry," keyboardist Hayden Wayne told *Mojo*. "Now remember, Jerry loves to be considered in the upper circles, nice clothing, etc. Jobriath picks up the cake and smashes it right into Jerry's face. I was shocked at the audacity of the act. Jerry kept very cool and laughed it off while trying to towel out the icing that was in his hair."

Elektra put out a second album, which they were happy to see sink without a trace so as to have an excuse to rid themselves of their latter day would-be Nijinsky. Jerry managed to get them on the road despite the lack of label support, but he was losing interest fast. Brandt abandoned the group halfway through the tour, "The farcical situation ensued where we, a managerless band without a label, were continuing to tour whilst charging everything to Elektra who thought they'd disowned us," the hapless Hayden continued. "Our final gig at Tuscaloosa University resulted in five encores, a screaming ovation and the fire brigade being called because the raucous behavior triggered off the alarms. We were starting to attract a following but it was too late. The band imploded."

I had occasion to experience the Jobriath phenomenon firsthand during that short time when it seemed possible Brandt would bring it off. It had been seven years since I last saw Jerry and I made a point of visiting him when I moved to New York in the early '70s. He had a floor-through apartment in a brownstone on 57th Street just next door to Bergdorf Goodman and Fifth Avenue. We were neighbors. By this time the scintillating host to thousands of revelers at the Electric Circus had come to devote himself to one extraordinary party boy in the form of Jobriath. The floor was dark yet inviting. In the middle of the sitting room, sub-lit, was a stage that was supposed to sell you on the actuality of Jobriath via its theatricality. Fuck William Morris, Jerry had morphed into Billy Rose. Whatever I saw that night I stored in my brain as something I could do with an artist of my own.

Meanwhile, I watched and listened as I realized somewhat awestruck that Jerry had once again sussed that the times they were a-changin'. The artist was nowhere to be seen, but Brandt's own aura suggested him. It was kind of unreal, yet real enough that David Geffen, whom Jerry had mentored in his own way when the King of All Media was but another mailroom apprentice at William Morris, would launch his career at Elektra Asylum cleaning up after what Jac and Jerry had wrought. And there seemed to be no need for the artist, at least not the man himself. Jerry's reality distortion field suggested him far more fully than Jobraith was capable of projecting himself.

A star has to have an intense inner desire; Jerry Brandt had it for him. Maybe all that Jobriath had was desire, the lethal kind which became AIDS and of which he died. I looked at these Brandt goings on and thought I could do this if I had the act, or was it non-act? A year later, John Lennon's dealer in Detroit introduced me to Brett Smiley and

I had my Jobriath. Like Jobriath, Brett fell over, but then so did I. Brett was straight; another element that didn't help it work.

It was the era of Glam Rock and David Bowie. But Jobriath, Brandt announced, was as different from Bowie as "a Lamborghini is from a Model A Ford (they're both cars; it's just a question of taste, style, elegance and beauty)." Jobriath had no past. According to Brandt he was a star of Garbo-esque proportions, and when was the last time Garbo spoke of her past? He'd been in *Hair* for a while, but was sacked; Brandt claimed it was because he kept stealing the show. But Clive Davis thought he was mad, while A&M Records thought he was a joke. There was scarcely a soul in America who could be paid to take Jobriath seriously.

But Brandt would not give up. He had vision, he had conviction, and he had that beautiful sense of arrogance that is the hallmark of all true hustlers—he refused to admit he was wrong, even when the entire planet was arguing otherwise.

Jerry was a man of bold ideas. When on one of our holidays in Paris, he turned up at our hotel with boxes and boxes full of ugly French jeans that he'd picked up somewhere, I could only laugh. But no sooner were we back in New York, then he'd also picked up a downtown store front and was selling them for $80 a throw, at his sensibly titled French Jean Store.

He toured the Voices of East Harlem around the world, and he brought us Carly Simon, knowing before anyone else that a girl who looked as good as Mick Jagger was going to sell to all the boys who were too butch to fancy him, or kept it hid.

But his greatest idea came to him the day he awoke from a sound sleep and decided to create Jobriath. So he went out and found this little boy from King of Prussia,

Pennsylvania, and he did just that. The most insane pop star of all time, a case study in making the most of what you have—such as when Jerry discovered that, as a chronic alcoholic, Jobriath would be unable to perform. Unable? There's no such word. Jobriath wouldn't perform, didn't perform. He was Garbo, remember? And when was the last time Garbo played the Marquee?

"It was a lot of fun," Jerry agrees. "It was very hard work, because it was all mirrors and acrobatics. But it was fun. He only played one show in his life, and that was at the Bottom Line, but everybody thinks he worked the Paris Opera House, and he worked the Albert Hall, and *et cetera et cetera*. What I would do, I'd hit three countries in a day and show the *Midnight Special* tape; we checked into a hotel in Paris and stayed two months, because they saw our show at the Opera House! So that was the life of a manager."

He had no idea, of course, how any of this would play out. "I made it up as I went along, which is like going to war with Bush, knowing how to get in but you don't know how to get out. And that was a bad thing, meaning I made critical mistakes, such as promoting a show before having a hit record, building the set before having a show, creating the costume and not having a record. It was all ass-backwards. But public relations-wise, it worked. To this day, Jobriath lives because I am Jobriath, and that's the truth."

How much of your own ambition and dreams were bound up in that package?

"I'd say 100%."

And how much of young Jobriath's?

"100%."

Snap.

Billboards were erected across North America, screaming Jobriath's name at passers-by. In London, every other bus carried his face on its front. "I don't know how to define hype," Brandt once said, "but if it means using the media to project an artist to the public, then I'm going to produce the biggest hype you've ever seen."

I prefer to think of it, however, as a hustle and one which takes us back to that earlier question. Is the money enough? Or do you need the fame as well?

It depends what you're looking for, dearie. "It's Bing Crosby, Elvis Presley, The Beatles and Jobriath," was one of Brandt's favorite remarks. "David Bowie? He's tacky and he can't pirouette." And while Brandt could find few folk who agreed with him, by that point, he didn't care. Why should he? The money was banked, even if it had all been spent, and Brandt moved on to other things. Jobriath, meanwhile, was doomed to a protracted demise, sinking deeper into obscurity before he died in the early 1990s, forgotten even by the caretaker who looked out for the frail, AIDS-ravaged nightclub pianist who still dwelled in a pyramid atop the Chelsea Hotel.

Jobriath was an object lesson, then, not in creating a superstar, but in creating a sensation; and, in that respect, it was about 30 years ahead of its time. Today, with that kind of muscle and marketing behind him, Jobriath would indeed be enormous, famed— if, for nothing else—for being famous, star of his own Surreal World series in which he and Andrew Ridgely are roommates, profiled on *Entertainment Tonight* every time he had another Botox shot.

Thirty years after the fact, Jerry waxed philosophical on his most successful hustle with his least successful artist. Asked what made the struggle to manage the unmanageable worthwhile, Jerry ruminated, "I think, in retrospect, because you became the act. I was Jobriath. It's the truth. It gave you a magic wand. But to answer the question, it's the lack of talent that makes a good manager. Either the act or the lack of entertainment talent of the manager, to be onstage himself. You supplement the act's talent with yours, and you supplement your own talent with the act's. It's a crazy thing, and then there's crazy money involved. But that said, I always hated management. Because you were the second banana."

Of course, although there was more to Jerry than his various roles as a booking agent, talent manager, clothing entrepreneur and nightclub host, the mystery of the hustle remains elusive even to the hustler himself. Brandt wonders how he became "one of those iconic people who didn't know why! I never knew who I was. Everybody else did. I always used to say I don't know anybody, everybody knows me. Which is also the lot of the performer, it's very inter-twined. If one admits it. People who talk about business, they're accountants, because that's not what it's about."

And in the finest tradition of Paul Anka's "My Way," asked if he'd do it all differently if he had the chance, Jerry replies, "Of course. Everything. But don't ask me why. I love people who say they have no regrets; I'd like to meet this guy, Mr. No Regrets. Even Jesus has regrets. I don't trust a man who can't be embarrassed and who has no regrets. Never trust a man you can't embarrass."

ADRIAN MILLAR

IT'S REALLY ALL about gangs. My attraction to the Rolling Stones had less to do with their ambitions, which were quite modest in the beginning, or my own, however much I may have emulated the grandiosity of my exemplar Phil Spector, than simply wanting to be in their gang. The Beatles' fascination for us all was even more elemental: we wondered secretly, "Would they like me if they met me? . . . I hope so." When I got to know Adrian Millar, whom you will now meet forthwith, I wanted to be in his gang, too.

Sometime in 1965, a rather obnoxious but not unappealing character parked his purple E Type Jaguar behind my Rolls Royce Phantom, opposite the Cromwellian Club in Kensington. Adrian Millar, I was to learn, came from the North London borough of Barnet, the same neighborhood where, on the day we met, George Michael was probably sucking on a dummy. It showed: Adrian was alone, aloof, arrogant and most probably in heat. I was with a couple of Rolling Stones and a sizable cast of supporting characters. We may have just finished a recording session at Olympic Recording Studios in Barnes.

"Oi! I wanna be a pop star too," he shouted at us, and we Stones, approaching the top of our game, smiled at this cheeky recognition of our success. Adrian was at once presumptuous, aggressive and quite amusing. But though he may have warranted a place holder in my mental rolodex, we did not henceforth become fast friends.

By early 1970, Millar was hanging out with his partner Patrick Meehan Jr. on the Caribbean island of Antigua, now notorious for online gaming and a complete disregard of U.S. intellectual property rights. Such high lifers as Giorgio Armani, Eric Clapton, Richard Branson and Silvio Berlusconi have also pitched their tent on Antigua, so life was good. Especially in light of the fact that Patrick and his dad had taken over management of Black Sabbath. Meehan Sr. had worked as a roadie for Gene Vincent and later as a stuntman on the Patrick McGoohan series Danger Man, so there was some muscle on Sabbath's management team as they geared up to rival Peter Grant's Led Zeppelin for the heavy metal heavyweight crown.

The Cromwellian

The Meehans had become friends with my partner in Immediate Records, Tony Calder, who was enjoying long periods of down time at Millar's home in the sunshine, while working less in London and New York. I was devoting less time and money to Immediate myself as my chronic state of manic depression demanded repeated stays in a nursing home in Highgate, where I daresay the cure was probably worse than the disease. As I breakfasted on runny eggs, Paul Anka's "Lonely Boy" would have provided a suitable interior soundtrack; I was both soft and toast.

Tony was seeking a divorce from Immediate and a large alimony payment from me and he thought Adrian could help him get it once we all got together to discuss the label's inevitable dissolution. In the event, Tony begged off our meeting in London, citing an attack of ulcers, and sent Adrian along to threaten me, which was happening with distressing regularity at that particular juncture.

Just a week earlier I had attended a launch party for Judas Jump, whom one of my other partners in crime, Don Arden, had sold to EMI. There I was ambushed by a violently unhinged Mrs. Tony Calder, who hysterically demanded I pay her long-suffering husband his due, no doubt to the amusement of Don, who knew full well Immediate had never shown a profit and took almost everything I had to keep afloat. When Adrian came to visit me at what was left of the Immediate offices at 111 Gloucester Place, he quickly got the picture and he departed without Tony's pound of flesh but with a new understanding that we had joined each other's gang of one.

Although it would be a while before Adrian and I bonded again, I certainly related to the extraordinary hustle he perpetrated on behalf of the Babys a few years later and empathized with how this cautionary tale ended for him. It all began with a chance meeting in a Fulham Road café in the middle of one night in 1973. Adrian and his chauffeur Mick had stopped in at Smalls, just about the only place open at that late hour. It so happened that Smalls Café was a second home to sundry local amateur musicians and it was with one of them that Adrian was instantly smitten, much the same way John Kennedy stumbled upon Tommy Steele.

Mike Corby was six foot two, eyes of blue and Rock Star Beautiful. He had charisma that he must have got wholesale. "Look at him. That's a fucking star," Adrian declared to Mick with typical understatement.

Mick shrugged. "I've seen him a couple of times before. He's a dopey bastard . . . he thinks he's Jimi Hendrix."

"No, he's got it. He's got magic."

"Why don't we just nick his guitar?" Mick joked.

Millar was already moving over to the young man's table. "Are you a musician?" he asked, though he already knew the answer. Gently playing the "ego" game.

"Yes, I'm a guitarist," Corby obligingly replied.

"That could make it a bit more difficult," Millar added sarcastically. "It ain't easy, but it ain't hard either. You're a star, kid . . . stick with me. Whatever you're doing, stop right now. I've got big plans for us . . . both of us."

And that was how the Babys were born.

Corby excused himself from whichever situation he was then unemotionally uninvolved and uncommitted to, and started work forming an outfit that would transport the two of them from boredom to stardom, Cricklewood to Hollywood, from skint to the mint.

After auditioning a series of absolute non-starters, a manic depressive human carrot named John Waite walked in the door. Although weighed down by one of the heaviest chips ever seen on any shoulder, he had an interesting voice, a passable image and he gave the impression that he would share a sleeping bag with the devil, just to climb up one rung of the fame ladder. He and Corby could have been made for one another and, sure enough, in front of the camera, something just clicked.

The problem was, Corby didn't like Waite and Waite didn't like Corby. Corby's plumby upper class accent and aristocratically flamboyant behavior bespoke a snobbery Waite couldn't tolerate. He hated everything about his ostensible co-star. But Millar's master plan for the three of them was compelling: a band of pretty boys who played like Led Zeppelin couldn't go amiss. It wasn't easy, but it wasn't hard either. In fact, it was simple.

With the addition of a drummer and another guitarist, a final line-up and a name were decided on. A couple of pictures were taken, and some demo time hustled out of a few fascinated onlookers, including Decca and NEMS Records, with whom Waites had had a brief flirtation via the Boys. Unfortunately, the plan had become very draining. As the stakes were going up, enthusiasm was coming down. The band couldn't write convincing songs together. The drummer wouldn't leave his old band or play without a salary and, to make matters worse, punk was just around the corner, with its wholesale disregard for both Led Zeppelin and teen idols.

The Babys were about to die a crib death. It was time for Plan B.

"You need four songs," Millar informed his charges. "That's all . . . But make them the four best fucking songs on earth. Better than Led Zeppelin, better than Deep Purple, better than Black Sabbath. Fuck, Free and Jethro Tull are all ugly bastards!"

So the process began. They wrote four songs, polished and honed them, and they were so close to perfection that Millar couldn't help but ask for a fifth. It was shit. So were the sixth, seventh and eighth. The band had but four songs. And that would have to do.

It did, too. The Babys were then offered to Warner Brothers for a cool million or, around twenty-five times the amount that EMI paid for the Sex Pistols, a band that not only had more than four songs (I'm told), but who had also generated a million pounds in free negative publicity. It was an absurd demand, an outrageous demand, and this is how it played out.

Former/future Beatles associate Derek Taylor was the Warner brother who'd be making the deal.

For four songs, remember.

"Millar, I LOVE IT! How much are you going to charge me?"

"It's any figure you want Derek, as long as there's six naughts on the end."

"I haven't got that type of money. Be serious. If you're talking a million, I just don't have it."

"Then you obviously can't play, can you? I don't want to have to deal with tin pot labels anyway."

Taylor smiled. He was enjoying the game as much as Millar knew he would—because no one goes to do battle without first finding out all they can about their adversary. "I think I can get the cash, but I'll have to go to the head office to get it approved by the big guys. Give me some time, come to the office tomorrow and pick up a check for £5000. That'll pay your rent for a couple of weeks."

The following afternoon, Millar collected the check and a bucket to go of Taylor's legendary charm, but he also found himself agreeing that it was going to take more than a demo and a photograph to convince the fat cats at Warners to part with a million.

"How about one of those new videotapes?" Millar ventured. "It's like a film . . . except . . . it's not."

"Absolutely great idea," agreed Derek. Chris Blackwell, over at Island, had a little studio with lights and a camera crew. Taylor would pick up the tab. "If you can get the boys over there early Friday, and get the tape to me Friday close of business, I'll leave for California on Saturday."

Except he never did. Or, at least, not for the reasons he thought. For the Babys were just a few hours into the shoot when an especially attentive head cameraman wandered over and told Millar that "the boss upstairs" wanted a word. "I've shown him some clips of the band from this morning and he wants to talk to you."

Ten minutes later, Millar was in the executive office of David Betteridge, Island Records UK Managing Director. "I'm not going to waste your time," Betteridge half barked, half apologized. "We've seen the band, and we know what Warners are offering you."

"Oh yeah . . . and what's that?" Millar snapped back.

"It's a mil."

"How do you know that?"

"It's my business. We have our sources," Betteridge smiled smugly.

"Well, you do have sauce, and you know more than me."

"Look, we haven't got Warners' money. But believe me, we're better equipped and hungry to do the job you need on these boys," Betteridge pitched sincerely.

"You're talking, but not saying anything. At least, nothing that adds up," Millar murmured.

"I'm saying six hundred grand, and you can have it right now."

"Well, at least you're making a noise . . . and not a bad noise at that. That's usually my job." Both men smiled as Millar continued guardedly, "But I can't do that, Warners are paying my bills."

"We won't charge them for today, and we can straighten out any other bits of 'outstanding.' What is it, a few grand?"

But Millar already had Derek's £5000 and felt uneasy. "I'll tell you what," he said. "Put your offer in writing and let me sleep on it." Such a document could only add to the band's value in the short term.

"You've got it," said Betteridge, convinced he was the cat who was about to get the cream, and at a discount price! These dimwits don't turn down six hundred grand when it's in their hand.

As David Betteridge finished dictating the offer to his secretary, he returned to Millar and left her to type out the document. But, as she prepared the paperwork, her boyfriend, Phil Cokel, production manager at Chrysalis Records telephoned her, to find out if he'd be seeing her later.

She doubted it. "It's all gone mad here. They're trying to sign a fantastic new band called the Babys. They're in deep persuasion mode. I might be here quite late if they can seduce the manager and tie up a deal."

"What's the manager's name?" Phil cannily enquired. And a couple of hours later, just as things were winding down in the studio, a telegram arrived for ADRIAN MILLAR c/o ISLAND RECORDS.

Cables usually arrived bearing bad news. Millar was apprehensive. He had no need to be.

"HAVE HEARD WHISPER THAT THE BABYS ARE ABOUT TO BECOME THE BIGGEST THING IN ROCK. IF THEY ARE ABOUT TO BE BORN WE MUST BE THE MIDWIFE. MY INTEREST IS GENUINE. PLEASE CALL ME ON THE FOLLOWING NUMBERS, ANYTIME. ROY ELDRIDGE, HEAD OF A & R, CHRYSALIS RECORDS."

"What can I do for you?" was Millar's economical opening line, when gentle giant Roy Eldridge immediately took his call.

"What can I do for you?" Eldridge replied, slightly thrown by the abrupt tone in Millar's voice.

"Nothing I can think of," Millar added dismissively.

"We want to sign the Babys."

"You haven't seen the Babys."

"It doesn't matter. We know all about them. We WANT to sign them."

"Is nothing fucking sacred? Nobody can keep anything secret. They're signing to Warners . . . or . . . eh, Island . . . Oh, who the fuck knows."

"Yes I know, but they haven't signed quite yet, have they?" reasoned Eldridge.

"I suppose you know the numbers, as well," added Millar sarcastically.

"Of course. But we'll compete with anyone. I promise you that money is not one of our problems," Eldridge replied with complete confidence.

"What is one of your problems, then?"

"Warner Brothers or Island getting the next Zeppelin to start with, and us not. We don't like being onlookers."

"I take your point. Keep talking. What's your proposal?"

"I'd like to meet, see the band and talk numbers with you and my boss."

"Nice idea, but I haven't got that amount of time to spare. I'm expecting to make a commitment to Warners, or maybe Island, but that's a very small maybe, by the beginning of next week. That only leaves this weekend."

"If I can fix it, can you deliver the band, not for an audition or showcase, more a 'viewing'—just to see them in the flesh, get the vibe?"

"I suppose I could. But where am I going to get a decent room on such short notice?"

"Don't worry about that. I'll chuck Bryan Ferry out of Studio One at AIR London. We own it, after all. Is Sunday night a date?"

"I suppose so," Millar replied resignedly, feeling himself being drawn into yet another mini conspiracy. This situation had more twists than a corkscrew in a whirlpool in a tornado.

"Let me know whatever gear you want in there. PA, mikes, lights, you name it."

"OK."

"Good."

"Done."

"See you Sunday."

"Yep! See you Sunday, seven-thirty or eight."

A lot can change in 48 hours. First, Derek Taylor rang to say he couldn't wring the money out of Warners—Millar hoped like hell he'd keep shtum on that news, at least for another few hours. Then Mike Corby turned up and fell straight into a ferocious and, apparently, final conflict with his band-mates, management, and anyone else in the room. The band essentially split on the spot. They would do this one last performance, and that was it.

Fortunately, Chrysalis were not witness to that display. But they threw their own wrench into the works when, having thoroughly appreciated the band's four song set, they asked if they could perhaps hear a fifth.

It was time for some quick thinking, but still Millar said the first words that came into his head. "If you don't know now, you'll never know, so piss off."

It worked. At nine-thirty the following morning, Millar was awakened by his ringing phone.

"Are you awake?" Dennis Muirhead, Millar's solicitor, inquired.

"Why?"

"Are you up?"

"Yeah. I am now."

"Well, you'd better sit down."

"What's going on?"

"I've just had Doug D'arcy on the phone. He wants to sign the band."

"Why am I sitting down?"

"You're sitting down my lad because the butterfly boys at Chrysalis have outbid Warner Brothers."

"Oh, I forgot to tell you," Millar said after a long pause. "Warners passed."

The ten-second pause was deafening and endless.

"Well we don't have to bring that up, do we?"

"I suppose not."

"They've offered well in excess of a million, and they want to do the deal today. Chris Wright, the chairman, is flying back from the South of France as we speak. Can you be at their office at two this afternoon?"

Doug D'arcy and Roy Eldridge materialized like two grinning Cheshire cats. "Chris Wright's en route, he'll be here any moment, but we can start the meeting in his office." Millar promptly sat himself down in the chair behind the chairman's desk—meaning that when Chris Wright arrived a few minutes later, he had to find somewhere else to sit. He chose a pile of cushions in the corner of his own office.

An understanding was quickly thrashed out, and both parties seemed content with the terms. However, in those grim days before we had computers to take all the fun out of everything, the formal contracts themselves would take up to six weeks to draw up. Millar was handed a letter of intent and £20 grand; now all he needed do was glue the Babys back together. Which wasn't that difficult, either—after all, it's amazing what a record contract can do to curb an ambitious young man's self-destructive

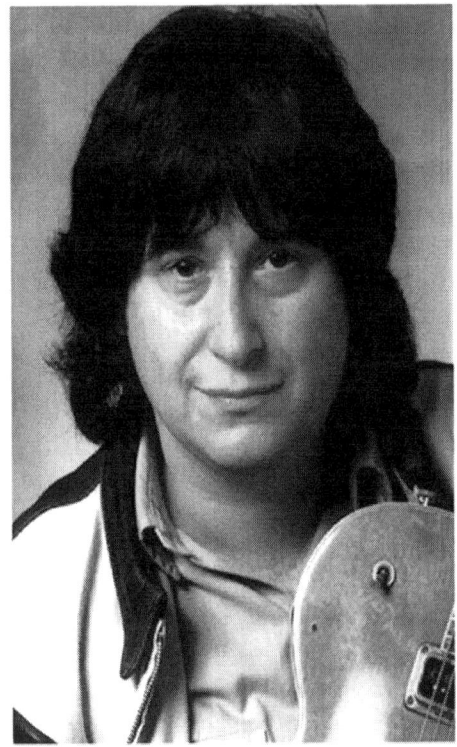

Adrian Millar

tendencies. Ask Brian Jones. Or on second thought, perhaps better not.

A publishing deal was set up with Carlin Music—those four songs were certainly proving their worth. Bob Ezrin was called in as producer, working around the edges of his commitment to the first Peter Gabriel album. And while the band certainly got the thin edge of that particular wedge and a less than stunning album to show for it, we have to remember that Ezrin was working with only . . . four . . . songs . . . .

Britain was never going to work for the Babys. It was too provincial, too fashion-driven, too engrossed in all things punk. The Album Oriented Radio format that propelled arena bands like Zeppelin and Aerosmith to the top of the charts in the U.S. without Top

40 singles didn't exist in the UK. Millar knew this, Chris Wright knew this, and Terry Ellis—Wright's partner in the whole Chrysalis operation—knew it. He was in the States, about to launch the label's newly independent American wing, Chrysalis Inc., but flew to London to cast his eye over what was in the pipeline, then went home with just one twinkle in his eye. The Babys.

Ellis immediately understood the notion that four photogenic faces attached to a rock band equaled a possibly gigantic sales angle. For Terry, the devil wasn't in the details, all he cared for was the Big Picture, which suited Adrian fine since he had no idea when his band might implode. What Adrian sensed but was reluctant to admit to himself, was that Ellis was thinking of himself not as a record man but as the manager he had been some years earlier, when he parlayed his management of Jethro Tull into a successful label. Terry saw in the Babys what he wanted to see and while for now, that was a good thing, Adrian realized that Ellis' ignorance would not remain bliss forever.

Adrian had another problem he wasn't eager to share with Chrysalis, although it was inevitable it would come to light. For whatever reason, the only band member signed to Adrian for management was the unreliable Mr. Corby. Chrysalis were suspiciously accommodating in resolving Adrian's lapse: Dennis Muirhead grandly suggested, "We'll just write you into the recording contract as a fifth member, until you tie up a new management agreement." Which gave Millar a neat 20% of recording income, equivalent to a typical manager's take. But only for the first contract term and completely recoupable against their outsized advance.

Fair enough.

The Babys, all four of them plus the fifth Baby, were now based in the States and having a wonderful time. Radio loved them, the concert circuit loved them, and even the Mafia, who appeared to be in charge of distributing their records, loved them. Now comfortably settled in at the Sunset Marquis Hotel on North Alta Loma, the Babys regarded their improved circumstances to be a fitting reward for a job well done as opposed to a job done well. They played the Dinah Shore and Midnight Special TV shows; now they were getting ready for a rare night out at the Rainbow Grill.

Millar's phone rang. It was Russ Shaw calling. A powerful Chrysalis promo man, Shaw also happened to be a very important member of Ellis' inner circle, one who spoke with the authority of Ellis himself.

"Hey ... HOW ARE YOU... great!" Shaw boomed with the fake sincerity cultivated equally by American radio DJs and the record executives charged with keeping them happy. "Terry asked me to call you. The guys up at The Monterey Peninsula Agency love the band, and he thinks it would be good if you went and had a meeting with them. So, we're flying up there this afternoon. I'm coming with you. I'll pick you up at one thirty—be ready!" It wasn't a request; it was a demand.

As they arrived at the departure lounge at the airport, Shaw said he had an important phone call to make and excused himself for a few minutes. But he was back in time for the 30-minute flight and made delightful small talk all the way. "These guys have the Beach Boys and Chicago and would be great for the Babys." Yet, throughout the dinner meeting that followed, Millar couldn't shake the impression that no one seemed to know why the other was there, and not once was there ever any mention of an agency agreement. He was still puzzling over that when he arrived back in LA the following morning.

Millar took the elevator up to his second floor suite. He entered, threw down his overnight bag and collapsed on the bed. On the second bed was the full length pigskin coat that he had given Mike Corby; he picked up the phone to call Corby and tell him to get his clutter out of the room. There was no reply.

He decided to call the other band members. No reply there either. "They must have gone out to eat," he thought, "or got lucky with some young girls who believe what they read in glossy magazines."

On his way down to the pool he asked at reception, "Have you seen any of my guys this morning?"

"They checked out yesterday afternoon."

At two o'clock the previous day, immediately following the phone call from Russ Shaw confirming their departure for Monterey, Ellis and a small group of assistants arrived at the Sunset Marquis, rounded up the Babys and laid it on the line. "It's this simple. You leave here now with us. Forget all about Adrian Millar, and do exactly what you're told, or your contract is terminated this minute. You've got ten seconds to make your minds up."

"Who's going to manage us?" Corby asked.

"That's my problem, not yours," replied Ellis, and that was the end of the conversation. Within half an hour, bags were packed, rooms were emptied and bills settled. The rooms were paid for up until noon the next day to coincide with Millar's return from Monterey.

Ellis had learned a very good lesson during his time as a manager—make your first punch a knockout blow, strike first and get out of Dodge before the going gets rough and tough questions have to be answered. But this was too easy. A few mild squeaks from the rock stars, not even whimpers, and a demoralized, dispossessed manager who wouldn't know his arse from his elbow when the shit hit its target.

Millar's first call was to Chrysalis, not knowing what had happened and half expecting a logical explanation. Maybe a TV show had come up or something. Russ Shaw and Terry Ellis were not available to take calls, but a lowly A & R assistant, Marley Brant, picked up the phone. "Hi Adrian, What's up?"

"Do you know where the boys are?"

"Yes I do, but that's classified information, and the guys don't want you to bother them anymore."

"What?!"

"You're no longer their manager and they'd appreciate it if you just left them alone."

"Where's Terry Ellis?"

"He won't talk to you."

"And Russ Shaw?"

"He's out of the office, but he won't talk to you either. These are the band's wishes, and Terry and Russ can't get involved. Hey, have a nice day."

Millar had obviously underestimated the Babys' importance to Chrysalis and overestimated his own importance to the act. Of course there were measures that could be taken—within a couple of weeks, the Babys, Russ Shaw, Terry Ellis, Chris Wright,

Chrysalis Records Inc. and Chrysalis Records Ltd. were all served with multimillion dollar lawsuits, charging contractual interference and inducement to breach of contract. And that was just the beginning of their woes. Days later, Ellis learned from the Chrysalis legal department in London that, whatever the outcome of the lawsuit, he would still have to account to Millar, as he was included in the recording contract as a full member of the band. He certainly hadn't bargained for that old chestnut. But for every hustler, there comes a time when "control" becomes more important than mere profit.

Millar continued laying the seeds of his revenge. He had been told to quit the Sunset Marquis and was offered a ticket to London in return for signing a disclaimer to any future earnings by the Babys. Instead, he put a call in to Don Arden, up on the Trousdale Estate just west of Beverly Hills. Don wasn't home but his daughter Sharon took the call.

"Hello my darling," she cooed. "What's happening? How are the gorgeous Babys?"

"To tell you the truth, the fucking gorgeous Babys have disappeared!"

Without a second's hesitation, Sharon stormed, "I hate that fucking Terry Ellis; this has got his fingerprints all over it. My dad will go fucking ballistic. Where are you?"

"I'm just checking out of the Sunset Marquis."

"Well, you don't want to stay in that karzi anyway. You wait there. I'm on my way over. You're staying here with the family. Fucking Terry Ellis. I can't believe it."

The first question was, as Sharon succinctly put it, where could those fuckers have gone? Not too far—Millar still had their passports, but Sharon didn't think that would prove too much of an impediment. "Terry Ellis is such a slippery git. He'll tell the British Embassy they've been lost and get replacements."

The legal position of Chrysalis and the Babys was pretty much hopeless but Terry Ellis didn't want to admit it and, more importantly, he didn't want to pay for it.

About a week after Millar had moved into a new Hollywood apartment, it was broken into. Amongst items taken were the welcome mat, $900 in cash and the four Babys' passports. Millar was absolutely convinced his apartment had been ransacked as he slept.

Soon afterwards, a friend called from London. It was Nigel Thomas, the former manager of Joe Cocker and a mutual friend of Adrian and the Chrysalis principals. "Millar, I think you should get this lawsuit over and let the band start work." He also informed him that Elliott Roberts, manager of Joni Mitchell, Neil Young, Crosby, Stills & Nash and so on, wanted to meet to discuss the situation and would he please take his call?

Millar, in his own self-interest, felt obliged to accept. With the insertion of Roberts into the drama, any leverage Adrian felt he might have had dealing with fellow Brits was vastly outgunned by Roberts' prominence in the LA entertainment cartel. It seemed that the Americanization of his boys was all but complete, like it or not.

Within hours the phone rang. "Can we meet?" asked Roberts.

"What for?"

"Well, let's try and work things out."

"We haven't got anything to work out," said Adrian with a tone of defeat creeping into his voice. Ironically, had a meeting with Roberts been offered under any other circumstances, Millar might have thought the occasion well met. But, though he remained bitter at events, Millar's sense of proportion prevailed. He agreed to a meeting the following day, and gave Roberts the address of the Arden mansion.

Roberts arrived in his gleaming blue Mercedes. As Elliott parked the vehicle on the huge forecourt, Millar opened the car door and deliberately towered over him.

"So you're Mr. Big," Millar barked at Roberts.

"I wasn't quite expecting this," said Roberts apologetically gesturing towards the magnificent residence.

"What was you expecting?"

"They told me a fish out of water—not a killer shark."

"What's your point?" Millar demanded.

"Look, I'm the messenger and this isn't any of my business, yet."

"That's completely right. It's none of your fucking business." A meeting in the living room was becoming more and more unlikely.

As if to try and pacify Millar, Roberts mumbled, "Terry wants you to get all the money you're owed and all future earnings you're entitled to."

"Well that's nice of him. He wants me to have what's already mine. Kinda unsteal what he's stolen. How considerate. Now let me tell you something, Mr. Elliott fucking Roberts. This was my painting—admittedly not a fucking masterpiece, but it was mine. And it should have my signature on it, not Terry Ellis' or Elliott Roberts', because any signature but mine makes it a fake, a fucking forgery. Comprendo?"

"Well yes, I completely comprendo, but here's his offer anyway. You get your commissions going forward and what you're owed in back commissions; my office will do the day to day donkey work, and we'll pay you under the contractual terms and conditions." Which sounded sweet until you actually thought about it. What it meant was that the band could work out the initial period of their contract—the first year clause that was pretty much standard across the industry, and which included him as a paid-up band member. And then when that agreement lapsed, they'd be free to sign a new contract without him as a party to it.

It was clever. Very, very clever. Act like the good guy. Neutralize the lawsuit, nullify the problem and pick up the pieces in due course. Added to which, the 'first year' contractual period would unquestionably operate at a huge loss, so no commissions would be due anyway.

"Let me think about your offer, before I reject it," Millar tormented Roberts.

Millar allowed his LA lawyers to tighten the screws while he returned to London, and was soon working with a zippy little punk group called the Wasps, who were everything that the Babys were not. A close knit, friendly, good natured unit, with more songs than they knew what to do with and a local buzz that could not be manufactured. By the time Nigel Thomas resumed his shuttle diplomacy on Chrysalis' behalf, Millar had virtually lost interest in the Babys and the lawsuit.

"Why don't you let me settle it for you?" urged Thomas. "Those fucking LA lawyers are holding out for a billion dollars. It could go on forever, and nobody's getting anything. Let the Babys start work and you start collecting some money. That will piss Terry Ellis off more than anything."

"That's all very well, Nigel, but the contract with Chrysalis is about to lapse and I'll be totally fucked."

"We can negotiate a way round it, lock in a timeframe."

"If you can do that, then do it. But I'm not sacking the lawyers, you'll have to do that," said Millar.

"Adrian, they're fucking useless anyway. This should have been settled ages ago. They're only bumping their fees up all the time it drags."

"Go on then." And so he did. Thomas negotiated what was the most predictable settlement. All outstanding sums were to be repaid, with Millar to receive his contracted management percentages paid quarterly in arrears. But Millar had one last ace to play. The settlement document was ready for signature, and Thomas and Millar were seated in the office of Chrysalis' London lawyers.

"If you'll just sign here, Mr. Millar, we have a rather large check for you," glowed Chris Wright's legal eagle.

"Hang on a second there, captain. Who said anything about a check? The Babys got my money in cash ... and that's how I want it back."

"But you'll need a large case to carry it."

"You get the cash and let me worry about the case. I'll be back in thirty minutes. If you're not ready, the deal's off."

Thirty minutes later, Millar's large black leather shoulder bag was full to breaking point, but he was also completely aware that a new adventure was just about to begin and it certainly did not include the Babys. It wasn't easy, but it wasn't hard either, as Millar had assured Corby at the beginning. It was a simple game when it came right down to it. And the name of the game was Getting Paid.

Under the terms of the settlement, Chrysalis Records Ltd (UK) undertook to collect, audit and pay all sums involved. But, sure enough when the first payment became due, no accounting appeared. Millar telephoned Thomas and, eschewing the common courtesy of small talk, he demanded "Where's my fucking money?"

Thomas was evasive, "Oh, just hang on, give them a minute to sort themselves out. They may have just overlooked things."

"Yeah, Nigel, you're right. I will hang on, until tomorrow morning. Then, if there's no accounting, there'll be a bad day at the office—a very fucking bad day."

The following morning, as he had expected, Millar's cupboard was bare. As was his mailbox. So he went to work!

He placed a series of ads in classified sections of the national press. Central London apartments with highly desirable garage parking: £25 per week. Low mileage Rolls Royce: £2000. Tickets for Wimbledon and top West End shows at unbelievably reduced prices; and, of course, the highly paid secretarial job working for a multimillionaire playboy and socialite.

The response was overwhelming—as the main Chrysalis switchboard could testify.

There was more. Burning up the telephone lines, Millar ordered thousands of pounds worth of items and goods, including a coffin, COD of course, to be delivered either to Chrysalis' office address or to Chris Wright's home—indeed, years later, running into Wright at Tramp nightclub, Millar was gratified to learn that "though I understood your strategy and reluctantly respected it, it really pisses you off when the postman knocks on your door at six in the morning to deliver the Ford Cortina Workshop Manual."

Finally, Millar received a frantic call from Doug D'arcy.

"What do you want?" Millar demanded.

"No! What do you want?" D'arcy demanded back.

"I want what's mine."

"If I get you what you want, will you leave us alone?"

"I don't like leaving you alone. Almost as much as I don't like you."

"You'll put us out of business, and that's not funny."

"Well, I think it is funny, so why don't you just fuck off. You should have thought about having a business to run when you stole mine."

The following day Millar met Nigel Thomas at the Four Seasons Hotel in Mayfair and a hefty brown envelope changed hands. No more payments were late.

Many years later, I asked Millar about his recollections and opinions on the whole incident. He smiled and said "I spent many years in hospital after the Babys and Chrysalis affair, trying to have the knives removed from my back, and I gave it a great deal of thought. I think the Babys were four boys who aspired to be extraordinary, but never had the talent. And Chrysalis were a label that aspired to have talent, but were always just . . . ordinary. The only good thing about my relationship with them all was—I didn't have one. I think we were happier apart."

And you know what? I believe him.

In the last few years of his life, Adrian used to come and visit me in Bogotá. He was bored, but as usual he always brought the edge with him. He would have me visiting parts of town I no longer hung out in looking for emeralds. It was like a huge drug deal revisited except this time the drug was solid and green, though the B players, the supporting cast, seem to be the same as those in the marching powder game. Once, outside the downtown emerald exchange, Adrian gave a street hustler one hundred dollars to leave him alone. The motley crew that came for late appointments in my apartment reminded me of my life in the '80s. Addiction as addiction.

Adrian was clean too, but he was bored. He was supposed to come out a couple of Christmas's ago for more emeralds, some sun, a rest from the English winter and to chase down an antique table he had spotted in our coastal town of Cartagena the last time he had been with us. He never arrived. He had chest pains in London, went into hospital, and fell into basic organ collapse. Although he died at the age of 56, he remains on the short list of people in my life who gave me life.

I always believed in Adrian. On one occasion when we were giving each other moral support about a business to which none of us truly belonged, Adrian played me a group, the latest thing he had come across that he wanted me involved in, for my own good, of course. Adrian was always trying to remove the lazy in me. The group sounded great—too great. I mean God bless Adrian, and he did, but Adrian in the second chapter of his life was never going to get anything really great because something really great just would not have put up with him. He made Don Arden sound like a hands-off guy.

Adrian not only addressed what might be wrong with the act, but what had been wrong with every act ever known. Anyway, the group sounded great. Adrian was pressuring me to join him. I asked if he could leave the room for a few minutes. I did not say why. Adrian left; I waited a couple of minutes for his energy to follow him and put on the cassette and pressed play.

They did not sound great anymore. The promise, the brilliance, and the money that I had thought I heard when Adrian was in the room was no longer there. It had gone out with Adrian's departure, it was all Adrian. Nothing without him. What an unbearable gift to live with. You are the act.

MALCOLM MCLAREN

"Malcolm was definitely the Brian Epstein of punk—without him it wouldn't have happened the way it did. I loved the guy; his birthday gift to me when I turned 21 was a hooker and some heroin."

— *Steve Jones*

Malcolm McLaren

ONE LATE SEPTEMBER afternoon I sat alone on a cold iron seat outside the Caffè Nero on the corner of Frith and Old Compton Streets in the heart of London's Soho, nursing an espresso I wouldn't drink and a sparkling water that I would. I'd had my espresso fix half an hour before and a few blocks east at the Algerian Tea & Coffee Store. You are not encouraged to dawdle in the Algerian gaff, but neither are you told not to. They do a brisk business in teas from India, China, Ceylon and Formosa, superlative White Monkey and Lapsong Souchong among them. The coffees are equally global in origin, from Sumatra to Ecuador, Algiers to Bolivia, and even Vietnam. The organic Colombian compares favorably to the cup I drink back home in Bogotá. There are artichoke teas for a healthy liver and licorice sweets for those heedless of their blood pressure.

The shop opened in 1887 and smells exquisitely from old wooden fixtures, aromatic and exclusive wares, and long hours worked at a refreshing craft. Artists, musicians and street walkers beyond count have passed by its inviting doors. Until they speak, the staff might remind you of Bryan Forbes, Richard Attenborough or Gillo Porticorvo. Those whose families fled from the prolonged insurgence against French occupation in the Fifties have been pretty well assimilated, but the premium they charge to serve you, quick and courteous as it may be, reflects the shrewd mercantile instincts of their native Algiers. A single espresso costs a pound, the same amount it costs to use the bathroom at Harrods.

I like espresso and there must be a brotherhood among those who prepare and serve it. I once dined at an Italian restaurant in Fairfield, Connecticut where I was told the proprietor had attended Don Paul Castellano just before he was gunned down outside

Sparks Steak House in midtown Manhattan. When my friend requested a double espresso, the well-travelled maître d' pursed his lips slightly and asked "Why?" There's something about strong coffee that gives those who sell it a self-confidence we all aspire to.

On the iron bench outside Nero's, my mind wandered among decades of memories lived in the neighborhood of Old Compton Street. I imagined myself downstairs at Mario & Franco's Terraza where Len Deighton, gourmet and novelist, lunched alongside filmmakers David Puttnam and Jules Buck while the prized table in the center of the room awaited the arrival of Sammy Davis Jr. The "Trat" was a magnet for Soho high society from its opening in 1959 and remained so even after Mario and Franco sold it in 1968 and moved on to open other successful restaurants. Once Mario had welcomed you into the club on your way up, his loyalty could be counted upon even if one's fortunes declined. When my Immediate Records imploded, taking my ready cash and much of my self-esteem along with it, Mario invited me to eat on the cuff until I got myself sorted. He only required that I pay for my drinks.

The Trat introduced "casual" dining to a London dominated by pretentiously plush and formal restaurants off the lobbies of the city's grand hotels. Its location in raffish Soho was perfectly suited to a celebrity clientele that reflected the diversity of show business, fashion and the arts of the time. International movie stars Frank Sinatra, Brigitte Bardot, and Laurence Harvey were joined in the exclusive downstairs dining room by British socialites such as Anthony Armstrong-Jones and his fiancée Princess Margaret, the future Lord Snowdon having caused Mario to reconsider his dress code of neckties for the men.

Laurence Harvey in 'Expresso Bongo'

We local lads, making a name for ourselves in the theater, photography or pop music, were pleased to be in such distinguished company. Composer Lionel Bart, photographers David Bailey, Terence Donovan, and Brian Duffy, Vidal Sassoon, Mick Jagger and the Shrimptons lent the room a lively youthfulness that was as much a part of

Swinging London as Carnaby Street. Conspicuous by their absence were the Beatles and their manager Brian Epstein. John, Paul and Brian, though business and fame necessitated they move to London, continued to patronize the same kind of old-fashioned eateries they had enjoyed in the unfashionable Liverpool of their pre-Fab days.

Soho and dissipation have always been somewhat synonymous and no one carried the flag higher than the painter Francis Bacon and his Sancho Panza Daniel Farson. I sometimes passed them on the street as they poured themselves into various pubs only to be flung out again once they'd outstayed their welcome. Our mutual friend Lionel Bart once introduced me to Bacon who even when relatively sober was the most frightening queen I ever met. To the extent that he was less talented than Bacon and even more licentious, Farson was as much to be avoided as he was perversely fascinating. Obese and dissolute, condescending and combative, Farson once passed me by with the force of a blond meteorite; I stepped off the curb to avoid his running into me, blind drunk as he was. Rough trade indeed.

Where else but Soho might Decca Records chairman Sir Edward Lewis on his way into Kettner's have passed Johnny Gentle or Cliff Richard en route to the 2i's Coffee Bar on Old Compton Street? And as I enjoyed a game of three dimensional chess in my mind where past, present and future once again proved there are no coincidences, I found I was waiting for Malcolm McLaren.

How is it we had never met, I wondered? True enough that by the mid-'70s when Malcolm was just beginning to hit his stride as a pimpressario, I had moved to New York and was enjoying my life as a newlywed. The obvious and invidious comparisons between his Sex Pistols and my Rolling Stones, so tritely trotted out by the tabs as if they'd discovered the Rosetta Stone of rock 'n' roll outrage, were reason enough for us to have avoided each other. Yet we both grew up in North London, a mere two years apart in age, fatherless, Aquarian and half-Jewish at that. Had we discussed it I'm pretty sure we'd have found Malcolm discovered the Rolling Stones before I did, although as a 17-year-old art student he wasn't in a position to do much about it. I've often said that had I met the Rolling Stones a week later in the spring of 1963 our fates might never have become entwined; a teenaged McLaren might well have seen the Stones perform a month before I did.

On my way to that cold iron bench in Soho I'd taken the tube south from Hampstead station. Back in 1962, might Malcolm have been coming up while I was going down on one of the longest escalators in the London tube system? When I met my first wife-to-be, Sheila, at a party, might he have been among the middle-class Jewish kids posing as French beatniks? I think not, our red hair would have given us away to each other. Some god of rock 'n' roll must have been protecting our still embryonic sense of singularity, which, in all modesty, was to have a huge impact once it found expression. Though we never met, and now it is too late for Malcolm has sadly passed, I found myself sharing with him memories of our youth that tied us together in spirit more closely than the bands we guided to fame and fortune.

In putting together the hustler's hall of fame that is this book, I found I could not ignore Malcolm McLaren, despite the fact that he is the only contemporary figure with whom I was not personally acquainted. While not exactly a manager, artist, or impresario in any fully realized sense, and although his DNA as a business person might most accurately be labeled "Shopkeeper," McLaren in his faith and enthusiasm for the political and social potential of Art has much in common with Diaghilev, begging the question if the doomed Sid Vicious was his Nijinsky. I rather consciously avoided him while he was with us, thinking his relationship to me was a bit too much like mine to Phil Spector's or Jayne Mansfield's to Marilyn Monroe. I now find that attitude somewhat rude, thoughtless and arrogant. Now that I am firmly committed to a contract extension on my own life, perhaps I can do a bit of justice to his, now that his run is over once and for all.

He was born in 1946 in London near Highbury, and his family ran a small clothing factory. Increasingly alienated from both his mother and his step-father, he was raised by his eccentric and well-to-do grandmother, Rose. Rose fancied herself a free spirit beyond the boundaries of conventional morality and liked to tell of the days when she and a painter friend sold fake old masters to the nouveau riche. A fitting exemplar for her swindler in the making grandson.

McLaren was eighteen when he met designer Vivienne Westwood, who would be the next most important woman in his life. Practical and down to earth, she helped to ground her restless boyfriend, rather like Mary Quant helped me to learn how to have fun getting it done. Despite his ambivalence toward their relationship, Westwood was loyal to McLaren to the very end, describing him as "fascinating and mad" as terms of endearment.

The pair took over 430 King's Road in Chelsea, and dedicated their retail clothing establishment to the Teddy Boy revival that was stumbling around at the time as an antidote to the hippie movement that had turned so much of youth away from rock 'n' roll. And there Malcolm might have remained, as did Vivienne via a series of name changes over the next few years, until she went runway and moved on from the youth market in '81. Malcolm viewed the shop and its wares as a means to an end. "The next

Archie McNair, Alexander Plunket-Greene, Mary Quant and staff. Bazaar, London, 1961

major movement in pop music," he declared, "would not merely be linked with a fashion; it would be physically created by one."

It was not an entirely original prediction: Mary Quant was aware of much the same thing in 1960, and Swinging London proved the wisdom of her words. The mother of the muses, Chelita Secunda, first wife of the notorious Tony Secunda, set such wheels in motion when she applied the first dabs of glitter to Marc Bolan's cherubic face; it was not Bolan's music, after all, that ignited the Glam Rock movement that was sweeping Britain even as McLaren made his pronouncements, it was his appearance. The music came later.

In 1972, McLaren met the New York Dolls when they dropped by the shop during a visit to London that was to prove fatal for their original drummer. Impressed by their street smart demeanor, the garish collision of five New York Bowery thugs and a red light Salvation Army thrift store, McLaren hitched himself to the Dolls' tour bus, first around the UK and France; then across to New York itself where, to an extent that is wholly dependent upon who is telling the story, he became their manager—and managed them into the ground. His time with the Dolls should have taught Malcolm that controversy is difficult, easy to create, impossible to control and often destructive. Even the Dolls' large and enthusiastic following in New York was puzzled and put off by his red plastic outfits and communist stage set. It was perhaps the greatest miscalculation since I allowed the Rolling Stones to wear matching hound's-tooth suits for their first TV appearance.

But when he returned to London in the spring of 1975, having totally failed at whatever mission he had in mind for his first management project, Malcolm's appetite for more was ravenous. He had left behind a shop called "Too Fast to Live, Too Young to Die" and quickly re-christened it "Sex." However, he had yet to learn that the things that get into the papers are not the ideas that the entrepreneurs hatch, it's the accidents that they cannot predict, but which they learn to manage regardless, especially in America. Ask Sid and Nancy. Be that as it may, whilst Don Arden was turning up the heat up under the chicken's feet and telling us they were dancing, Malcolm started dancing himself.

Murderers murder, inventors invent, terrorists terrorize and McLaren, no matter how highly or otherwise you regard his achievements, was at least savvy enough to take half a dozen disconnected statements and string them into one cohesive sentence. According to chronicler Johnny Rogan, "what separated the Sex Pistols from the young acts of the period was their unwillingness to respect their elders on the rock circuit"— Johnny Rotten famously sported a Pink Floyd T-shirt, upon which he had scrawled "I hate." But of course he hated Pink Floyd. What is the point of starting a band if all you want to do is recycle, unquestioningly, the same sounds that are already available from a thousand others?

McLaren tells us in the ill-fated film, *The Great Rock 'n' Roll Swindle*, "How to form a band." Take four kids, "make sure they hate each other, make sure they can't play. . . ." So far, so typical. Another early scene insists "anybody can be a Sex Pistol," and that may also be true. Anyone could. But not everyone was, and the chemistry that developed, however fleetingly, between Johnny Rotten, Glen Matlock, Steve Jones and Paul Cook was certainly inflammatory enough to spark Rotten, the lyricist, into sufficient frenzy to turn out at least a handful of anthems—"Anarchy In The UK," the Sex Pistols' first record, is a lovely burst of noise, even if you don't appreciate its dynamics and sentiments. Steve Jones was a great rock 'n' roll guitarist and Lydon/Rotten, wrote, in terms of the articulation and shout called for in the day, some very good lyrics. And later, of course, they had Sid.

Swindle, unfortunately for Malcolm, provided ample evidence of his shortcomings as a manager, if not as a hustler. It is the kiss of death to dance in the same spotlight as your band. It does not matter whether they are breaking up or you are breaking down; it is just inexcusable. Rule #1 is never to do anything that is not about the band. My own weekly columns in the music press were for the most part daft and presumptuous. I even had myself retiring in 1964 "due to pressure." What a cunt and embarrassment I must have appeared to my boys. Any band with the killer instinct required to survive is always looking for their manager to fall; failure confirms the manager's incompetence, success breeds the suspicion that the manager is unnecessary.

In hindsight, we can admiringly recall how all McLaren had to do was sit back and let things happen. At the time, that was all he was capable of doing—even the Sex Pistols' greatest masterstroke, releasing "God Save The Queen" a mere two weeks before Her Majesty's Silver Jubilee (and thus soundtracking the event for every anti-monarchist in the land) was a glorious accident, a fluke of timing. Had McLaren's original intentions come to pass, the record would have been released a full four months before the happy event, and might even have been forgotten by the time the street parties started. Which might have saved the band members a few trips to the hospital, as royalist rabble took to jumping them on the street.

Yes, there was a Great Rock 'n' roll Swindle underway. But, contrary to almost everything that has been written since then, it was the industry that was doing the swindling, building Punk and the Pistols into such a phenomenon that, from the Clash to the Police, from Squeeze to Paul Weller, the music industry had its next decade's worth of superstars handed to it on a newsprint-coated plate.

It would be spring 1977 before the Sex Pistols finally found a home that was willing to take them as it found them. McLaren tumbled between the figurative sheets with Virgin's Richard Branson. Branson understood the value in the Pistols' status as pariahs—indeed, he'd actually tried to sign the band immediately after the EMI incident, only to be brushed aside by McLaren's continued conviction that the band needed a "real" record label. It was desperation that finally prompted McLaren to accept Virgin's offer; but it was Virgin's encouragement that finally allowed him to shake away his fears, and learn to enjoy his band's notoriety.

Despite the storm of disapproval and violence that swept over the Pistols and McLaren, they really had it too easy and it ruined any chance they had to be legitimately great. Bands are hardened by the road, yet promoter cancellations and pissant club dates ensured that often the Sex Pistols' greatest performance was their misbehavior upon arriving at an airport. As McLaren himself would say years later, he had a cart when what he really needed was a horse.

Malcolm did manage to take in about 700,000 pounds, just under a million as Johnny Rotten chortles in the Swindle movie. And it's that 700,000 pounds that became the undoing of both band and manager. It's always about money in the end, isn't it? Lydon, increasingly in competition with best mate Vicious for the title of nastiest punk, grew tired of being held at arm's length from Malcolm's machinations. The outrage he felt at anyone who condescended to him was now turned on a gambler he felt was dealing from a marked deck.

McLaren had neither accounted for nor paid the band from the money that had come in, and a lot of it had been sunk into his own little Heaven's Gate. While legal proceedings against McLaren's company initiated by Lydon and eventually joined by Jones and Cook took ten years to resolve fully, there was hardly any doubt that the court would find the principal "adult" in the matter to be in bad faith. Perhaps it cannot be said that greed was McLaren's deadly sin, but his competence was sorely discredited. Ultimately, all assets in the business, including the film that seemed dated and quaint the moment it was screened, devolved to the band. By that time it had been years since Malcolm McLaren had considered artist management a rewarding use of his time and talents.

As a cultural catalyst, Malcolm's own career as a recording artist from 1983 on, when he almost single-handedly launched hip-hop as an international phenomenon, has far better stood the test of time than his "management" of the Sex Pistols and Bow Wow Wow. It is true he pulled both groups together and prodded them into record contracts and notoriety, but once the artists were toddlers, so to speak, he became redundant, if not also bored and a little intimidated. Both acts were so ephemeral, albeit entertaining, that it's hardly likely their short careers would have been greatly extended or more significant if "managed" by anyone else. Perhaps in the end, Malcolm McLaren was far more like Andy Warhol, the filmmaker, than pimpresarios such as Tony Secunda and myself.

Which comparison leads somewhat naturally to a consideration of what I feel to have been the Sex Pistols' most important contribution to rock 'n' roll, Sid Vicious.

Lionel Bart and John Lennon

As a young boy, just before the "dawn" of the rock 'n' roll era, I was greatly taken by Tony Curtis, particularly his 1955 performance as a bad boy bank robber in *Six Bridges to Cross*. His exotic, gypsy-like looks and cocky confidence were like nothing on offer in Britain, still drab and downtrodden by post-war privations. Tony gave us young lads a glimpse of a world beyond the foggy streets of Big Smoke. Twenty some odd years later, I got the same thrill from Sid Vicious. To most observers, Sid seemed pathetic and doomed; to me, he embodied all the hope and possibility buried deeply within every alienated and lonely kid. Had I been closer to Sid in age, he would have become my secret friend, someone who did all the things that I dared not, who I might hope to become should danger threaten me and I found I was suddenly fearless.

Pete Townshend wrote, "Hope I die before I get old." It's hard to imagine Sid even conceiving of life beyond his next fix. Allegedly a virgin when he met groupie siren Nancy Spungen, the attention she paid him and her neediness came to define his terribly narrow, yet somehow noble, short life. He was no more a bass player than Malcolm was a "manager," but just as Malcolm succeeded as an agent provocateur, Sid was surprised and pleased to find he was a somewhat better musician and certainly a better front man than anyone had ever assumed he could be. When Sid attempted to cover Eddie Cochran, most people were amused or horrified but I saw in Sid the spirit of one of my earliest idols, Jet Harris, and found it was good.

A rock 'n' roll generation is about seven years and every seven years a new generation takes it upon itself to rewrite history. Sid was born in 1957, or two generations later than I. He was a starry-eyed fifteen-year-old when Bowie's "Rebel Rebel" became his alpha and omega of a rocking good time. Crosby, Stills & Nash, Cat Stevens and James Taylor had passed him by. Jim Morrison and Jimi Hendrix had been dead a long time. As for the Sixties, Bowie summed them up for the likes of a young John Beverly in his anthem "All the Young Dudes":

"My brother's back at home with his Beatles and his Stones

We never got it off on that revolution stuff

What a drag too many snags"

At first, Sid was merely the Sex Pistols' greatest fan, who invented the pogo dance that gave way to the mosh pit of the next generation. He delighted in terrorizing "journalists" who weren't sufficiently enthusiastic about his gang. Raised by a mother who herself was an on-again, off-again junkie, the Sex Pistols became Sid's family and

Malcolm McLaren the wily Fagin who told the spiritually homeless boy, "Consider yourself one of us," when original bassist Glen Matlock proved to be too normal to remain a Pistol.

McLaren's latter day take on Sid may be cynical but it is almost certainly accurate. "The idea and the whole notion of the Sex Pistols was to be totally irresponsible and struggle for immortality," he told an interviewer in 1989, a decade after Sid's death while awaiting trial for the murder of his girlfriend Nancy. "That was the dream and it so happens that reality sometimes forces its way through the door and you meet your maker. Sid met his maker. He got it. He wanted it that way. He was a fan of the group, originally, and then he became a member of his favorite group, which is something most fans dream of. His dream came true, so what was he going to do then? To be, in his mind, the greatest Sex Pistol. And how was he going to do that? Die! And who was going to kill him? His mum. She was a junkie. She scored for him. He asked for it."

So in the end, perhaps Sid Vicious was the only true Sex Pistol. The others, including Lydon, were no more than ruder versions of Glen Matlock. McLaren certainly seemed to think so, although at the time of this conversation, the wound inflicted by the court settlement was still fresh. "You know, the final and fatal tour of America was such that Sid was paraded as the ultimate and total icon of rock 'n' roll. And Johnny Rotten was extremely jealous. Rotten called Sid a circus act on stage . . . .

"Well, these parades were the ultimate, man. How far could you go? He didn't want to survive because Sid was a major star. He's there in the rock 'n' roll hall of fame alongside all the other punks—Marilyn Monroe, Jim Morrison, Elvis Presley. Sid's there. Johnny Rotten? Nowhere, man; just a face in the crowd, just a suburban kid who tried desperately hard to be a bad boy and never made it, guilt-ridden, toying with rock 'n' roll. He's pathetic, just pathetic. Sid was a total star. Because he never feared tomorrow and he went through that door . . . ."

I couldn't agree more and yet . . . Malcolm's bitterness toward Rotten is as oddly and disturbingly familiar to me as his admiration for Sid. It bears more than a passing similarity to my failed friendship with Mick Jagger and my enduring affection for Keith Richards. Is it possible that the disillusionment we both had thrust upon us is what we have most in common, after the notoriety has been put aside as yesterday's news? A disillusionment not with show business or temporary wealth but with the bond we thought we shared with our secret friend?

I sit on a cold iron bench in Soho and I find I am waiting for Malcolm McLaren.

DON ARDEN

"I grew up surrounded by violent people and violent behaviour. It was not unusual to see my dad threatening someone or brandishing a firearm."

— *Sharon Osborne*

Don Arden, 1968

I HAVE LITTLE use for the past and do not give it too much thought. I decided that whoever our God is, He listens to our thoughts if He chooses to, and therefore as a matter of decorum one should attempt to distil the fruit cocktail of mindmatter down to clear running water whenever possible. It's not that I do not have a healthy respect for my past actions, but it could be mighty unhealthy to rely on them as the reason behind each new day. Of course, my past became my present when I set about producing my books, and that's an acceptable glance back.

Having lived through it, I do not consider my life to have been a work of art, even less a publicity stunt. What to others may be a wonder, dazzlement or aberration, to me is most properly the accumulation of causes that I either enjoy or suffer the effects therefrom today. I do not play "Paint It, Black" at home or whilst driving, but I'm very pleased to hear it at my supermarket or the cinema. The one exception I make as regards my past has to do with fondness, which nourishes the heart and is good for us as long as it is a fondness based on a real experience as opposed to an imagined one. A fondness is more than an experience we share with another. It's a nice strong wooden match illuminating time, a meeting with one which usually gives off an aura that you were meant to meet, or had done perhaps in a lifetime whose karma, if not one's memory, one shares in present time. And by that criterion, I'm very fond of my next guest, Mr. Don Arden.

I always wanted to be in show business—standing next to Don Arden, you were. The first time was at the Granada, Harrow in 1962. Don was promoting a Brenda Lee tour; I was hustling for the PR gig. Either Chris Hutchins or Keith Goodwin already had the job. The damp dark backstage walls were as unattractive as a bunker, but the halls were alive with laughter and music as Don held court. His youngsters Sharon and David scampered from one dressing room to another and Don enjoyed bringing a night of entertainment to a theater near you.

It was exciting and intoxicating. Alive, ambitious and brash. I was in the valley of the kings, with those who traveled like gypsies weaving homiletic fables and singing songs, who having warmed themselves in the footlights found a home there. Above all, it had something going that not much of late Fifties Britain had—it was cheerful. Don and his family opened their hearts and home to me and let me in. Later, I worked the press on the Little Richard/Sam Cooke/Jet Harris tour. I lasted ten days whilst the tour ran a month because I had sent out a press release inviting the newspapers to come see the Teds literally rip it up in their enthusiasm for Little Richard. The Granada tour circuit managers told Don that either I went or the tour closed. I went.

Don Arden was born Herschel Levy. His mother was from Latvia, in what became the Soviet Union. Her parents were Jews, two of the millions forced from their homes. Walking to the nearest place they could board a boat, they landed in England and remained in Liverpool for a year, then followed the opportunity for work to Manchester. Don's father's parents were Polish Jews, as was my grandfather, Militar Schatkowski.

As I studied show business and came to work in it, I often found myself attracted to and connecting with those of the Semitic tribe. I think I subconsciously admired the Ardens' embrace of their Jewish heritage; my mother, raising me on her own, took some pains to present us as perfectly neutral in that regard. Her beauty and her unmarried status made some wives of her acquaintance uneasy, so it was best to blend in as much as possible.

Such anonymity was not to be had in the poor neighborhood Don grew up in. "We lived in a ghetto," he said bluntly. "Since everybody was so poor, the only way to discriminate between the inhabitants' faiths was to watch which church or synagogue anyone attended. As we grew older, friends turned into enemies." This was the key to who he would become. There were no after school boyhood friendships between religions, just fist fights and bloodied noses. The hierarchy was based purely on muscle and intimidation.

He joined the Synagogue's choir at the age of six, making him the center of attention in his family. They all wondered how he'd gotten in and where he learned to sing, as no one else in the family was musical. Within the first month he was having arguments with the Cantor because he felt he was ready to solo alongside adults with many years' experience. Little Harry already had an agenda: if he was respected as a singer, he'd meet the king and queen, "this was obvious." Newsreels at the local cinema convinced him that the Royals were the only family in the land to have a garden. He'd never known anyone else who had one and it was a milestone when he and his sister got a little patch of green to call their own.

His mother was ambitious for herself and her children, but his father's family scoffed at her attempts to better her lot, and young Don picked up on the negativity. His father, Lazarus Levi, did piecework, putting raincoats together. He worked all the time, leaving home at five in the morning and coming back at eight at night. His wages were 3 pounds a week, which had to make do for the four of them. He encouraged Don to take up a trade. Don worked for his father for three months before drifting off to a life of his own.

His mother was in love with the theater; it was what she lived for. She would, as often as time and money allowed, take Don and his sister, Eileen, up to the cheap seats where they sat enthralled. And in his own way, Don became quite the student, making notes from the newspapers about the headliners of the day. Somehow, the precocious eight-year-old found the pennies to purchase sheet music and was literate enough to learn the lyrics. His model was a South African who went by the name of "Afrique," a musical impersonator whose Caruso was renowned. By the time Don was 13, he could perform all of Afrique's routines.

There was no rehearsal space; imagination and daily life became his stage. Walking to school, he acted to an invisible audience and planned. At the intersection one could catch him going on: "You dirty swine, I'm going to kill you, you dirty rat." Everyone thought of him as a "loony." He was unaffected by their ridicule, caught up in his goals and fantasies. He described it as having a "double-active" brain, teeming with schemes and angles. I lived out a similar fantasy life when a tween in the better cushioned enclave of Hampstead NW3. We didn't have intersections; we had balmy leaves and avenues of trees. I didn't do Cagney; I didn't play tough. I played Marlon, Monty Clift and James Dean, and an actual audience would have been superfluous.

His mother was the pillar of their home and kept the little house spotless despite the dirty streets just outside her doorstep. The walls were so thin, Don joked, that after they said their prayers the kids next door would say, "Amen." Sometimes they would hear Don singing from within the outside loo. The purchase of the family's first radio was another milestone in their slow struggle to improve their lives.

They left the ghetto when he was seven and moved up the street to Bury New Road, a Jewish area. In the new home, Don and his sister had separate bedrooms and the house had two bathrooms. Life had improved. It was a different world, going from the box and a single tap that they shared to this almost excessive luxury. Simple things like electric lighting fascinated them. They would wander around the house turning the lights on and off, utterly amazed.

Don's parents scraped together enough to send the children to Hebrew school after their regular school was over for the day. It was in some ways one of the most challenging aspects of Don's young life, even more so than the poverty they shared with all of their neighbors. The demands of the Hebrew school's instructors and the unwanted extra attention that his attendance there drew to him as a Jew toughened him up. It was necessary for the Jewish boys to gather together for the trip to Hebrew school, lest one of them walking alone be ambushed by the Christian lads. And leaving after their lessons in the ancient language, they'd find a jeering little mob of urchins itching for a fight. Though often outnumbered, the five Jewish lads found an equally combative leader in Don.

In Don's streets you were either a fighter or a victim. There was no middle ground. Don was born a fighter. His father belonged to the Young Jewish Brigade, determined adversaries of the local Oswald Mosely gang of British fascists. These wannabe Nazis made the mistake of holding their meetings on street corners before running amuck through the Jewish ghetto. The Young Jewish Brigade were led by men who were often champion boxers. The Jews and the Nazis had been brawling in the streets since Don was still Harry and only four.

Both of Don's parents supported his show business ambitions. When he had his first professional audition as an under-aged 14-year-old, his mother willingly put his age as 16. The family paid for him to attend the Manchester College of Music part-time where he studied opera and grew into the solo turns in the Synagogue he coveted. He had a presence that the classics required as much as musical ability.

When he was 17, Don's parents divorced and he got engaged to Rita Marlowe, seven years his senior and already an established entertainer. While he was performing in her show, he was called into the service and denied leave in order to marry Rita. Unwilling to wait for Don, she married someone else four weeks later. Decades passed and it happened that Don learned Rita was singing in a piano bar in Los Angeles, where he was living at the time. After her spot, he went up to her and said "Hello, sweetheart." She didn't recognize him, as she was blind. Overcome, Don left $100 in her cup and slipped away.

Don wasn't a good soldier. He despised the army, hated taking orders from his "superiors." Jewish medical officers helped him to fake recurring illnesses, but his malingering was resented and brought more trouble on his head. Didn't matter—Don got very sick with pneumonia, which got him honorably discharged.

Don: "After the war I became a talented thug. I fell in with the artist crowd at Huddersfield, at the Hippodrome's Green Room. The Green Room was where the artists, managers and a few of the better connected patrons drank and socialized. I became well known due in part to my talent and partly because of my physical strength. I was the brawler from the Jewish ghetto. I got into a fistfight on the set once while an act was on and was kicked out because of it."

He was banned from the circuit and out of work for nearly two years. Eventually, Don returned to his roots, singing in Hebrew to a primarily Jewish audience, this time with an orchestra replacing the local choir. He worked at the London Palladium for two years. It was the first time he had been paid as a star, with his name on posters and the marquee. Every agent in the country was calling him. —

At around this time, Harry Levy became "Don Arden." He was getting too big to be stuck with a name so obviously ethnic. If he'd been a comic it might have been different, but as it was Don was already thinking of expanding his opportunities beyond performing. In his early twenties Don had enough financial independence to strike out as an agent himself. Within a few years he'd become the complete package: artist manager, booking agent, record promoter and concert producer.

Throughout his rise, Don prided himself on his physical fitness and wanted nothing to do with drinking, let alone drugs. If he had the time and the inclination, he'd drag his heavy suitcases from the hotel to the train station himself. His competitiveness was born of a deep mistrust of his fellow man. Neither the audience nor his colleagues in the business were spared. "If (an audience) wanted to start on me, I'd belt them 'round the fucking ears,' he exclaimed." Even less sentiment was wasted on his rivals. He remained certain they were liars, cheaters and jealous whores. They "would kill you if they could."

Don married his lifelong companion Paddy when he was 24. He and his wife lived in Brixton, back then the residential center of showbiz. He started a business from his front room. Before they could afford a phone, he used the phone booth on the corner and had business cards printed with its number on them. Eventually, he had two

Saturn Returns—with Ruby, Max and Esther

telephone lines put in, which in those days was unheard of. They left Brixton in '62 or '63 for Barclay House in Mayfair. Paddy was ten years older than Don and an acrobatic dancer. She already had two children, Richard and Dixie. The Ardens had two children together: David, born in 1951, and Sharon, born in 1952. Both entered the business.

"I got a contract with the American Army for their bases in Germany. The German agents had a serious problem in that all of the stars were controlled by Jewish managers, who saw no particular reason why they should enrich their former oppressors. That was no problem for me, of course. I placed myself between America and Europe. All the rock 'n' rollers had to go through me to get to the U.S., and vice versa. I was the sole European rep of the William Morris agency, which at the time had the biggest stars in the world. This was how I got into the Star Club and rock music."

Don heard rock 'n' roll as opportunity knocking; he appreciated that young GI's and their European peers wanted something new. He traveled to the States on a talent hunt at a time when both rock 'n' roll and American artists were anything but mainstream in Europe. His risk paid off when the Morris Agency designated him their man in the old country. Upon his return, Don booked Gene Vincent's first tour of the UK.

"Gene was miraculous. He had never studied music formally in any sense but I thought that he was the best at that genre of music. There was no doubt about his completeness as a performer. His voice, mannerisms and delivery were all perfect, dark and sinister. Gene asked me to manage him after the tour." For all the success Don would later have with groups like the Small Faces and the Electric Light Orchestra, like Larry Parnes he was really most comfortable with solo acts. What made the Beatles so attractive to Brian Epstein, that they were a kind of gang you wanted to join, somehow evaded some of the sharpest operators of the time.

Gene's sheer belligerence, fueled by alcohol abuse, caused some of the staff to quit or break down. He was capricious and arbitrary. While on tour in South Africa, Gene bedded the 15-year-old sister-in-law of the promoter, Mickie Most, who threatened to kill him. Understandably, Don and Gene cut their stay short but eventually Mickie made his own way to England where Don helped Most launch his dubious career as a performer.

He struggled along at the bottom of a bill headlined by the Everly Brothers and featuring an as yet little known rock 'n' roll band, the Rolling Stones. Mickie soon decided to try his hand at "production," which was ambitious because the vast majority of English pop records were made by the record labels' in-house A&R executives.

David Arden picks up the story. "Don liked Mickie and although he was a terrible act used him on his tours as often as possible. It is a fact that Mickie realized he was going nowhere and told Don and Peter Grant he would like to become a record producer. Don basically said 'Great, you're a record producer. Peter, you and I will form a record company.' At this time, Don had begun to realize that records were where the big money would be. I was there the first time Mickie, his wife, Peter and Don first saw the Animals at the Scene Club off Great Windmill Street. Everyone was ecstatic over their performance, so we went to their dressing room after the show and Don introduced Mickie to the group as their record producer. We all left, but Mickie returned to see the Animals, as he had forgotten to ask them something.

"The rest of us continued to our car, and the next thing Mickie comes running up to us and tells Don that Ian 'Sammy' Samwell is in the Animals' dressing room telling them he wants to produce them. Don returned to the club with Mickie, leaving Peter to look after Mickie's wife Chris and me, and politely told poor Ian that the Animals already had a producer. But Don had nothing against Ian personally and later had him produce "What'cha Gonna Do 'Bout It" for the Small Faces. After the Animals, Don gave Mickie the Nashville Teens and along with the Animals and Herman's Hermits, by August 1964 he had produced three UK Top 10 hits."

Gene Vincent remained an irredeemable alcoholic. Much later, Don had him taken in for an examination, but Gene wouldn't speak with the doctor. He was awash with "free" drinks from hustlers trying to make good with him. The doctors couldn't understand how he was still alive. Don tried to talk him out of it. Although they were very close, Don being like a father to him, Gene refused to listen. He died of a bleeding ulcer, still drinking, in October of 1971 at the age of 36. He had been born in 1935 the same day as my mother and Mary Quant, February 11.

Don became a partner in Hamburg's Star Club, which confirmed his reputation as the go-to guy for American rock 'n' roll acts, but even the street savvy Arden found the scene there tough and intimidating. German partner Manfred Weissleder was responsible for policing the club and keeping the local authorities happy, despite outbreaks of violence that at least once lead to a patron's death. It was in this crucible that the Beatles were forged into a steely band of brothers, but they were as babes in toyland surrounded by the worst sort of pimps and spivs. They probably found Hamburg comfortably similar to Liverpool. Both cities were busy seaports with a constantly changing population of drunken sailors. Don recognized that the club created a venue for rock 'n' roll that no cinema turned concert hall could hope to duplicate.

Don insisted that "the time the Beatles spent in the Star Club developed their sound. People think of it now as the 'Liverpool Sound,' but it came together in Hamburg." As an outlet for the boys' adolescent high spirits, Hamburg had it all over their home town, where their hijinks would never go unnoticed. One Sunday morning, John and Paul dressed up like priests and went to an old church, where they "anointed" the communicants with their urine. They were arrested, but Manfred got them out without charges.

Pissing on civilians was something Don could live with, but he never came to terms with recreational drug use. Though most of the white Southern rockers Arden promoted had a taste for booze, he found their dabbling in speed and reefer distasteful. "When I first found the drug scene going on, I was already in my forties. I never associated with that crowd. I didn't tolerate it." He resented them spending the per diems he advanced on drugs.

Among his other problems, Don found himself challenged by a different kind of bootlegger. Outside his shows, rings of ex-convicts hustled unauthorized photos of his stars. Don's solution appeared in the form of a widely feared thug named "Mad Tom," who dealt with the pirates quickly and violently. Since the victims were ex-cons, the police never bothered him or Don.

Because he was receiving threatening letters from his enemies, particularly the lowlifes dealing to his artists, Don quietly moved from Brixton to Mayfair. Once, when his wife had taken ill, he received a letter of condolence for her passing, even though she was alive and well. They sent a hearse to the Brixton address, which Don hastened to turn around. He didn't need any more notoriety in the neighborhood.

After this, he decided that he would get rid of the drug dealers. A certain woman was running the whole operation. She bribed hotel staff to look the other way and bought police protection as her crew made deliveries to the artists, under Don's nose. Don foiled her plot to kill him by having her committed to an asylum by completely legal means.

Don now had all the action he could handle. From the late '50s to the early '60s, Don promoted UK and German tours by the Kaye Sisters, Brian Hyland, Little Eva, Screamin' Jay Hawkins, Carl Perkins, Duane Eddy, the Shirelles, Bo Diddley, Chubby Checker, Freddy Cannon, Johnny "Running Bear" Preston, Little Richard, Sam Cooke, Ray Charles, the Everly Brothers and Sophie Tucker. When Little Richard requested the Beatles appear with him on his Liverpool show, he was dismayed to find himself opening for them.

Before Little Richard famously turned to Christ and turned his back on rock 'n' roll, he kept an odd sort of diary that was accidentally discovered by 12-year-old David Arden. He travelled with a large Bible in whose margins were found descriptions of Richard's sex life, which could be said to be various, vigorous and polymorphous. Apparently, he considered these bawdy jottings to be a "message to God."

Richard had a certain ambivalence toward his conversion, no doubt because while Christ might be King, Little Richard was most certainly still a queen. Perhaps he regretted throwing his jewelry off the Sydney Bridge while touring Australia because, despite his fervent wish to spread the gospel through song, he agreed to open Sam Cooke's Arden-promoted UK tour with his rock act. Richard broke his promise and gave the punters a taste of that old time religion, who, unconvinced, rioted in that all too familiar fashion Don found expensive and distressing. Don showed Richard the error of his ways and thus chastened, Richard reverted to form and "slaughtered them."

In Sam Cooke, Don discovered another great artist for the ages. "The only performer better than Gene Vincent was Sam Cooke. He was asked if he wanted to play with Sophie Tucker on one of his nights off, to which replied that he'd love to. Going on before her, he out-performed her, leaving her humbled, if painfully so. She was Sam's big idol."

Don found the transition from the rocking '50s to the swinging '60s challenging. By late 1963, he had six UK package shows topped by American artists ready to roll that he couldn't give away. The "revolution" that had made Jerry Brandt a force to reckon with in the U.S. had precisely the opposite effect on Don Arden's fortunes. "We all died because of the Beatles. They killed all interest in the American acts, the roles had reversed. I lost a great deal of money because of bad timing. The only act that continued to draw was the Everly Brothers, who I managed to make something of on a tour with Little Richard and Bo Diddley. Due to their publicity, I gave the Stones a spot at the bottom of the bill, which attracted attention to the package although they weren't yet a draw in themselves." Don's losses were said to have amounted to as much as £100,000, a medium-sized fortune in those days.

Because the Beatles and the Stones were so vocal in their enthusiasm for Chuck Berry, he was likely to prove an exception to the American curse, while presenting Don with another set of problems. Having spent two years in an American prison for transporting a minor girl across state lines, no reputable agency would book him. Comparing him to his idol Gene Vincent, Arden felt Berry wasn't up to much and only worked with him because the Beatles had given him some commercial cachet. Don thought Berry a one-trick pony as a musician and was revolted by his selfishness and cruelty.

When it came to abusing women, Berry gave Ike Turner a run for his money. "To say he 'mistreated' women would be an understatement; he liked to drag them through the gutter." Of course, Jerry Lee Lewis' career had been even more dramatically ruined when he insisted on bringing his 13-year-old second cousin with him to Britain, albeit they were legally married in the States. In perspective, the antics of the early Stones really were child's play by comparison. But this was the world in which Don Arden reigned supreme. His rival Robert Stigwood was not so prescient and went bankrupt meeting the "evil" Chuck's demands. Although his relationship with producer Joe Meek and EMI chairman Sir Joseph Lockwood had helped Stigwood become one of the first independent record entrepreneurs in Britain, his instincts as a tour promoter paled in comparison to Don Arden's. Other victims of Stigwood's fecklessness were the Rolling Stones, whom he stiffed when the money ran out while they were mid-tour.

What bothered Don about Chuck Berry was certainly not informed by any taint of racism; it was the guitarist's arrogance that tweaked him. Don had experienced too much discrimination in his own life not to have a certain sympathy for artists of color. His affection for John Lee Hooker, riding his first hit "Boom, Boom" while on an Arden tour, was reinforced when the bluesman stepped off the sidewalk into a busy Tottenham Court Road to allow three white men to pass. The spontaneity with which Hooker needlessly humbled himself struck a chord with Don.

 Stigwood wasn't the only stone in Don's shoe. While promoting the Animals, whose showstopper, "House of the Rising Sun" ran a cutting-edge ten minutes in performance, Don learned that members of his own team were not wholly to be trusted. "I sent Peter Grant on the road with the Animals to the States and when he returned he told me 'there's no money left for you, Don,' but he'd found a way to pocket thousands he thought I'd never discover."

Gene Vincent

"I first became acquainted with Peter Grant when he was peddling rock 'n' roll to the American forces," Don recalls. "He was nothing. I put him to work as a road manager and chauffeur for Gene. The biggest lie in rock music at the time was that Peter was a wrestler. He was 6'2" and 300 lbs., but he was always sick and couldn't walk very far. In the business, needless to say, it was all about image. Grant was destroyed by his wife. We parted ways when he stole some money and lied about legal issues. On the other hand, he did tell people that 'he learned everything from Don Arden,' so given the second Bank of England that Led Zeppelin became, perhaps he was a better student than I gave him credit for."

While a physical confrontation between Arden and Grant would have been worth the price of admission, when Stigwood went too far in wooing the Small Faces, he suffered a technical knockout in the first round. "The Small Faces were the hottest group around," as Arden himself tells one of the most infamous tales from the mid-'60s. "Stigwood wanted to manage them. Guess he fancied Stevie (Marriott). I got a group of men together and they almost threw him out of the 24th floor of his building. He shat himself and from that point was completely terrified of me."

Don's delight in the retelling is infectious and displays the timing that must have stood him well when he trod the boards so many years earlier. The confrontation wasn't the least bit spontaneous; it was choreographed with the professionalism of a vaudeville sketch, sort of Fred Astaire meets Humphrey Bogart.

Arden had Wilf Pine take two steps forward on a silent count of three, pick up the huge glass ashtray Don knew Stigwood kept on his desk and smash it down with such force the wood cracked. Next came the famous scene where the five angry giants lifted Stigwood from his chair, carried him over to the window and upended him there from. Arden asked his colleagues as they held the squirming and scared shitless impresario over the street if he should forgive the interloper or drop him. In unison they thundered, "Drop him!" The only problem was "the cunt was wearing slip on boots instead of lace-ups and we had to make sure we had a firm grip on his ankles while he squealed like a stuck pig lest he fall without our permission."

When the police came round to find out what all the fuss had been about, Stigwood redeemed himself somewhat in Don's eyes. Either out of fear, resignation, graciousness, or all three, Stigwood told them that Don and he did have a dispute, but that Don had been a perfect gentleman and they had settled their differences amicably.

Any affront to one of Don's artists was likely to be taken personally and acted upon aggressively, particularly if the lapse involved money. If Arden decided that by his own lights he was on the right side of a disagreement morally, he seldom let legal niceties get in the way of a forceful resolution. After one Small Faces show, the promoters wouldn't pay them or let them pack up their gear. Don and twelve colleagues made a somewhat bloody example of the miscreants, which prompted a protest from other promoters on the tour that Don ignored, knowing that henceforth non-payment was one spot of bother he needn't trouble himself about. Later, the Small Faces accused him of destroying their careers, but even then they acknowledged a unique loyalty to the artist on Don's part.

It was also to Don's credit that he took advantage of a phenomenon the Who only half-harnessed and the Stones were given cultural cred for but never thought of. The irrepressible Small Faces, easily bored and liking a bit of upset, started throwing bits of their own clothes out to the paying public. A delinquent version of Chanel's "gift with purchase," as you might say. Cheaper, though, than destroying a full Marshall amp rig every night with assorted microphones, thereby dragging your spendthrift manager into massive debt and concurrent debauchery in the name of art. The Faces' stunt was far more in keeping with the Nice burning American flags; flashy, but relatively cheap.

Still, Don wasn't quite comfortable with paying to replace the boys' clothing, and he knew a few people who knew a few people in retail on Carnaby Street. Doubtless, Don understood rags instinctively. Soon enough deals were struck to provide the replacement gear gratis as long as the original labels remained intact as they flew into the punters' eager fists. And a small taste for Don was not amiss given that this fortuitous product placement brought the Faces-loving lads back through the door for more clobber. Pace Paul Weller, that was mod.

But the working-class suss and longing for financial security Don shared with the Small Faces led to their parents trying to kid a kidder. It was as if most of the boys' relatives had a bad case of Brian Jones disease—the compulsion to take with both hands what one should be grateful to accept with one. Double dipping between the band and their near and dear was frustratingly common, as each would claim not to know that the other had received funds that now must be given again to the petitioner at hand.

While Don might have grudgingly admired their front, he resented what he sensed was an unjustifiable arrogance in their demands. He had worked too hard and endured too many setbacks to brook this Fredo-like pretense of entitlement. Not that he wished them to be actually intimidated, although that was a frequently useful arrow in Don's quiver, but it was disrespectful, after all.

When the boys appeared to be spent, wasted and wanting after another spell of touring, the parents accused Don of child labor violations. Having learned better than to try to influence his artists' lifestyles, Don knew that hard work for good pay was the least of the Small Faces' problems, but his hints in that direction fell on deaf parental ears.

While overwork was a constant complaint, occasionally someone would outdo themselves.

Having some time on her hands, Mrs. Jones, mum to Kenney, found that he had some 85 suits stashed at her humble abode and further, that she had nowhere to put them. Don rather got the idea she thought the solution to this variation on a theme of Imelda Marcos was to buy her a larger house. He dryly suggested Master Kenneth come to live in his own many roomed mansion where closet space would cease to be a bother for her.

Don's management proposition added value in two indispensable ways: first, it never occurred to him that he wouldn't need to pay music journalists, radio DJs, and TV producers to hurry his act up the chart. And second, he knew whom to pay, when, and how much, so that they never thought they'd got over on him even though he was paying. Don Arden was an investor protecting his investment, not a john. Pity the fool that took commerce for familiarity. For anyone to feel entitled to Don's good will was a quick way for his back to turn. The police were not completely oblivious to Don's powers of persuasion but they hadn't a grasp of the facts that would warrant questioning him. By now it should be obvious that everyone in Don's universe had either been invited in and knew the rules of the house or else had invited themselves in and found themselves rather brutally unwanted and unneeded.

Though Don had little use for the alleged mobsters he would meet in his travels, probably comparing the Italian toughs unfavorably to the Krays, his own sense of extended family was worthy of a Godfather. In the early '70s, I was in England recording Donovan when Arden strongman Wilf Pine (destroyer of Robert Stigwood's ashtray)

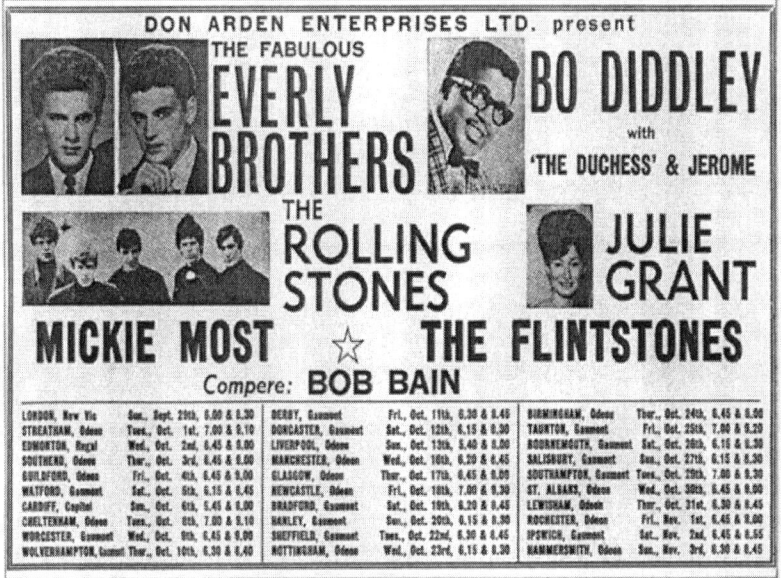

Poster of concert presented by Don Arden

called me about producing Jimmy Helms. Though I agreed Helms could sing well enough, I balked when Wilf insisted I record only songs from which he might derive some publishing loot. His demands were jarring to one immersed in Donovan's mellow yellow.

All the more so because he tended to call one in the middle of the night, his tattooed knuckles gripping the telephone handset as they might one's throat, Robert Mitchum-style in Night of the Hunter. I knew Don greatly appreciated Wilf's pit bullish loyalty, but something had to be done. He had me come down to the Arden estate in Wimbledon the following Sunday for tea. Wife Paddy was all smiles, oolong and cucumber sandwiches, while Don acted hurt on my behalf. Wilf was the Rottweiler in disgrace: "I never meant I was going to kill you, Andrew," he explained, diplomatically omitting all his options against me short of murder. Don seemed pleased with his role as peacemaker, so I accepted Wilf's apology and chewed on a biscuit instead of my tongue.

Despite Don's well-deserved reputation as a tough man to beat at his own game, some continued to try. Patrick Meehan Jr. waged war with him over control of Black Sabbath for years with neither able to effect unconditional surrender. Those of us who were caught in the middle of their quarrel were lucky not to become collateral damage.

In January of 1975, I found myself at the Midem music festival in Cannes, France, accompanied by my wife-to-be Esther, and rather not looking forward to a meeting with my erstwhile business partner Tony Calder and his new business partner, the aforesaid Patrick Meehan Jr. The dodgy duo were eager to launch Immediate Records Mark II, and despite my reservations about both them and the project, they hoped to obtain my blessing, if not my participation. I was vaguely aware of Meehan Jr.'s Black Sabbath troubles, and although I had no dog in their fight, I sided instinctively with Don. I have found "Jr." to be a diminutive its bearers usually live up to and it was not a point in Patrick's favor as we began our mating dance. Don was at Midem because in those days, if you were in the music business, you had to be.

And so it came to pass that at the Casino at Cannes, an employee of Meehan Jr. made the mistake of offending Don, and all hell broke loose. Don was nutted on the forehead while his daughter Sharon, then decidedly daddy's little girl, attempted to murder his assailant with a marble coffee table. I'm not sure why I allowed myself to be drawn into the subsequent peace talk between Don and Patrick, when I had my own uneasy business with Jr. to conduct. Probably Don relied on my loyalty to him, and he was entitled to it. Perhaps Don thought that if he brought along innocent Andrew, he could escape further injury while his stitches were still healing.

I'm sure I reluctantly enjoyed the noirish circumstances of the meet, which was set for a moonlit evening on the yacht Meehan had in port, as if he were Cary Grant in Mr. Lucky. Don was attired in his Mr. Big best. He'd decided against British houndstooth and dressed in a powder blue suit more suitable for an evening on the French Riviera. Our friend Nigel Thomas had agreed to play the part of the "honest broker." He had a few words of sobering advice for Don: "When we pull up by the boat, you must not get on it until we've turned the Roller around. We may have to make a quick getaway."

While the Rolls made its way down the Rosette to the marina in a fog out of central casting, I considered whether I preferred to be Jean Gabin or Alain Delon in this scene. As it turned out, I was never called upon to be a "serviceable villain." Don power blued his way out of the Rolls alone while Patrick waited on the dock in a fur coat and five days of stubble, like a stand-in for Don Johnson in Miami Vice, as his rented captain glowered at us as if he had a machinegun hidden under his pea coat. We never learned what came out of this mano a mano, but Esther found it an interesting variation on the testosterone-laden confrontations of her native Colombia.

If anything, Don's life became more colorful and complicated as he enjoyed even more financial success in the go-go '80s. ELO became the biggest act he'd ever had, but doing business in America with the likes of Walter Yetnikoff and Morris Levy took a lot out of him. He held the American Mafia at arm's length and entertained new friends like Cary Grant and Tony Curtis in a Beverly Hills home previously occupied by Howard

Hughes. For fun, he continued to play a fiercely competitive game of tennis, winning by attrition, if not sheer skill, most of the time.

But what utterly unmanned Don in his later years was his estrangement from his daughter, who far more than his son shared his ferocity, cynicism and obsession with control. No one is more aware of their bond than Sharon herself. "If he'd been a butcher," she once told an interviewer, "I'd be slicing lamb chops now." Once again, it was a dispute over Black Sabbath that roiled the Arden family business: in 1979, when the band fired their iconic lead singer Ozzy Osbourne, Sharon became "romantically" involved with the feckless front-man and then took over his management.

Don was appalled. This was a betrayal of Shakespearean proportions and he could not abide it. She later claimed that when she attempted a rapprochement, he let loose the dogs of the estate and she miscarried Ozzy's child. Confirming that trouble comes in threes, in 1986, both Don and his son David were arraigned on felony charges for blackmailing and falsely imprisoning an accountant, of all people. In another twist worthy of Greek tragedy, the son served time and the father was acquitted. Such bittersweet "freedom" was small consolation for Don. Sharon's fury so dominated their lives that twenty years after they first fell out she spat, "The best lesson I ever had was watching him fuck his business up. He taught me everything not to do. My father's never even seen any of my three kids and, as far as I'm concerned, he never will."

It so happened that I was inadvertently drawn into Sharon and Don's quarrel early on, once again as an innocent bystander. Don flattered me by suggesting I write the script for a horror film in which Ozzy would star. I'm sure that, already sensing which way the wind was blowing, Don's agenda included having someone loyal keep a watchful eye on

Osbourne and his daughter. I served Allen Klein in a similar capacity when I "produced" the unmanageable Bobby Womack.

By the time I joined Ozzy and company on the road, Sharon had crossed the Rubicon and there would be no more discussion of a film in which Don was involved. Ozzy had not yet found his feet as a solo act. The Randy Rhoads line-up of the time was selling out concerts, but the records Ozzy was releasing through Epic were falling flat. It is a fact that most record company executives have very little use for a performer who bites the heads off bats unless that performer is selling very very well. You can ask Iggy Pop for a second opinion on this.

Still, merchandise was being sold by the truckload on their tours. Ozzy had seemingly turned Iggy's potential for self-destruction into a marketing campaign. Surrounded by an organization now under the total control of his wife Sharon, Ozzy was on lock-down during the daylight hours only to emerge more insane each night to the delight of his fans. Miniature bottles of booze of the kind served on air flights were particularly banned; easily concealed and downed severally in an instant, even one was said to trigger tremors and hallucinations in the star.

And a star he was. The show was impressive — the rapport Ozzy has with his fans is relaxed and total. Despite the wildness in his eyes, he's in control of his act, if not quite himself, adding a delicious suspense to the proceedings that is rock to the core. When he comes offstage to rest before an encore, he steadies himself on an equipment box and rather incongruously does a few easy limbering up knee bends, as if their common interest in fitness would make Oz and Mick gym pals. Richard Simmons' heart might swell with a hustler's sense of accomplishment. Dazed, confused and charming,

Ozzy takes time to ask after "Mick and the lads," as if we were still all one big happy family, before inquiring slyly, "Does your wife still smoke pot all the time?" Meaning Sheila from whom I had been separated years hence. I told him I didn't know about Sheila, but I continued to enjoy a toke.

Sharon eventually called to formally end our creative relationship, although I might have wished she'd saved herself the trouble. I couldn't help but take it personally when she snarled, "I've fucked my father's acts for him for years, now I found someone to love, so fuck him." The Ardens had done more than open the world of entertainment to me as a teenager; they had made me a part of their once seemingly happy family. In retrospect, in many ways the Ardens were far more committed to their Byzantine family ties than to "success."

Years went by and Don continued to think of me as a friend and potential collaborator. In 2002, he got a yen to tell his story in his own words and called me to Park Lane to discuss my co-writing his memoirs. I already had the perfect title: Once Upon a Time in Showbiz, its not so subtle allusion to Sergio Leone reflecting Don's alleged reputation as a hard case.

As it happens, I was having a long overdue reunion with my own elderly mother whom I had not visited in some years. Disoriented by her long struggle with Alzheimer's, my mother was living out her last days in Oxford, attended to by the devoted husband she always deserved, Janez. Though I'd straightened myself out some time before the trip, I'm not so sure that sobriety made the month we shared one bit easier. Little did I know at the time that Don would come to share the same indignity as Mother, once a proud and steely mind became inexplicably addled.

Back at Don's flat we shared smoked salmon and bagels, while I tried to balance my excitement over his project with some reservations about whether I could tell his story as well as I felt I had told mine in *Stoned*. It's been said that "memoirs are the liar's biography," a concept I acknowledged when at the outset of my first volume I wrote, "There are three sides to every story: mine, yours and the truth." True to form, Don was already insisting that his screed would be the whole truth and nothing but the truth. My own life might have been much easier had I been able to live it solely in that one dimension Don claimed to inhabit.

At one point, Don sent his son David out of the room on an errand and suddenly turned to me, smiling slyly with an almost licentious gleam in his eye: "Well, Andrew," he beamed, "have you heard . . . ?" I knew that almost anything could spring forth then, since Don shared with Allen Klein a compulsive need to know everything about everybody and an almost equal compulsion to share these tidbits. With a wink as good as a nod, he stated with great finality, "The Ardens are back together," meaning Don and Sharon, who by that time had come to resemble the Macbeths. I could not shake the disconcerting thought that Don's agenda was not altogether paternal and forgiving. It was in him to wish to even the score with Sharon and she would do well not to let her guard down even yet. Don had his son-in-law Ozzy to thank for an introduction to his grandkids; the artist who had nominally been the cause of war between the Ardens had insisted his wife make the first move.

In the event, the book was begun but never published. I delegated the responsibility of conducting interviews, including those with Don, to Simon Dudfield, who had performed the same role so admirably in the preparation of *Stoned*. Don never warmed to Simon, perhaps because he could sense the fear and awe the much younger man betrayed when they met, or perhaps simply because the older man couldn't be bothered to explain who Sophie Tucker was.

When we would see each other from time to time, the Shakespearean quality of Don's personality loomed as large as ever, though now he resembled Lear more than Richard III. Like Albert Grossman, he had lived long enough to outlast most of his enemies, but unlike Albert, Don never seemed to retreat. A lifetime's worth of grudges seemed to keep him young; while to those he considered family, I among them, he remained the most affectionate, if unusual, of father figures. If Albert had the mind of a brain surgeon, Don had the heart of a lion.

In 2003, Allen Klein invited me to the Bel Air Hotel to record my early memories of Sam Cooke for a cable television special he was making. As Esther, Max and I were saying goodbye to producer Iris Keitel, I saw this familiar figure coming towards us, seemingly aglow in the perfect mango-tinted light of a late afternoon in fall. The silhouette screamed showbiz; the gait was equal parts Edward G. Robinson and Buster Keaton. It was Don.

Esther he knew, and I was proud to introduce Maximillian to him. Max was duly impressed. Don was bespoke and gracious. Later, Allen told me that Don seemed to remember so little from the UK tour Sam had done with Little Richard that the interview was all but useless. I thought nothing much about it at the time. I had lunch with Don a few days later and he told me that he was at the first stages of Alzheimer's. The point here is that he told me.

Conflict, even if only in his imagination, kept Don game and engaged in living. He was not complaining, but he was at the first chapter of sad. I thought I understood. When the page is turned on the last hustle, we can spend our lives bullfighting ghosts. I still occasionally forget myself and brace for war with an opponent who long ago ceased to impact my actual life. But for the most part I am lucky; I remain still, deep Colombian waters engulf me, and the beach of plenty is wife, mother and child.

Conventional wisdom has it that he with the most money wins, but it's easier for a camel to pass through the eye of a needle and all that. The hustler, above all, requires of life that it allow him to be his own man, and the richest among us seldom are. Don would have made a poor politician; he just couldn't be beholden to anyone for the sake of a good deal for very long. It was distressing to see the lion in winter beset by personal and professional slights that diminished his essential greatness not a jot. The mind controls the body, as men of wisdom have urgently tried to counsel us, and while outwardly, Don remained robust, inwardly, the hell he had created in his soul was eating him from the inside out.

One day after we had lunched together in Beverly Hills, we strolled about Rodeo Drive, silently acknowledging how far we had come from very different British backgrounds to be able to take all this luxury and superficiality in stride. It was nice being busy doing nothing in tinsel town. We hugged and agreed to meet again in a few days.

After we parted, I collected the rented white pickup truck that allowed me to indulge yet another of my American fantasies without the obligations of ownership. For me, life was good, and I sincerely prayed that it might be so for Don. I drove down

Burton Way and saw Don walking. I had given no thought as to whether he'd be driving or driven, but he seemed to be taking no particular route home, zigging here and zagging there like a token on a child's board game.

Like Philip Marlowe on a $100 per diem, I followed him. I drove around the block so as to keep him at a discrete distance and watched him enter a little gingerbread house off 3rd, once the home of a single, perhaps happy, family and now divided into small apartments. The thought crossed my mind that had Don's ancestors landed in America, he might have ended up in Hollywood anyway but lived the life of a Mike Todd instead of becoming the "King of Rock 'n' roll."

I took a break from writing this book in my sometime home of Vancouver to visit my son Max, who was living in Los Angeles at the time. I enjoyed seeing Max feel his way towards the man he would become in the town that has been so good for me, but which I could never truly call home. Once again I gave thanks for what little peace is accorded us in this life.

David Arden took me to see Don in the assisted community in which he now lived at almost 80 years of age. Appropriately, the grounds overlook the Hollywood Bowl. Don is feisty, immaculate, and the cock of his walk. Happy to see David, he liked the idea of me, even if he cannot quite place me. His room in the home is one I fancy Larry Parnes might have liked, mementos of the real deals and family keepsakes neatly displayed.

His posture is amazing, and I'm tempted to hope that the body can control the mind rather than vice versa. Years of prideful discipline support a razor straight spine that

Mike Todd and Liz Taylor

still obeys his original will. Don likes this room and seems happy to have me in it, so while I'm there with him I'm happy for him.

The ghosts of Morris and Velvel have taken up their rightful place in the nether world, and Don's aggravation with his fellow man seems confined to a normal distaste for his neighbors. One imagines that should he meet one of the more annoying sorts on the way to the dining room, a stern glance and a straightening of the shoulders will serve notice that Mr. Arden is not to be trifled with. On the other hand, if he feels like singing, he might lure his next door neighbor to the piano and enjoy arrangements once created at the behest of no less than Frank Sinatra.

Within months of our meeting, Don was gone. He passed on July 21, 2007. I have frequently said that there are no coincidences, but I must say I was amazed to get a call from David Arden while I was hosting "In the City," a Manchester music festival founded by the late Tony Wilson of Factory Records. His father was to be buried in the city of his birth and fate had permitted me to pay my final respects in person.

Sharon was not in attendance, but not for lack of caring. Once they were reunited, the bond between father and daughter became stronger than ever; the bills for Don's nursing care were paid by Sharon. In the years following their reconciliation, Sharon had become a uniquely successful figure in show business, and like her father, nobody's fool.

Star of her own reality TV show, talk show host, concert promoter, artist manager, and judge on the X Factor and America's Got Talent, Sharon's autobiography sold over two million copies while the memoir Don eventually published was barely noticed. Despite the many cruel assaults each visited upon the other, it would be hard to imagine Sharon Osbourne becoming who she is today had she been anyone else's daughter.

As I stood in line with the elderly Jewish Mancunians who had known Harry Levy when he could lick his weight in bad boy bigots, I knew there had to be a vaudeville gag in there somewhere. And when I dug the spade into the damp dank earth, I heard Don whisper to me, "Not too close, Andrew. I wouldn't want you to scuff your shoes."

PETE KAMERON

THE BOOK YOU are reading might have been written almost 30 years ago had I been patient enough to learn how to type and smart enough to insist that I write it myself. In 1983, at a dangerous time of my life, one of my dearest friends suggested we work together on a different kind of book. Though he never had anything but my best interests at heart, Pete Kameron was at heart a hustler.

In fact, Pete was a Zen hustler.

It's almost, but not quite, too bad that the book in question was never written because what you're reading now would have been the "behind the scenes" bonus content. There was no such thing in 1983, of course, so what we were going for was the Main Event. Never was anybody I loved so much connected to a project I was so glad came to naught. I'm very glad I got to live, learn, love and write again.

Although I like to think of myself as a man of parts, that is, I can appreciate and even contribute to the arts in more than one form, I am at my best and most effectively, a man of music. In 1983, both I and the business I loved and loathed were on the ropes.

By the early '80s, the bubble blown by the success of the *Saturday Night Fever* soundtrack and all the disco drek it dragged onto the charts had burst. Punk had petered out, although it never gained any commercial success in the US to begin with, and the "New Wave" with its Duran Durans and Simple Minds was just beginning to lap the shores of the album charts. MTV was in its infancy and the compact disc was a shiny gleam in Philips' eye. As a result, the industry contracted painfully, creating a smaller scale template for the dot.com burn-out and the real estate bubble of later years. It was not a good time for an old hand from the '60s like me to be looking for work.

To make matters worse, artists, producers and managers had been suckered by the record companies into accepting half royalties on cassettes, and now cassettes were rapidly outpacing vinyl as consumers embraced Walkmen, boom boxes, and auto cassette players. Frankly, if people were going to be satisfied by the sound of a cassette in a boom box, all those 24 track studios that had been built at great expense were pretty much pointless. The situation is much the same today, only arguably worse now that any aspiring *American Idol* contestant can make a reasonably good sounding record in his bedroom (no need for even a garage), which if it ever hit would be experienced almost exclusively in a compressed lossy format on cheap earphones. No wonder *High Fidelity* magazine is out of business.

It's amazing that we fell for it again when contracts were amended to pay smaller royalties on the as yet insignificant Compact Disc. By the end of the decade, vinyl was hard to find and the record companies were gorging themselves on inflated sales of music people already owned on vinyl which they had repurchased at a huge mark-up. Of course, the label execs gave themselves unwarranted credit and big raises, thinking they were responsible for what was really a one-shot windfall. Maybe those of us who actually made records should have unionized, like the Directors' Guild.

My own professional and financial situation rendered me especially vulnerable during these uneasy times. I depended almost totally on Allen Klein's good will for the food on my family's table and the coke I put up my nose. I had sold my recording rights in the Rolling Stones to Allen in 1969 and most of my publishing interests by 1972. What

I didn't reluctantly sign over to Klein usually found its way into his pocket by machinations I didn't always understand and probably could have done nothing about.

On the other hand, Allen was the only person who would employ me to do what I did best, produce records. Along with albums I produced for Donovan and Bobby Womack, he employed me to remaster reissues by Sam Cooke, Herman's Hermits, the Stones and Marianne Faithfull. Even this welcome offer of work was a mixed blessing; revisiting the Marianne Faithfull material reminded me of just why I had left her after only one single, though I loved her personally. The Womack album didn't even require much of me in the way of production. I was there to be Allen's eyes and ears in the studio, while Womack waved guns and did drugs. When he eventually got down to work, he was brilliant and didn't need me to tell him so.

While hit producers in the '80s were increasingly recording engineers hired by artists for their technical expertise, in a lot ways I was still the guy who thought you plugged electric guitars into a mains socket. I got results, but I often took the long way around to get them. When I remastered Sam Cooke, I used the RCA studios in New York on Sixth Avenue, which had been designed to have the same dimensions, and therefore the same room sound, as the RCA studios in LA where Sam had recorded often. I thought the similarity in venues might enable Sam and me to commune over the project and so I organized a séance to find out if he were interested. You see, I was working on *Sam Cooke at the Copa (Live)* and I wanted to ask him how high to mix the cutlery.

Given my dependency on Allen, I couldn't tell if he was really treating me like shit or I just felt like it. I did realize that in many ways Allen wanted the best for me, which was nice since he'd already had the best of me. There was a Stockholm Syndrome quality to our affection for each other, and when I looked at myself in the mirror I didn't really fancy seeing Patty Hearst staring back at me.

Pete Kameron knew Allen Klein personally and professionally, was just as tough as Allen, and even more in my corner, as he frequently reminded me. What Pete wanted to do was take me back from Allen. Allen and Pete had locked horns over the Who in the late '60s, and ever since one of them was always trying to get over on the other. It was a game of badminton and I was the shuttlecock.

Pete's first helpful suggestion was that I join forces with publisher Howie Richmond, who as the very successful founder of Essex Music had done serious business with both Pete and Allen. I didn't relish being the mole that would enable Richmond to get back at Klein for turning Richmond's partner David Platz against him. It's nothing against Pete Kameron that this scheme had a real down side for me; all these guys operate in the grey zone and either learn to live with it or learn to love it. What Pete offered was love at a percentage.

Not to be denied, Pete had another idea, one his better angels whispered would allow him to make a deal for my written take on the '60s and the Rolling Stones, bring in some well-deserved loot, and employ my wit, intelligence and vanity. I'd be back in the game. Some game, anyway. The problem, as you'll learn, was that we were not to be a duo but a trio. Pete's other recruit to the Gang of New York was his friend, Kevin Eggers. Kevin is as deserving of a place in this book as any of our other lovable villains—Jean Luc Young, Jerry Brandt, or Adrian Millar. A lot of what he talked himself into thinking was ok was breathtaking. But first some background on the real protagonist here, Pete Kameron.

By the time I met him, he was global in a way director Peter Medak suggests the Krays wished to be in his movie of the same name. He was living in London, where he was perfectly placed at the nexus of movies and pop music. Since finding the right film vehicle for the Stones was a priority in those days, it was natural that we met.

In fact, Pete was as New York as New Yorkers come. As Lenny Bruce once had it, "Here's the truth. If you're from New York, you're Jewish, even if you aren't. And if you're not from New York, you're not Jewish, even if you are." Kameron was a New York Jew.

However, Pete was not a stomach Jew. I'd not be surprised if he knew more Kabbalah than Madonna. He'd read and taken in Ouspensky, Gurdjieff, and Freud along with Chairman Mao and Bhadwan Shree Rajneesh. It's not hard to imagine Pete Townshend being fascinated by the way Pete K. could suavely change the subject and keep Pete T. entranced. Love, wisdom and a percentage.

A hustler doesn't have to have a talent for relationships or an engaging personality but both give him a leg up. Pete didn't presume to know the meaning of you but he brought to any encounter your whole history with him. He not only remembered it but depending on how he sensed you were feeling could bring out all this seemingly extraneous encouragement that put you back on a positive footing. Pete Townshend knew that this was the kind of guy who gets presidents elected.

So when Pete Kameron introduces you to someone and says, "He's a friend of ours," you're naturally curious, eager, nervous, alive. That's why Pete is the Zen hustler. He's altogether there in the moment, but with a paradoxical grounding in past, present and future. At least in theory.

One afternoon as we sat down to black lychee tea, some cupcakes and a shared morphine derivative, he quoted the Maoism "remember old bitterness." He was warning me and reminding himself that bitterness was an attachment we could ill afford. It was a time at which I was apart from my family and skidding off the road. Pete could bring you back to why you'd gotten into the car and turned on the ignition to begin with. The positive results of my meetings with Pete overcame Esther's intuitions that he was up to no good. I often came away a better Andrew.

Pete was born on March 18th, 1921 on the Lower East Side of New York, of a Polish father and an Austrian mother. Of course, he was much younger than the most notorious alumni of that ghetto, among them Arnold Rothstein and Meyer Lanksy, but undoubtedly Pete's childhood was steeped in the atmosphere captured so well by Sergio Leone's *Once Upon a Time in America*.

While he was still in high school, Pete ran numbers and experimented with small-scale scams. His tales of those days were delivered in a severe scatting style worthy of Annie Ross and his frequent "Y'know's" gave his storytelling a rhythm and groove. This was not a conversation, it was a performance and the only time he'd permit the "M" word to pass his lips as he described wise guys who had probably gone to their Maker long ago. If he caught himself going perhaps a bit too far, he'd smile, wave his hands that did not do dishes, shrug his shoulders and get out of jail with a Y'know card.

Late in life, after Pete left New York for Beverly Hills, he loved it when I called him from Manhattan. Neighborhoods like Times Square or the Village were invariably associated with memories of who fucked who and where, who played what and when.

He'd hint the characters he so enjoyed remembering were made guys and he trusted me to keep shtum about it.

Pete Kameron

I never really knew how connected Pete himself may have been, and in a way it doesn't matter. He was a product of his times and the place he came up in as much as someone my age living in London would have identified with Carnaby Street and Soho. He reminded me in some ways of a much more highly self-educated version of my pal, Peter Meaden, who would see his beloved High Numbers achieve success as the Who under the guidance of Kit Lambert, Chris Stamp and . . . Pete Kameron. The struggle to escape the poverty and discrimination that came with a childhood lived in the slums informed his world view ever after. One deep, dark evening in Manhattan, under the influence of a skinful of smack, he lost patience a bit with what he must have thought was druggy naiveté on my part. Quietly, without menace, he declared that there were only two kinds of people, those who had killed and those who had not. That shut me up for a while.

Fortunately for his longevity, Pete preferred art to vice, and as a young man hooked up with legendary music man Milt Gabler. Just as a young Brian Epstein took over part of the family furniture business and started North End Music Stores, Gabler inherited his father's radio business in midtown Manhattan and renamed it the Commodore Music Shop. He was the first retailer to sell "cut-outs," buying excess inventory of jazz releases from the "major" labels and selling them to his growing following among musicians and fans.

He also anticipated reissue labels like Rhino and Legacy by leasing discontinued titles by such greats as Bessie Smith and Bix Beiderbecke. When Billie Holiday complained to Milt that Columbia Records would not release "Strange Fruit," her controversial side condemning racism, Gabler got permission from Columbia (with the blessing of Billie's mentor John Hammond) to record it for his own Commodore Records. Would that my friend and nemesis, Jean Luc Young of Charly Records, had taken a page out of Milt Gabler's book and avoided taking short cuts with the catalogues he licensed and then exploited without any moral restraints. When Gabler moved on to production and A&R full time at Decca (not the same Decca as the Stones signed to in the UK), he was responsible for signing the Andrews Sisters and Bill Haley, while producing hits for Brenda Lee and Sammy Davis Jr.

So Pete couldn't have asked for a more talented or sincere patron as he began to make his way in the world. In 1949, a friend took Pete along to the Village Vanguard in New York to hear the politically controversial folk group the Weavers, which included the legendary Pete Seeger. Kameron took the Weavers on for management and spent much of his time defending them against McCarthy era witch hunts.

Once again Milt Gabler showed what he was made of and signed his protégé Pete's act to Decca, where they had hits with "Goodnight, Irene," "Tzena, Tzena, Tzena," "So Long," "Around the World," and "The Roving Kind." Not only did the Weavers pave the way for the Kingston Trio and Peter, Paul and Mary, but after he left the Weavers, Pete Seeger championed a young Bob Dylan and his manager, Albert Grossman. Though similar in their devotion to musical quality and character, Grossman had a much easier time of it than Pete Kameron, who eventually saw the Weavers dropped from Decca when Seeger refused to testify before the House Committee on Un-American Activities. So you see, unlike many hustlers, Kameron was always a stand-up guy.

A recent online article about the Weavers describes Pete as a "suave charmer." In appearance he was dapper, short, calm and gnomic. He radiated a conservative air of importance which disguised the turbulent waters just under a quiet surface. He was meticulous in his attire, favoring blazers by Brioni or Dougie Hayward. His accessories were flawless, particularly his jewelry, which he changed depending on the time of day. He could wear a Cartier watch that was decidedly feminine without the faintest suggestion that he was unmanly. Pete Kameron was bewitching, unbothered, and occasionally bewildering. Women loved him and he loved women. His hands (and oddly enough those of Allen Klein) always reminded me of Vivien Leigh.

He moved to London at the beginning of the '60s, and we met for the first time in 1965. Filmmaker Donald Cammell had spoken to him about an idea he had for the Stones or, more precisely, for Mick Jagger. Pete was supervising the music for the James Bond films at the time, but was always open to new movie projects. He and Cammell came to see me at my Ivor Court office and my fight or flight instincts instantly went onto Red Alert.

A scary, skunky darkness wafted off of Cammell that was almost palpable. I didn't know at the time that his father had written a biography of Aleister Crowley, who was a family friend and neighbor of Donald's while he was growing up wrong. Cammell was creepy enough to give drugs a bad name and thought his indulgence in them gave him license to purvey uncommercial crap. I saw no point in biting the hand that fed me and got Kameron and Cammell out of my office as quickly as possible. The film, *Performance*, would eventually be made, and made very well, probably due to Nick Roeg's co-direction. But while Jagger was still there, I wasn't. So actor James Fox played out our relationship instead.

Pete arrived in London at just the right time; the first few years of the '60s were a lot more exciting and creative than the last few. He helped structure the European arm of Essex Music, which would come to own all the Stones, Who, David Bowie, Marc Bolan, Lionel Bart and Anthony Newley copyrights. He set up a worldwide publishing structure to handle the musical side of the James Bond franchise. Paul McCartney, Sheena Easton, Shirley Bassey and Duran Duran et al should be forever grateful, as émigré Bond producers Harry Saltzman and Albert R. Broccoli must have been. Some of the theme songs from those movies have stood the test of time far better than the movies themselves.

Although throughout the '60s and early '70s Pete and I traveled in overlapping circles, our friendship took root when I moved to New York with Esther in the late '70s. He could see that I was having trouble gaining traction in both my career and my emotional life (apart from my happy marriage) after my attempt to launch the Werewolves as their manager/producer was unsuccessful. Hence his enthusiasm for the book project. Kevin Eggers had recently shepherded a commercially successful "celebrity bio" of Elvis Presley by Albert Goldman from development to publication, so he became the third leg of the stool.

It wasn't hard to see why Pete Kameron was attracted to Kevin Eggers. As Irish-American as Pete was Jewish, Kevin had kissed the blarney stone and found it good. He cultivated a Norman Maileresque persona and considered it his mission to preserve the legacy of American music without much regard to commercial success. Nevertheless, he was a hustler and, as his former partner Giorgio Gomelsky described him, "a collector," which was not a term of unalloyed approval as Gomelsky applied it. They had been partners in Tomato Records and the experience had not made Giorgio any less cynical.

Kevin left his Brooklyn home when he was 14 and made his way to California, where he got a job caddying for Fred Astaire at the Bel Air Country Club. He also caddied for Fred McMurray—who, Kevin confided, was the meanest man in the world. Kevin would tell me about McMurray with such a forlorn look on his face that it was apparent that there was more between them than stingy tips. As Bobby Darin was to

Allen Klein, Fred McMurray was for Kevin. The kind of wound that sends you back in the ring with blood in your mouth and vengeance on your mind. I have had a few of those in my life and can tell you the emotions stirred can become obsessive and toxic.

At a weekly touch football game near Beverly Hills, Kevin met Elvis Presley and that was where he first encountered the gofer Lamar Fike. Years later, Fike would become Elvis biographer Albert Goldman's grass courtesy of Eggers. By the age of 19, Kevin had worked his way up from the mailroom of the GAC agency to become assistant to Sid Bernstein, the booker who would go on to be the New York promoter of the Beatles and the manager of the Young Rascals. Kevin had it that he also worked for Sid when the Beatles and, later, the Stones were presented by Bernstein. We decided to make nothing of the fact that I did not recall meeting him then. He might have been there, I might have not noticed him, we moved on.

In 1966, Kevin formed his own record label, Poppy, which later became Tomato. His first album was the debut of the Texas songwriter Townes Van Zandt, whom Kevin and his brother recorded until the singer's 1997 death. He also released John Cage's Four Walls, and an inspired, eclectic assortment of music by Albert King, John Lee Hooker, Nina Simone and Philip Glass.

"Their importance in the music community, in life, our society and our culture far outweighs any of these platinum sellers," he said of the artists he favored, but who probably sold fewer records than my Werewolves. Unfortunately, as of this writing, the surviving family of Townes Van Zandt have a different view of Kevin and the still raging legal acrimony over who owns the Van Zandt masters, and who should and who hasn't been paid, persists in making lawyers richer than ever from Austin to Nashville to New York.

Kevin has represented and/or misrepresented Elvis Presley on two occasions, both of them after the King was silenced by death and could not defend himself: the aforementioned Albert Goldman book, and the 2003 effort to dub contemporary musicians over Presley's classic recordings. In a piece of 2003 promo hype, Kevin was quoted as saying that he was inspired by the desire to pass a musical legacy on to his daughters, now in their 20's, who know Presley best as a sad, fat man in a white rhinestone suit. Now that is unmitigated blarney, but if you knew Kevin (who may be the Irish Jerry Brandt), you would know how he could spin that story and make the gullible believe it.

Goldman's book vomited up a detailed account of Presley's final days, his drug problems and sexual predilections. Fans were appalled by the book's lack of reverence for Presley's place in popular mythology, but nonetheless made it a best seller. Presley expert Greil Marcus in the *Village Voice* accused Goldman and Eggers of cultural genocide. While Goldman's slightly less provocative bio of Lenny Bruce had established his credentials with a press always open to controversy, Elvis made him a celebrity in his own write. Elvis and the even more execrable *The Lives of John Lennon* provided the template for tabloid fodder that Brits such as Andrew Morton and Philip Norman have made their bread and butter. At least Norman tries to provide a factual timeline for his subjects' lives, but Andrew Morton takes a schoolyard bully's delight in destroying the reputation of his betters.

So why was I willing to shack up with Eggers when I knew full well he was an unindicted co-conspirator in Goldman's hatchet job on Presley? Whatever professional and financial difficulties I'd had since leaving the Rolling Stones in 1967, I'd been careful not to exploit my insider knowledge of their personalities and missteps. I had to have realized that the book Eggers hoped to get from me was not going to be an homage. But I was no longer the boy who wet himself the first time he heard "You've Lost That Lovin' Feelin'." It was gone, gone, gone and not coming back. I needed a win, and Kevin and Pete seemed to feel I had one in me. I would write my autobiography, Kevin would package and sell it, and Pete Kameron would look out for us both. I would make a lot of money. I said yes.

Kevin was a family man who encouraged both Esther and I to hang out at his comfortable home in Brooklyn's Park Slope. His hustle was transparent but I enjoyed watching him work it on me. Although I was the mark in round one, I was pretty sure I'd get to hustle him back in round two. Did I find it illogical that Kevin had spent more money on Milton Glaser designed album covers than he had on the records themselves? Yeah, and at the time, it amused me.

Only a couple of years earlier, I had conned RCA Records into a full range of Werewolves' promo tchotchkes designed by Mick Rock to look as if they'd been filched from a stateroom on the Queen Elizabeth II. The way I looked at it, Eggers was going to get us paid by a deep pocketed third party and if he wanted to practice on me, it was ok. Making our way back to Manhattan we'd stop by Pete Kameron's East Side pad for some more good conversation and better cocaine. I can't say I didn't enjoy the attention and respect, even if part of me realized these two old hookers were telling their john how big his dick was.

Kevin cleverly countered my objections to his complicity in the Presley debacle. He claimed he had been shattered and screwed by the deal he'd made with Goldman. Goldman was a drug addict, a liar, unreliable, practically a major label music executive, to hear Kevin tell it. When you hear someone disparage a former partner without restraint, remember, you'll be next. So what kind of deal between us did Eggers feel would be fair? He wanted a third of everything since he felt the twenty percent he'd made from Elvis wasn't enough. With the numbers Kevin and Pete were throwing around, I felt I could be generous. There was a lot more feeling going around than thinking. And oh yeah, I wasn't actually going to write the book. A "professional" would be paid to do that. A little detail that would take care of itself.

Eventually, just as we were going to contract, I was asked whom I would like as a writer. Super agent Mort Janklow was now on board, representing either the publisher, Kevin, or me. I was never sure. What was good enough for Janklow clients such as Pope John Paul II, Jackie Collins and Danielle Steel was certainly good enough for this tyro auteur. So I asked them to get me Michael Herr. "No problem," they replied.

I was elated and relieved. Herr had written the universally acclaimed account of the Vietnam War, *Dispatches*, as well as the narration for Francis Ford Coppola's *Apocalypse Now*. He was anything but a hack and would surely treat my story with more integrity than Goldman had Presley's. I was even more chuffed when I got my first check.

I kept asking Kevin when I would get to meet the lady who had cut the check, Gladys Carr, the senior editor at our publisher McGraw Hill. Kevin told me "all in good time." I never did get to meet her; there never was a good time. Slowly it dawned on me that I was not wanted as the man who had uncovered, managed, promoted and produced the Rolling Stones during their first great run. Rather I was to be Lamar Fike with an English accent, the roadie, gofer and PR schmuck who would reveal to all the world where the Rolling Stones had buried their bodies, throw open the closet wherein they kept their skeletons, and maybe if McGraw Hill got really lucky, prove that Brian Jones had been a suicide or a murder victim. Kevin, in particular, was not looking to redeem the sacrilege of Elvis; he was looking to repeat it for a higher percentage.

And where was my dear friend Pete Kameron in this rapidly metastasizing cluster fuck? In the midst of it all, I did not pause to consider, although I did notice I was not pausing. If Kevin had his way with me, Pete and I would betray the high esteem in which we had always held artists, something that had bonded us to begin with. Perhaps I couldn't admit to myself that Pete was assuming that I would shit on something even more near and dear to me than my time with the Stones: my own legacy, the part I knew I had played in their greatness despite all the rough spots I'd hit since parting with them. And the worst of it was I knew I only had one shot at this. There would never be a second chance to make it right.

My heart, which unhappiness had led me to freeze with coke and numb with morphine, was broken. Despite asking me for input, Kevin prematurely issued a press release announcing the ultimate kiss and tell on the Rolling Stones, their prodigious abuse of drugs and sex along with the details of their wealth down to the Middle Eastern oil fields that gushed money 24/7. Thinking he'd win me over, Kevin directed me to an item in the *New York Post's* Page Six gossip column that claimed breathlessly that we'd obtained a $1.5 million advance. The last thing Eggers, Kameron or Janklow needed was for me to confess to McGraw Hill that it was sixteen years since the Stones and I had been intimate. Kameron knew the history well enough to realize that once the band caught wind of the pre-release hype around the book, no one who ever wanted to speak with them again would speak with us. What were we thinking?

We never did get Michael Herr, which was his good luck. I'm not even sure he was ever approached on the project. I couldn't afford to return the money I'd received and probably thought my own talent and fortitude might still prevail if only I found the right partner to write with. This wasn't my first rodeo; I'd been in the music business for twenty years and I'd been lied to before. Frequently. But as the saying goes, "Fuck me once, shame on you. Fuck me twice, shame on me." I was at the end of the plank and the pirates I was in business with were behind me on the deck waving cutlasses in my direction.

Enter Michael Number Two. I had picked up *Hospital: The Hidden Lives of a Medical Center Staff* by a fellow named Michael Medved. It was structured as an oral history and resembled in format one of my favorite biographies, *Edie*, about the ill-fated Warhol starlet Edie Sedgwick. Michael flew to New York to meet with us, and what a piece of work he turned out to be in person. An orthodox Jew, he was pleasantly enthusiastic about cinema, food, writing and just about everything else life had to offer—except music. I mentally cast him as Zero Mostel in *The Producers*, dizzy and cuddly and altogether a happy bloke, except that his wife and he were having a hard time getting pregnant. Which he insisted on sharing with me in too much detail.

Pete Kameron at home

We set him up on the 27th floor of a five-star hotel on Central Park South, forcing him to live up to his orthodox faith, which forbade him from using an elevator from Friday afternoon until Saturday, twenty-four hours later. I looked forward to schooling Medved in the details and nuances of my life in the '60s, which I'd shared with the Stones. I brought him books by George Melly, Nik Cohn, David Dalton, Tony Sanchez and Robert Hewison. I insisted he steep himself in the Rolling Stones catalogue and the vital blues records that had influenced them. Plus videos. Magazines. A crash course for the ravers. It was like asking Jackie Mason to replace Mick Taylor.

While Medved was busy taking in data that would have been second nature to any actual fan of the Rolling Stones, I asked Pete and Kevin when Medved and I would leave for London. I wanted to revisit the physical locations that were the setting for our story. It crossed my mind that the more I had my co-writer to myself the more influence I'd have on what he'd eventually write on my behalf. I'd been hustled so much so far that you'll forgive me if I'd decided it was my turn. When it became obvious even to me that my partners had no intention of sending us anywhere, I became uncooperative. I didn't know exactly how I would change things to be more to my liking but I was getting tired of being a bit player in my own drama.

Of all the dozens of tracks I had produced with the Stones, many of them worldwide Number Ones, Medved was most eager to discuss "Andrew's Blues," which had never been released because it was, frankly, obscene. The Stones had been joined by Phil Spector and Gene Pitney at Regent Sound in London's Denmark Street at the same session at which they cut our first real hit, "Not Fade Away." Phil had brought along a bottle of good brandy to loosen the boys (and me) up since I'd confided I could use the moral support. "Andrew's Blues" was cut amidst considerable jollity by all those in attendance, and the lyrics when they weren't dirty, satirized my relationship with Decca Records chief, Sir Edward Lewis.

Well now Andrew Oldham
sitting on a hill with Jack and Jill
He fucked all night

and he sucked all night

and he taste that pussy

till it taste just right

Whoa whoa Andrew

Oh oh Andrew

Come and get it little Andrew

Before Sir Edward takes it away

from you

Medved wanted to know if the Jack and Jill thing was a bisexual innuendo. Subtle, wasn't he? I don't know where he got that idea from a vocal delivered by three such renowned cocksmen as Messrs Pitney, Spector and Jagger. I asked Medved whether he knew that this was the first time Pitney and Spector had been together in the studio since the classic "Every Breath I Take." Nah. Not a clue.

One hysterical Central Park afternoon, Pete Kameron and I stopped off at our mutual dentist, Pete for some work and me for some gas. As we walked the block east to Medved's hotel for tea, I asked Pete to please do drugs in front of the guy so he would get over thinking I was some kind of addict freak.

"Just bring out half a Percodan and offer it to him," I begged. I was very keen on Percodan at the time, despite the fact that 13 years of its abuse drove Jerry Lewis to the brink of suicide. By my calculation, I had years and years to go of numbed out bliss. In those days I liked to admit sardonically that I was a serial abuser of drugs but at least I rotated through them. I thought of making up bumper stickers that read "I brake for Percodan," but decided I'd rather spend the money on drugs.

"Or you could do a line of coke on his coffee table," I hissed. So he and we did. We did our drugs in front of him; we talked about drugs and their place, and waste, in music. We were poster children for the stoned, not the Stones. But Medved still did not get it. Whose idea was it again to bring in an orthodox Jew?

Eventually, Medved had had enough of me and my Stones, and he was paid off and flew back home. I was pissed, reckoning that for the same money we could have flown to London and got the work done. I'm sure that Michael's concerns might have had to do with flying with someone who was already flying, but he should have koshered that one before he signed on. I was glad when he was gone.

McGraw Hill and my partners were getting fed up with my rants about quality, accuracy and control. But I still had no idea of how to extricate myself from the mess, especially as I had already taken their 30 pieces of silver, so I stayed at the table and made up my mind that whoever they came up with next as a writer would have to be fine with me. I certainly wasn't going to tell them that Keith made the records, or that the moon was blue.

I knew Kevin was frustrated with me, but I didn't really know how McGraw Hill felt because I'd never met anyone there. The only time I met Mort Janklow, he spent more time admiring my vintage khaki shorts than asking pertinent questions. Would it have concerned him that I only worked with the Stones for four and half years and was basically persona non grata for abandoning them during their 1967 drug bust? Did any of the players except Pete Kameron even know there had been a bust? Or that despite the Stones' druggy reputation, that Keith and Mick were essentially innocent of the charges against them?

Safe to say that although we never discussed it, I knew McGraw Hill was paying for dish on which jet set socialites Mick had bedded (preferably married) and whether Keith had really gone to Switzerland for a total blood transfusion. I could make a pretty good case that although after my departure, Allen Klein, Bill Graham, and Prince Rupert may have made the Rolling Stones a richer and more successful band, they had not made them a better band than I had. Any credit for that would go to the Stones themselves and perhaps Jimmy Miller. But the unavoidable truth was that after 1967 it all had nothing to do with me. If a super 8 film existed of Lord Snowden snapping Mick shagging Princess Margaret, they'd have to get it from someone else.

Even Pete Kameron was getting miffed with me. He hinted it was childish of me to refuse to trash my legacy when lucrative opportunity knocked. Had I asked him if he would do the same to former partners and clients such as Kit Lambert, Chris Stamp, Pete Townshend and Terence Stamp, I'm sure he would have beamed a Zen smile my way and said, "But Andrew, you're the writer in our partnership." And there was always this notion that Pete was my White Knight who was carrying me off on his charger away from the evil Black Knight, Allen Klein. I didn't like being cast as Guinevere any more than I enjoyed playing Patty Hearst. I had told Eggers and Kameron I'd write a book with them; I hadn't offered to give them my balls for safekeeping.

I was really caught between the devil and the deep blue sea in the words of that wonderful oldie by Louis Armstrong. I was a little too sensitive to how Pete Kameron was feeling about me on a given day because I was so miserable under Allen Klein's thumb. So I had a lot of displaced anger and a very short fuse. There was the time I used a Brill Building studio belonging to the scion of a famous R&B songwriter to do some pre-production on a Klein project. Since I'd brought the brat some business and Allen had paid him, I telephoned him to ask for the customary kickback. He refused and then he went a step too far. "I'm going to do an Allen Klein on you," he smirked.

I cannot remember whether I had twelve dollars and four Pampers or twelve Pampers and four dollars. But I needed the kid's money and felt fully entitled to it. I put the phone down, did a line, and slid a stiletto into my pocket.

I was in the Brill Building in five minutes flat. The young laddie who was going to Allen Klein me was sitting down when I entered the room. He made the mistake of raising his hand as I treated him to a little kabuki with the knife. Big mistake: I cut him and it felt like a kiss. Today, the kid would probably call the Post and put us both on the front page.

I thought we couldn't do worse than the sweetly dopey Medved, but I was as wrong in this as I'd been about everything else. I was now offered A.E. Hotchner, who I grew to detest as one of the most distasteful characters I've ever met. I okayed Hotchner because he had written a book on Doris Day, and I didn't do any more vetting on him than McGraw Hill did on me. His relationships with Ernest Hemingway and Paul Newman were certainly to his credit, but what they saw in him escapes me.

Hotchner's celebrity targets were not always as All-American as Doris Day. Long after we agreed to disagree, to put it mildly, he and *Vanity Fair* were successfully sued for libel by Roman Polanski in London High Court. Hotchner claimed that Polanksi had tried to pick up a model at Elaine's restaurant in New York by telling her he could make her into "another Sharon Tate." Of course, Sharon Tate was Polanski's pregnant wife at the time she was murdered in 1969 by the Charles Manson "family."

Hotchner was pleased to inform *Vanity Fair's* readers that the attempted pick-up occurred mere months after Tate's grisly death. Hotchner wasn't quoting the model in question directly, but a magazine editor who was dining at Elaine's on that evening who testified that he had heard Polanski proposition the girl. Polanski denied the entire encounter ever occurred in a videotaped testimony from France where he was in exile avoiding extradition to the US on an unrelated statutory rape charge. British law requires the defendant in a libel action to prove their allegations and since *Vanity Fair* was unable to do so, Polanski prevailed. One doubts "Hotch" got in touch with Roman to apologize.

Well, give Kevin Eggers a dubious kind of credit. In Hotchner, he had found a co-writer the equal of Albert Goldman as a voyeur and cad. His home in Westport CT, a stones' throw from Paul Newman's and close by where Keith Richards lives now when he is not falling out of trees, was quite nice but reeked of a sense of entitlement that did not comfort me. Sex, drugs and rock 'n' roll were the total sum of his agenda and rock came in a pretty distant third. I grew to hate the expression his face took on as he tried to pump me for dirt he'd no doubt been promised by Kevin I'd spout like a broken fire hydrant. If I closed my eyes, a vision of Hotchner as a gargoyle in tweed staring down from his ivory tower haunted me. In fact, it was ok if I didn't want to be quoted as the source of this trash talk. He'd prefer to hear it from Mick or Keith themselves and when could I arrange that for him?

But I was not going to play. I gave him the background material we'd provided Medved, and told him that getting anything from the Stones depended entirely upon which side of the bed they got out of, and he had better not count on Mick Jagger getting out of bed at all. He asked me which of the other Stones I had lined up for him to talk to.

I thought about getting the same spiritualist that had tried to put me in touch with Sam Cooke to contact Brian Jones. It would have served Hotchner right. And Brian would have loved the attention, dead or alive.

I laughed and lied and did my best to outrage him. If Kevin had portrayed me as a monster to pique Hotchner's interest, I would do my best to live up to my bad name. I made a great show of taking various drugs in front of him, hoping my "the part of Mickey Rourke will today be played by Sid Vicious" routine would turn him off and drive him away. It figured that my misbehavior only turned the prick on.

Yet Hotchner had a sterling reputation as a philanthropist for his work on Paul Newman's various charitable businesses. The only parts of our conversations I enjoyed were the Newman stories, particularly how Paul's extensive collection of performance motor cars were all built to order. As a car buff myself, I appreciated the custom hatchback Newman had lent his pal Hotch. But although Paul Newman was a fellow Aquarian, I would have loved to meet, A.E. Hotchner was the last person I'd have chosen to introduce us. I had to be satisfied with one of my favorite Newman quotes. When asked what his nightmare was, Paul replied, "To wake up without blue eyes."

No surprise, Hotchner came to dislike me as much as I disliked him. I later heard he told a mutual acquaintance I was the most horrifying work experience he'd ever had. It's true that once I'd decided I could not win him over or turn him away from his mission to slander the Rolling Stones, I really outdid myself. I had a friend of mine, who happened to be a dark-complected Afghanistani filmmaker, costume himself as a Palestinian terrorist and stalk Hotchner's home.

I would call him from odd places all over the world at inconvenient times with terrifying advice. One time his wife answered the phone and I asked her if she knew where her husband was. When she told me she didn't, I suggested he might be next door sucking Paul Newman's dick. Hotchner's charitable deeds probably gave him some spiritual protection against his sleazier tendencies, but my grasp of cause and effect was getting mighty shaky.

One day, Hotch was set to do an interview with Marianne Faithfull at a downtown hotel. Marianne demanded an eighth of blow before she would talk. I popped out to Queens and provided the eighth, and Kevin, having unobtrusively enveloped it up, passed it on to Hotch, who may not even have known what the contents were. He passed the envelope to Marianne, who disappeared into the bathroom with it, then reappeared moments later to demand, "Do you call this real blow? This is shit. Come back with the real thing if you want me to talk." Hotch for sure knew by now. I was glad that Marianne still knew what good blow was, but I can only guess that Kevin, or someone, had stepped on it, because what I delivered was the real Colombian deal. He tiptoed around that suggestion with a leprechaun laugh, but no wry Behanesque comment.

I may have underestimated Hotchner; he could give as good as he got. He finally had an off duty cop raid my New York hotel room, looking for guns and drugs. He found the gun but not the drugs, and the hotel which I had patronized for years did not invite me to stay with them again. Over seven years after we parted ways, to the great relief of us both, Hotchner published a rather tepid book based on interviews with "friends" of mine and the Stones he managed to arrange for himself. One pal called to ask me what was going on and stated his interview with Hotchner was like discussing jogging with Chet Baker.

A year and a half had passed and my book was obviously going nowhere. Kevin and Pete Kameron were exasperated with me, Kevin forever and Pete for a while. I called up Allen Klein, and told him the whole tale. He got me out of the deal, and even extracted some more money from McGraw Hill on the proviso that I would not write another book for a year. Pete was certainly disappointed in me and his feelings were hurt by my turning back to Allen in my hour of need. We never spoke of it.

With it all over, I took time to count up how much I'd have earned had the original deal gone through. Kevin had his third, the agent 15%. Pete would have got his. The writers, maybe a quarter. After taxes, I would have ended up owing them. A long way from what the *New York Post* had promised me. Hotchner proved to be the only pro in the room; he got paid twice.

My friendship with Kameron did not suffer any permanent damage, because I made sure it didn't. Pete became an investor in the *LA Weekly* where he was both inspiring and business-like. Mike Sigman joined the paper in 1983 as general manager and has written that Kameron kept the paper from sinking under from its own terminal hipness. "When I arrived at the *Weekly* . . .," Mike recalls, "the staff featured a brilliant mix of punks, anarchists and malcontents who did not, shall we say, take kindly to authority. It was Pete more than anyone else who helped me see both the vast potential of the *Weekly* and the hilarious absurdity of the often horrifying chaos that ensued. It was Pete's Zen attitude that kept me grounded"

Does this not sound like Allen Klein marching into the Beatles' Apple HQ at 3 Savile Row, when the band reportedly had only enough cash to keep the doors open for one more week? Klein set about installing his own soldiers and getting rid of anyone who had a heart. The only difference between Allen's involvement with Apple and Pete's with the *LA Weekly* is that Pete did not march, he strolled.

Sigman goes on to say, "Pete knew everyone. Whenever I was with him, people from every imaginable background, gangsters and gurus, movie stars and rockers, rich bank presidents and needy friends rushed to embrace him. We all valued his tough love. You could always count on Pete to nail your weaknesses and tell you how to be your best self."

In June 2008, having spent some time in Vancouver, I returned to Los Angeles on my way back to Bogotá, to say goodbye to Pete. He had emailed in his usual flippant but careful way that his liver cancer was not responding to chemo. About a year earlier, Kameron had asked me to put him in touch with Pete Townshend. Kameron had been the business brains behind Kit Lambert and Chris Stamps' management of the Who and particularly the establishment of the Who's label, Track Records.

Kameron told me he had been going through old files, and had found some correspondence between him and Townshend that he thought Townshend would appreciate having. I was not buying this, even from my Zen mentor. Pete didn't want to give Townshend documents, he wanted something else. But the tone of his request did not invite any queries, just acquiescence.

Giorgio Gomelsky once remarked to me that it was surprising that I remained so fond of some of those who have done me wrong, because I am not generally known as a turn the other cheek kind of guy. I replied, simply, it takes two. Somebody has to be offering you what you want in order for you to give up what you have, and if they take more than agreed, as long as it's not the food off my table, fuck them, because it's them that will get killed by their greed, and it's not even just them, usually it's their children. Anyway, I will not allow it to be any other way; it would be bad for me and certainly bad for my family. Whether your God asks you to buy bottled water, tie a red string around your wrist, denounce homosexuals or trust Christopher Hitchens when he tells you there is no God, it does not pay to accumulate more baggage than you can carry in this lifetime.

So there was something more to this "I wanna get in touch with Pete Townshend" reach that will remain an unfinished matter between the two Petes. Almost forty years ago, a Kameron deal on the Who's behalf went so far bad that Pete Townshend remains bitter to this day, although I think he'd have done better to forgive. After Kameron's death, Townshend emailed me, "Thanks for letting me know, but for me he died a long time ago when he sold us out to Allen Klein." Always the lyricist, that boy.

Allen took one stab at getting the Who, ostensibly, but not really, on my behalf, way back in 1965. That attempt failed, but Klein was to succeed more subtly a few years later in a maneuver that remains obscure to this day. Pete Kameron had it that he let Klein win because he just could not be bothered. It was an oddly unsatisfying explanation from a man with an endowed chair at the UCLA School of Law named after him. I respected Pete's privacy and memories too much to press him.

His entire career, Allen set up and manipulated corporate shells in a game of three card monte that only he could win. My guess is that just as he tied my publishing interests in knots so that I no longer recognized my own deals, he found a way to cut out

Kameron, Stamp and Lambert, to Townshend's everlasting regret. The details almost don't matter; it's a matter of get out of the kitchen if you can't stand the heat. There's that Dave Clark wisdom again.

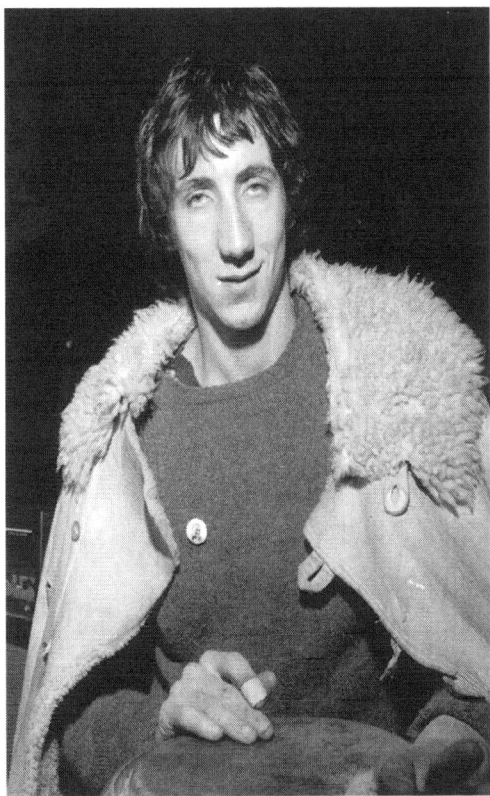

Pete Townshend

Pete Kameron had one more lesson for me that last week of his life. I left him on Monday night, saying I would call him the following day to say "goodbye" before I flew home. I called him as planned. He sounded a bit rough. Obviously, not even the pipe was working.

"I'll see you in August, Pete," doing my best to cheer him.

"No, you won't," he replied, very matter of factly, with no strings attached, no buttons pushed or pulled. "I won't be here."

He was not. He passed the following Saturday night, having been sung into the next life, by another of his friends and students, the ultimate pied piper of peace, love and psychedelia, Donovan.

Nice way to go, Pete. You even got to pick the songs . . .

Someone's going to take your money, better that you call them friend.

ALLEN KLEIN

BY THE TIME Allen Klein passed away on July 4, 2009, we had known each other for 44 years—almost half a century marked by his rapacity, generosity and unerring instinct for the weaknesses of those with whom he was in business. To say I was ambivalent is to greatly understate the complexity of my feelings toward Allen, who had completely altered my relationship with the Rolling Stones, virtually from the day we met. I could have wished he'd picked another date on the calendar; July 4th is my wife Esther's birthday and now we would have to share it with Allen.

I flew from Bogotá to New York the next day for the funeral in a disembodied state reminiscent of some mushroom trips I'd taken in the distant past. I could not say with certainty I was feeling the sense of closure many others who knew Allen may have felt on that day. At least I could tell myself with conviction that straight was better than stoned. That Allen Klein and I would share karma for the rest of my days seemed inescapable and had I been high when considering this, it might have sobered me.

When I arrived at the funeral home for Allen's memorial service, I was greeted by the photographer Mick Rock, perhaps my closest friend among the many mutual acquaintances in attendance. Ever the lad, Mick's mourning attire seemed to emphasize the fact that Allen Klein had been a businessman in a very unbusiness-like business. Although more conventionally dressed myself in a black suit, I couldn't help but be amused by Mick's Varvatos denim jacket, Harry Palmer inspired bins, and standard issue Converse classic "Chucks." Despite the seeming casualness of his dress, Mick Rock could be said to have been among the most sincere of those who had come to condole with Allen's nearest and dearest.

For many years, until a heart attack felled him in his Staten Island home, Mick had been the oddest kind of vegetarian, believing that a diet of dairy and eggs, rather than fruits and veggies, was sufficient to maintain both his health and his morality against the evils of meat consumption. This despite the fact that at the same time he also consumed prodigious quantities of less healthy natural substances. The disastrous result was that Mick needed an immediate triple-bypass to survive, and without health insurance his prospects for recovery didn't look good.

By the grace of beneficent providence, I happened to call Mick's home from my own in Colombia on the very day he had been taken to the hospital by ambulance. Sheer instinct had me ring off determined to save Mick by calling on the one man both of us knew had the best doctors in the world at his beck and call. Mick and I had worked with Allen on various re-issue projects and Allen was fond of him. In fact, his response was as gracious as if Paul McCartney had called to enlist his aid in rescuing Northern Songs from Michael Jackson.

Allen sprang into action, moving Mick from the charity ward to one of New York's finest hospitals, where his personal physicians were told to spare no effort in getting our friend back on his feet. After his brush with death, Mick rearranged both his priorities and his diet, and his gratitude toward Allen was boundless. So much so that Allen and I sometimes grew weary of Mick's appreciation for the helping hand. I had to admit, though, that Allen's response to the one thousandth time Mick had thanked him rang true as a bell: "Well, Andrew," Mick told me, "now when I bring up the subject,

Allen tells me to leave it alone. Helping me, he says, was his ticket to heaven." As we waited for the memorial service to begin, Mick and I wondered if Allen had been right.

People often speak of a "great weight" having been lifted from their shoulders on the occasion of various kinds of break-ups and losses. If I had felt disembodied on the plane over, now at the service I felt weightless and somehow purer. After the last handful of dirt had been shoveled into Allen Klein's grave, I felt somehow reborn, as if I'd just come out of a prolonged fast. Stone free, so to speak.

While Allen was often ruthless, he was very seldom vindictive. His affection for me was genuine and existed side by side with his undeniable need to always come out on top. He might have made me sit and stay for my "emergency" checks before handing them to me just minutes before the bank closed for the day, but I was an addict in the making and something of a tortured soul long before I met Allen. Even when I was outraged by his latest sharp-elbowed sortie against me, I knew that. It didn't keep me from enjoying the tennis in Sicily or the golf in New Orleans. Allen shared those pursuits of the rich and famous with me in a manner both natural and without condescension. Say what you will about the man, there was fun to be had with him.

I started this chapter long before Allen Klein passed away, and in the first weeks after his death it seemed unnecessary to finish it. But in time I realized that with Allen gone I had yet another opportunity to celebrate both my survival and my faith in the future. That was a good thing, the result of which I share with you now.

* * *

Given Allen's campaign to corner the English Invasion market in '64, '65, it was inevitable that we would meet eventually. But fittingly, one of the hustles I had going myself brought us together. Early on, I realized that song publishing provided an income stream more direct and timely than the royalties paid by the label on records sold. In the days before Mick and Keith began to write their own singles, it hurt my professional pride to produce hits out of obscure R&B tunes and not profit from it. So I would habitually contact the publishers of the "covers" we recorded and suggest that for 20% of their share they could catch a ride up the charts by England's Next Big Thing. What might be called "extortion" in another context was business as usual for the music business.

Our version of "It's All Over Now," originally done by Bobby Womack's Valentinos, was looking like our biggest hit yet, and pursuing the kickback led me to Allen Klein, who was consolidating his control of all things Sam Cooke, including the aforesaid copyright. Allen was in London at the time and our first meeting quickly enlarged in scope to include my embryonic Immediate Records and a particular pressing problem I was having with my partner Eric Easton.

Recall that when I first met the Stones in 1963 I was barely 19 years old, too young to sign contracts on my own behalf, let alone become licensed as a booking agent. In those first few weeks after the band agreed to let me manage them, I had two urgent needs: an office to work out of and gigs to keep the Stones busy and money coming in. At first we were all happy to allow Easton to provide both. But soon enough Eric tired of baby-sitting a teenquake and began to apply his decades of show business experience to screwing us. Allen was all too ready to take Eric on while the band divided over who to go with. To cut a long story short, in the end Easton had only Brian Jones' signature on a new arrangement and that was insufficient for him to carry the day. In his first at bat, Allen had delivered a base hit.

Meanwhile Klein was sizing me up like a professional poker player testing the new kid with a hot hand. My notion of what kind of success might be possible for the Rolling Stones was totally defined by the Beatles. When Allen asked me what I wanted most out of life, my naiveté led me to answer him in a manner that did not enhance my stature in his eyes. My wants and needs were very simple and deeply superficial at that time and, as to what I wanted, I had no doubt.

In the spring of 1964, I had taken a break from the often unrewarding ballroom gigs by which the Rolling Stones hoped to overcome northern resistance to their London-style R&B, and instead joined the Beatles in Blackpool. The Beatles were performing in the UK for the first time since their triumphant first tour of the U.S., and John and Paul offered their old London PR a lift back to the smoke in John's spanking new Rolls Royce Phantom V. I thought I'd gone to heaven even before we got stoned. So, when Allen asked me what I wanted I just said, "I want a Rolls Royce like John Lennon's."

This response, although truthful, was not productive. Allen must have been pleased to think that I could be bought off so cheaply, much as one imagines Chicago's Chess brothers kept their charges happy with Cadillacs instead of cash (though, in fairness, Elvis himself used his RCA advance to buy his mom a pink Caddie). Allen's preference for money per se would stand him in good stead when dealing with emotional types such as myself. He would meet his match in the equally avaricious Mick Jagger, but it took Mick a while to appreciate what he was worth in cold hard currency. By then, of course, the sorcerer Allen had his mitts in the business as only an owner can.

When Allen achieved his ultimate goal of controlling the business affairs of three of the four Beatles, even John Lennon was not immune to manipulation despite his relative worldliness and cynicism. To a point, Allen was willing to indulge John and Yoko's rather eccentric self-image as patrons of the Arts, with a Capital "A." Keith Richards, you may remember, always maintained that "Art" was short for "Arthur," which certainly kept a lot of rubbish at bay.

Allen Ginsberg had introduced the Lennons to Alejandro Jodorowsy's *El Topo*, an all but unwatchable mess of a movie, with which they were inexplicably enchanted. So Allen Klein bought the U.S. rights and inflicted this monstrosity and its successor, which he financed, on various art houses across the land to which young American Beatlemaniacs dutifully flocked as a result of John's endorsement. Knowing Allen, he probably made money in the end, although all John and Yoko were likely to have gotten is the satisfaction of being avant garde. And that might just have been enough for all concerned.

* * *

Allen Klein was born in Newark, New Jersey, on December 18, 1931. Keith Richards was born on the same day twelve years later, so Sagittarians both, with some karma together. Sagittarians are rather expansive and yet jolly in their cheek; if they are caught out, they tend to politely say, "Sorry, where were we before this?"

Keith himself has said rather recently of Allen, "I can never get a hard-on against Allen Klein. He did raise us to the heights, in a way. He's an operator, man." Less recently, Keith opined that he only needed to see Allen Klein twice a year, and a signature would do, the two days being paydays. Somewhere between the honeymoon and the divorce, Keith noticed Allen at a pre-show meet and greet (the Stones are too big and too jaded to do "after parties"), and asked, "Who left the barn door open?"

For although it was by now and for always Keith's party, he'd never bothered to nail shut the dog door that let Allen in. Keith may have "99 problems" but money ain't one so he can afford to be generous in his judgments, even though in a candid moment he did say something to the effect that the Stones got the silver and Klein got the gold. There are other Rolling Stones for whom Klein remains anathema, but they tend not to greet visitors before showtime. They probably worry more about money, however much they may already have. They have no book, they have no memory. It all works out.

Keith, it might be said, is something of an idealist. How else to account for his perpetual affection for the irascible Chuck Berry, who begrudges the Rolling Stones every dime they ever made. While Allen, on the other hand, despite the soft spot he had for artists, could scarcely be called an idealist. From Allen's perspective, expecting the worst from people was both normal and usually correct. His objectivity was uncanny, untainted by emotions such as rancor, sadness or disdain.

Allen's early life was marked by greater hardships than the Depression he grew up in. The son of two Jewish immigrants from Budapest, Hungary, his father was a butcher. His mother died within a year of Klein's birth, and the boy was sent to live in an orphanage by his impoverished father.

Following a stint in the Army, Klein developed his aptitude for numbers in night school, paying his way with odd jobs. In 1956, he graduated from Upsala College in East Orange, New Jersey. Finding work as an auditor, he drifted into show business as a bookkeeper, a career that introduced him to the seamier side of record company accounting. Auditing the books of various labels on behalf of his clients, he was astonished to discover just how much money was being withheld, sometimes under the flimsiest of pretexts, but very often for no reason whatsoever, beyond the fact that the labels tended to have better accountants than the artists. Assuming the artist even had accountants.

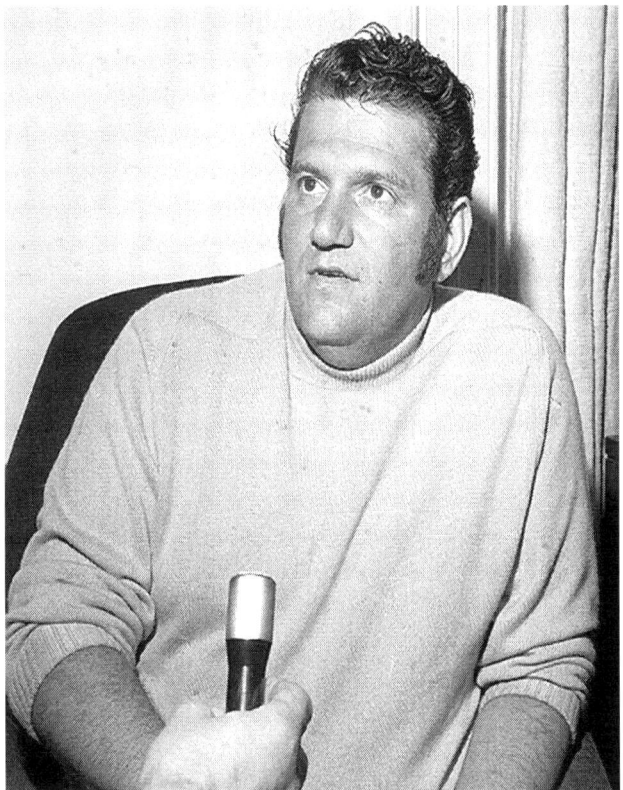

Allen Klein

Business trotted along nicely for a few years, but Allen was never satisfied with trotting along. His eye was always looking for the main event and, attending a friend's wedding sometime around 1961, he spotted it. Singer Bobby Darin was among the guests and, having started talking, the suave young vocalist was amazed when Klein asked him if he'd like to make $100,000.

"What do I have to do?" Darin asked suspiciously.

"Nothing," replied Klein, and it was true. Allen waded into Atlantic Records, with whom Darin had released almost five years' worth of hits, and extracted $100,000 in sundry unpaid amounts. But when Allen tried to up the ante by renegotiating Darin's deal with the wily Ertegun Brothers and Jerry Wexler, they were having none of it. Nevertheless, all concerned were impressed with Allen Klein's doggedness and marked him as a force that would need to be reckoned with.

Soon enough, however, Allen was cut out of Bobby's next big move. Disdaining the Top 40 success of such light pop fare as "Splish Splash," Capitol Records was pleased to offer Darin a make-over as the heir apparent to Frank Sinatra, with whom they had enjoyed some small success throughout the Fifties before Sinatra left to form his own record company, Reprise. The "Sinatra crown" and the million dollars that went with it suited Darin down to the ground so *au revoir* Atlantic and Allen, and thanks for the hundred grand.

He did have a couple of hits with Capitol, but they were not "Mack The Knife" or "Beyond The Sea," and while he continued to earn big bucks, his restless spirit did him no favors as he moved into a trailer, smoked pot, and grew a stash that looked no more authentic than his hair. He had awful denim jackets tailored in Vegas and renamed himself Bob Darin. Atlantic eventually took him back into the fold and in 1966 he hit a last time with Tim Hardin's "If I Were a Carpenter."

Allen Klein looked askance as Darin's career faltered, faulting not so much his new image but his business decisions. Klein always believed in the act staying in one place. Hits were unpredictable but an artist's catalogue provided the leverage that made both the artist and his accountant business partners with the label. I agree with him. It was disconcerting over the years to watch the Rolling Stones section of the record store racks become an ever more confusing jumble of prices and packaging, as the group meandered from London to Atlantic to CBS, then EMI and Virgin. Basically, whomever was offering the most cash with a CEO willing to finance Mick's unhelpful and unsuccessful solo projects or listen to his movie ideas. We had come a long way from the pristine purity of their first album cover.

I would stroll down to "B" and see the Beatles' CDs like little ducks all in a row and bite my tongue. I would go to "D" and see Dylan, too, all neat and tidy, with the exception of a couple of discs that dribbled out to David Geffen. Allen would have been gratified to see the Rolling Stones now on Universal, the only label they'd not yet exploited, their entire catalogue finally in one place for the first time since 1971.

As regards *l'affair* B. Darin, Allen once admitted to me in a rare instance of what passed for honest intimacy, "It's the only time I have ever been hurt by an artist, Andrew. I vowed it would never happen again." When I brought the Darin subject up some years later, disingenuously hoping to spread some of the hurt I was doubtlessly feeling myself on Allen's sandwich, his eyes didn't go cold, they just went away. His lips pursed as if he was about to speak, he shook his head and just said, "Never happened." Then he waited for me to change the subject.

Allen was good at waiting. His sound of silence summoned all your anxieties, all of the fears that he would then take care of. So I changed the subject, still hoping in my ambivalence towards Allen that I had inflicted just a bit of pain with my dart.

Allen successfully tidied up the books for Steve Lawrence and Eydie Gorme while making his management bones with crooner Bobby Vinton, whose hit "Blue Velvet" set a new low standard for pop in the largely uninspiring years between Elvis' induction into the Army and the Beatles. He was ready now for something really big: he set his sights on Sam Cooke, the first, but not the last, of the superstar black artists who would "cross over" in more ways than one (particularly apt given Sam's gospel roots):

Sam, Marvin Gaye and Michael Jackson all died too young in circumstances that screamed bloody murder. But in the late 1950s, unless you were listening to Alan Freed, you'd think Ricky Nelson and Pat Boone were the crown princes of rock 'n' roll rather than Fats Domino and Little Richard. At least Ricky had the good taste to employ guitarist James Burton since Elvis wasn't needing him much at the time.

America had not come all that far from the Jim Crow days when black orchestras playing to white audiences had to put up in a network of private homes because no hotel in the Mid-West would take them in. As late as 1964 when the Rolling Stones toured with Patti LaBelle and the Bluebells, the girls were still being denied equal accommodation. But nightclubs in some cities at least had become integrated, and Cooke became one of the highest earners in the business while his records were pop enough to get played alongside of Darin's.

Jerry Brandt was Sam Cooke's agent when he was at the William Morris Agency and managed by JW Alexander (who was, incidentally, one of the few men ever allowed into a Rolling Stones session; he played tambourine on *December's Children*). According to Jerry, Klein promised to make him a partner in Sam's management in exchange for an introduction, but in the end Brandt remained at William Morris where both Allen and I were happy to give him the Rolling Stones as a consolation prize.

"When I first met Sam, he didn't have a dime," Klein famously declared, and Cooke's own people have since conceded that. Diving into the accounts at Cooke's label, RCA, Klein emerged with $150,000 worth of previously undisclosed royalties, a sum that was more than sufficient to prompt Cooke to demote JW and install Klein in his place. Klein renegotiated Cooke's existing RCA contract, obtaining a $450,000 advance spread over four years. He then signed Cooke to a new company of Klein's invention that Sam Cooke may or may not have owned for a few days. The new entity was named for Sam's daughter Tracey. Why wouldn't the artist have thought it was his?

All of Cooke's performance fees and a healthy ten percent of all records sold would be funneled into Tracey Ltd, which in turn licensed future recordings to RCA for a period of 30 years. The company's ultimate owner, of course, was Allen and, following Cooke's death and a brief stewardship by the singer's widow Barbara, Allen "relieved" her and the extended Cooke family of all responsibility for the estate and became sole proprietor.

Cooke was allegedly in the process of firing Klein when he was murdered under still controversial circumstances on December 11, 1964 by the night manager of the Hacienda Motel in South Central LA. We have no idea if this was true; there is no evidence to support it, and it may just be the wishful thinking of Anti-Kleiners. Although the death was ruled a "justifiable homicide," the condition of Cooke's body suggested he had taken a beating far more severe than Bertha Franklin could have meted out with her broomstick and pistol.

It was supposedly in the late fall 1964 that Cooke first came to the conclusion that Klein was "no fucking good." A lot of little things had seemingly fallen into place recently, including the discovery that various expenses that he believed would be handled by RCA were instead being charged to Cooke. His questions concerning Tracey Ltd were being met with evasion, and the blunter Cooke's requests became, the more vague became Klein's responses. Cooke may have known that by firing Klein, he would probably be bound up in litigation for years to come, and might even be prevented from recording or working at all. But he was determined all the same. Or so his friends said after the fact. Klein just kept on doing what he did best, which included reducing anyone else who assisted in Cooke's career to the position of unworthy serf (or removing the riff raff, depending upon your point of view). Eventually, the rights to Cooke's entire legacy were firmly in Allen's grasp.

Arthur Kempton's *Boogaloo* painted an alarming portrait of how that played out. "Rather than its proprietor, Klein thinks of himself as the vigilant steward of Cooke's legacy, whose beneficence towards the family he dispossessed surpasses any reasonable claims that they might exert on his conscience, since owing them nothing, he provides money now and again when they are needy." Allen could be extremely generous when it suited him, usually when he had papers he needed you to sign.

Many years after all the bloodletting, Allen asked me if I wanted to know why he had not taken everything from me. I couldn't wait. Anyway, I had no choice in the matter. Allen had just given me a few grand for the rights to all of my Rolling Stones sleeve notes. And we were being super-pally.

"No, Allen, I have no idea," I replied, "Do tell me."

I braced myself since Allen could be so brutally tactless in the name of candor.

"Because, Oldham, if I had taken everything then I would have had to support you," he replied, touching a similarly raw nerve to the one he plucked when he told me on one occasion too many that his former lawyer had bedded my former wife.

When Sam Cooke was posthumously inducted into the Songwriters Hall of Fame in 1986, his widow Barbara closed her acceptance speech by thanking Allen for the hamburgers she put on her table. She delivered the line so well one could not discern if her vermouth was dry, droll or merely factual. Her former lover, driver, and Sam Cooke protégé, ex-Valentino Bobby Womack, was the entertainer that evening.

Now, I am not knocking Allen here. He was just doing what we all asked for along with a good deal more than we had asked for. Allen would get you back your kingdom, then pocket the keys. He was so damned brilliant that one can only believe that somebody's God was on his side. For many years, nothing ever went wrong for him; he met the Stones in May and we cut "Satisfaction" two months later. Sam was going to sack him in January, but died in December. After the Stones signed up with Allen, they resumed their endless touring and had little time to consider whether their new business partner was leveling with them.

What's in a name? As you'll have noticed it, was Klein's m.o. to give the shell companies he formed titles he knew had sentimental value to the artists he handled, Tracey Ltd being a case in point. Just as Sam's company was named after his daughter, the company that Klein formed to look after the Rolling Stones' master recordings, the masters Phil Spector had advised me to keep under our personal control at all costs, was given the same whimsical name as the publishing company that we owned in England, Nanker Phelge Ltd., itself named after the Stones' notoriously noxious roommate from their squalid Edith Grove flat.

In every legal sense, Nanker Phelge (U.S.) was the property of Allen and Betty Klein rather than the Rolling Stones and myself who owned the UK corporation. Over the years, Allen assured me that we went together to get advice on that score and were told the US company should be set up in Klein's name for tax purposes. We could hardly blame Allen as an accountant, since he wasn't one. Unfortunately, he sounded less convincing every time he reminded me of that tax nonsense. It didn't help that one of Allen's first moves was to fire the lawyers and accountants we'd been working with, carefully replacing them with people whose first loyalty was to him. Almost overnight, we became completely dependent on Allen for "objective" advice.

Ironically, only Bill Wyman, third up from the bottom in the hierarchy starting with Ian Stewart and Brian Jones, felt we should protest any of this. The rest of the Stones, myself included, told him to shut up and not rock the boat. "Satisfaction" had just topped the chart in thirty-eight countries, "Get Off Of My Cloud" was number one at the time. How bad could it all be? True, the Stones and I saw the Nanker Phelge U.S. corporate share certificates in our six names, but they were never actually filed, remaining in the firm possession of the Kleins.

In the event, there was a kind of fatalism in the relationship between me, Allen, Mick and Keith that is very hard for me to argue with despite the pain it evokes over forty years on. In 1967, when Mick and Keith found themselves arrested and jailed on the flimsiest of charges, I was self-stranded in the U.S. I knew that my return to London under the circumstances would almost inevitably see me joining the Stones in the dock. Worse, I knew the press might go easy on the "kids" but their money grubbing manager would be fair game.

Who could blame Allen for rushing to their side and attending the trial? Who could blame Mick and Keith for feeling betrayed? Yet despite the fact that the Stones were anything but stupid, and by this time had taken the full measure of their American manager, Allen Klein was seen by them to be the solution rather than the problem. Though as a matter of fact, I "quit" before I was "fired," the truth was always that a big piece of what made me what I was in those days died then. If only our split had brought any of us any closure. Thanks to Allen's magical maneuvers Mick, Keith and I are still hurting to this day, though Allen himself has gone to his reward.

By the time Allen landed the Stones, he'd had some experience of rejection at the hands of the newly risen British rock establishment. Early 1964 found him in London, introducing himself to Brian Epstein by suggesting that Sam Cooke be given the support slot on the Beatles' upcoming U.S. tour. Epstein may or may not have been intrigued; probably not, closer to insulted I would surmise. But any hopes Klein entertained of catching this particular fish were ended when he also suggested that he be appointed to handle the Beatles' finances.

Eppy may not have been the shrewdest businessman ever to walk the walk, and a lot of the financial decisions he made on the Beatles' behalf have since been revealed as naïve to say the least. But Brian operated at a time when a naïve belief in your artist got you into the game. If you had known any better you may not have bothered. Epstein recognized a poacher when he met one, and sent Klein packing without a second thought. Brian, bless his heart, may have been a Jewish furniture retailer, but he was a snob as well after his own fashion, especially when it came to who was allowed near his boys.

In fact, Brian might have felt he owed it to Great Britain herself to defend his wards against the depredations of the new barbarians. I don't think he was ever as enamored of America and Americans as were I and the Stones. In short, Americans were not gentlemen. Better enjoyed as Hollywood stars than business associates. End of story.

To console himself after failing to snag the Beatles, Allen made an immediate beeline for the first band to displace the Beatles at the top of the British charts, the Dave Clark Five, whose hit "Glad All Over" put the capital "I" in the British Invasion. The DC5 proved the Beatles weren't a fluke and opened the floodgates for funny hair and unintelligible accents.

The Dave Clark Five might have been about as cool back home as Kiss at Max's Kansas City but whilst the "Invasion" had its share of classic one-offs like "Go Now" and "She's Not There" the Dave Clark Five had 12 singles in the U.S. Top Forty between April of '64 and the end of 1965. If the Beatles ever looked over their shoulders at that time, it was the Dave Clark Five they saw, not the Rolling Stones. And the only mop-topped toothy grin they might have seen on the horizon belonged to Peter Noone, not Mick Jagger.

Clark had been in a group before and his early efforts appeared on the lowly Ember label. But the Dave Clark Five was his creation alone and no democracy. He placed the band on wages and produced the records with his own money. He hired only two outsiders, agent Harold Davison and ace publicist Leslie Perrin. By contrast, the Rolling Stones were purists and snobs in their own way, as was so much of musical England, and though history has proven whose music has been the more durable, perhaps at the time we were not nearly so superior as we thought.

The Dave Clark Five were yet another example of how the major labels worldwide were caught napping when "guitar bands" evolved beyond the Shadows into something unprecedented. It's well known how persistent Brian Epstein had to be to get a hearing at Parlophone, using his stores' record sales as leverage, and I, of course, was not above reminding Dick Rowe at Decca that he had passed on the Fab Four and might not want to let the Rolling Stones get away.

Although Capitol, EMI's division in the U.S., had rights of first refusal on the Beatles, they couldn't hear it (in fairness all they had were the sides backing Tony Sheridan) so "Love Me Do" ended up on the black-owned independent Vee-Jay, also home to the Four Seasons, who with the Beach Boys, were the hottest of the pre-invasion groups. "She Loves You" was licensed to the small Philadelphia label Swan. Within days of the Beatles' appearance on the Ed Sullivan show, all the Vee-Jay/Swan sides were in the Top Ten with a bullet and Capitol was suing anybody and everybody to get their rights back. Much as Apple and EMI do to this day. That's the record biz.

Similarly, the DC5, for slightly different reasons (for starters Clark owned the masters), appeared on Yank independents Laurie and Jubilee until Klein allegedly sold the band to Epic, a subsidiary of the giant CBS. Klein was already in business with CBS over Bobby Vinton, so it's possible the label had already signed Dave Clark and "gave"

Klein another of their artists to keep him happy. Regardless, after conducting a bit of bookkeeping business on Clark's behalf, Klein offered to renegotiate his contract with Epic.

The two men differ in their telling of that tale, Klein having it that Dave Clark was an Allen Klein artist, but one thing that Dave says certainly rings true. Allen offered to make him two million dollars. "No thanks," answered Dave, "I'd rather sleep at night."

This circumstance is also important because, in as much as Klein was somebody to get away from, Dave Clark did just that, the only artist of that time to do so. He walked away with exactly what he walked in with, save whatever commission he paid Klein for the work done. Both men played things close to their chest. Allen never once, in all our time together, ever said anything really good or bad about Dave Clark. In any event, Dave certainly proved to be a better business person and a more even-keeled well run fella than his musical "betters" who preceded him into the Rock and Roll Hall of Fame.

Allen found his first UK ticket to ride with producer Mickie Most. Mickie himself was not one to be trifled with; it was said he put a contract out on his sister-in-law's defiler, who happened to be handicapped. Mickie's world was growing fast at that time. He produced the Animals, Herman's Hermits, and the Nashville Teens, and one week in August 1964 all three acts were in the UK Top Ten. This was unheard of and an incredible feat for a man who, just eight months before, had been bottom of the bill on an Everly Brothers tour, along with the Rolling Stones. What made his accomplishment more impressive was that almost none of his acts performed their own material. Mickie had to go out and find the hits and then produce them.

For me, Mickie Most remains the most prolific and gifted British producer of all time, in that even George Martin and myself depended on the output of our artists for our hits (once I'd persuaded mine to write). Mickie needed only his ears. Mickie's Rak Records continued to be successful through the early '70s, by which time it could honestly be said that George and I had been marginalized. The Jeff Beck Group, Hot Chocolate, Suzi Quatro, Kim Wilde, and Mud made up an incredibly diverse roster. If all Mickie was known for in his career was giving Nicky Chinn and Mike Chapman their start, he'd be part of history; '70s glam wouldn't have existed without them, pace Ziggy Stardust and T. Rex. For those of you who like the Kevin Bacon game, you can get to Blondie via Mike Chapman in two from Mickie.

Perhaps it was because Mickie Most was so distinctively British that he was attracted to a partnership with Allen Klein, who was certainly his equal when it came to ambition. While Dave Clark had apparently decided to be self-sufficient, there was something missing in Mickie's approach to America that he felt Allen could provide. But it was a love match that left little room for the artists.

Those who have followed Peter Noone in the decades since he wooed Mrs. Brown's lovely daughter know him for an old soul and wise in the ways of the world. A great entertainer with a flair for impressions, he does Mick Jagger better than anyone this side of Tim Curry. Peter is philosophical about what he got out of selling over 50,000,000 records. "I've been through periods where I've started to get into the Allen Klein thing, and it's just very negative, a waste really. So I never bother about it. If a check comes, great. If it doesn't, it doesn't matter."

Other musicians, the remainder of the Hermits among them, have never tired of inquiring just where their earnings ended up. Allen used to claim to me that his deal was with Mickie, and it was Mickie who had to account to the artist. Nonetheless, although Mickie slipped away from Klein at the beginning of the Seventies, he had to leave a forfeit behind, his Animals and Hermits masters, which Allen Klein's ABKCO Records release to this day.

Klein was sharp. Accruing copyrights was second nature for him, and his portfolio bristled with potential hits for the artists who now seemed to be flocking towards him. The Sam Cooke catalogue remained dear to his heart, especially once there was no artist to get in his way, and it was a source of joy and extra jam when the Animals cut Cooke's masterpiece "Bring It On Home To Me," and the Hermits covered the Sam Cooke, Lou Adler and Herb Alpert wonderditty, "Wonderful World."

And then he got the Stones.

For reasons known only to himself, Allen perpetuated the notion that had I not goaded Mick Jagger into a lucrative career as an androgynous entertainer, his London School of Economics "training" would have led him to become Chancellor of the Exchequer. Allen liked to remember that "Mick would read every single page" of the contracts Klein asked him to sign. This is pure bollocks. Mick might have "read" the documents but that doesn't mean he knew what was actually in them.

I remember the high-pressure sessions at the Hilton Hotels in New York and London. While the band and Klein were in one room getting writer's cramp from merely signing, forget reading, a veritable avalanche of some of the most complex paperwork imaginable, lawyers like Marty Machat finalized the instruments of both our enrichment and destruction in another room. Apart from everything else going on, we were simply too busy to spend time reading and asking questions; we always had someplace we had to be next.

The Stones had got what we all thought we wanted and now the train had left the station. Soon enough "Nanker Phelge" would become a pseudonym for "Allen Klein and Co." and we would learn the true price of success. There is something, however, in the cliché that time heals all. Record companies are a lot bigger and smarter than they used to be, having themselves mastered the divide and conquer approach Allen pioneered. The Stones' distaste for their former business manager eventually faded as they realized that important parts of their legacy would forever be under Allen's control and the better strategy would be to stand together, as I'm sure they did when considering the implications of the recent "unification" move under Universal. With Forty Licks, there was enough dick to be sucked for everyone to enjoy a "happy ending." Or as Marianne Faithfull said to me just this year, "Isn't it ironic, Andrew, that Allen's record company is the only one that pays me."

Allen was quite the collector, of rock bands, that is. Like the Mikado he had a little list. I find it interesting that in the telling Allen always tied his interest in the Who into his "management" of yours truly. Of course, in short order I was as out of the loop as the late Sam Cooke, so who knows?

Allen did fly Pete Townshend first class to New York to meet us and, when interviewed by Dave Thompson in November 1994, Klein mused, "Now, how did that happen? Let me think. I had two occasions with the Who, once when we were on a boat in New York and I was trying to make a deal for Andrew to produce them. I seem to remember that Andrew introduced me to [them], I think their deal was over and I was trying to make a deal, but only if Andrew was the producer."

Whether Pete Townshend caught a vibe off the Stones that warned him off Klein, or whether he's simply extremely distrustful, Allen got nowhere with the Who at a time when they were building their reputation as the Third Greatest Band in the World one single at a time. Much as Allen loved artists in his own way, sometimes dealing with them was not the shortest distance between two points and, if that were the case, he was happy to do without them altogether.

Ten years later, publisher David Platz was the object of seduction on yet another of Allen's boat rides. Platz sold his Essex Music share of Townshend's songwriting catalogue to a company owned by Klein, at the same time technically removing any claim to ownership that Lambert, Stamp, Pete Kameron and their Track Records label may have had. Much, it might be said, as the Stones and I used Klein to cut out Eric Easton. No more than Easton were the Track principals let in on the deal and so today, ABKCO controls one-third of Townshend's publishing for the iconic Who Sell Out, the monumental Tommy, and the megalithic Who's Next with its advertising cash cow "Won't Get Fooled Again."

Who's next? The Kinks. Isn't it kind of obvious? Allen was simply starting at the top and working his way down. A month after he was rebuffed by the Who, Klein was sizing up the Kinks. According to the Kinks' co-manager Robert Wace, it was Peter Grant, Mickie Most's right-hand man (and later Led Zeppelin manager), who first suggested that Klein be brought on board in order to sort out the Kinks' own parlous finances. He failed. Wace told Kinks biographer Johnny Rogan, "We neither made nor lost in the Klein situation. His . . . job was to get a hell of a lot of money from Warners in the States, and he never really brought it off. Allen never did anything harmful to the Kinks."

He did resolve some scheduling problems that they were experiencing with their UK label, Pye, but ultimately, the staunchly upper class Wace concluded, "I think he was put off by our background, that is to say that Grenville and I were of a different sort than he was used to dealing with in business." Wace, after all, had initially hired the Kinks to back him while he crooned a version of Gerry and the Pacemakers "How Do You Do It?" at a deb's coming out party. Perhaps Wace was protected in his naïve conceit that managing a rock band could be a gentlemanly occupation. Benny Hill crashes Ladies' Day at Ascot as it were. Not done.

More likely, Wace and Collins were put off by Klein, but for the sake of the Kinkdom had to go through the motions and hear Klein out. Shel Talmy, however, who crafted a sound for the Kinks, the Who and a very young David Bowie, has cause to recall the day Klein breezed into the Kinks' life, if only because a sizable portion of his own income breezed out of it.

"I still don't know how Klein did it but he got himself between me and a large part of my Kinks royalties from Warner Brothers. I sent in accountants, I did some preliminary things with lawyers and they got nowhere because it's so well hidden and it would have cost fortunes so I had to drop it."

The UK was not alone in offering up to Allen's hungry heart potentially profitable low-lying fruit. In 1967, he acquired the rights to the Cameo-Parkway group of labels, a company that had been around since the mid-Fifties, but whose hits dried up around the same time as the British Invasion changed everything. It was not an especially noteworthy purchase. Among American acts, only the Four Seasons and the Beach Boys remained competitive enough to string a series of hits together, although the Motown Sound was coming on fast. Former million sellers such as Cameo-Parkway's Chubby Checker, the Orlons, the Dovells, Bobby Rydell, the Thymes, Dee Dee Sharp, Clint Eastwood and Jo-Ann Campbell were suddenly relegated to the "oldies hour" that opened some of the evening Top 40 radio shows. For that matter, you wouldn't be likely to hear Chuck Berry on the radio any longer until the Rolling Stones and the Beatles made him hip once more. Just before they went bankrupt, Cameo signed Bob Seger; "old time rock 'n' roll" indeed. Question Mark and the Mysterions' "96 Tears" was the label's last success of note, the latest act to define "one hit wonder."

In early 1969, Klein gathered all his acquisitions under the ABKCO logo, releasing and re-releasing Sam Cooke, Herman's Hermits, the Animals, Marianne Faithfull, the Stones, and the Cameo-Parkway roster as if he had been responsible for the original recordings. He might have dropped a stitch here and there, but not many. The Nashville Teens, for instance, were signed to Decca directly rather than to Mickie Most and escaped Allen's grasp.

Allen's method was pretty consistent and pretty consistently successful: he would endear himself to the artist by offering to squeeze the record label for more money, at the same time evincing an empathy for the artists' art that appealed to their vanity. The incumbent manager, if there was one already in place, would be made to look redundant, or vaguely accused of the very overreaching Allen planned to do himself once the ball was in his court. Then when he had bullied the record company into giving up more than they ought to keep the artist "happy," Allen went after more, more for himself that is. He schmoozed and then bruised London Records, the U.S. arm of Decca, who had signed the Stones worldwide in 1963. In actual fact, the Stones were not signed to Decca at all in the usual sense. They were signed to Eric Easton and myself, who in turn leased the recorded masters to Decca. Ultimately, ABKCO accrued to itself all the U.S. rights that had previously belonged to London, Eric and myself, to become the sole controlling entity of the catalog produced between 1963 and 1971. I said he was a sorcerer. It was nothing personal, just business.

Allen thought in terms of "market share" long before that kind of thing was tracked by record companies. There were only so many superstar acts and he felt entitled to make a play for them all. Thus, he never forgot his failure to snag the Beatles, but as I've said, patience was one of Allen's virtues.

When Brian Epstein died of a drug overdose in August of 1967, ironically as "Sgt. Pepper" was altering the zeitgeist's consciousness once again, Allen knew his time had come. NEMS, headed up by Epstein's brother Clive, had been taking care of the band's day-to-day business, but the band itself seemed increasingly rudder-less. Of all Epstein's greatest services to the Beatles, his ability to say "no" when it needed to be said was perhaps the most valuable. He was, after all, the only person who would have dared say it, and the group listened.

Now they could do what they wanted, spend what they liked. But the whimsical *Magical Mystery Tour*, a McCartney-flavored Christmas confection that aired on British TV at the end of 1967, seemed a rather self-indulgent follow up to the most influential album of all time. The Beatles announced the formation of their own multimedia atelier.

Apple Corps would be more than just a vanity label for the Beatles' own releases; it would show the world how much it needed the Beatles to save it from itself. Not coincidentally, John Lennon's relationship with Yoko Ono grew committed at around this same time, and business was shown to the back of the bus while Art took the Rolls out. You didn't need the third eye of a Maharishi to notice the Beatles were spinning out of control.

By 1969, it was obvious that somebody needed to call up the cavalry. A variety of names were suggested for the role of über-minder—one of the first was Lord Beeching, the former government minister whose name lives in infamy for his ruthless cuts to the British rail network in the early Sixties. Another was Lee Eastman, a respected New York lawyer who might even have got the job had he not also been McCartney's father-in-law. Given all that the Beatles put themselves through before the mess that became Let It Be, it's ironic that at the time it was thought that giving Paul his own way would upset the balance of power within the band. Besides, the three Beatles not named Paul had a suitor of their own.

Allen got his foot in the door via Apple publicist Derek Taylor. Tony Calder, my partner in Immediate, was surprised to receive a call from Allen asking for an introduction to Derek, all the more so since Tony and Allen were not particularly close. Tony and Derek were neighbors in the Weybridge enclave of Surrey, an affluent bedroom community just outside London. Tony arranged to pick up Derek one day and drive him to work. Whatever was said did the trick and Allen was soon getting his second bite at the apple.

Lennon had given Klein his opening when he lamented publicly that the Beatles would be "broke in six months" if something weren't done to right the Apple cart. By the time they met, Klein could quote Beatles lyrics casually, as if he listened to "Norwegian Wood" in the bath, while carefully distinguishing between the songs that were primarily John's and those that were Paul's. His proposal did not seem greedy on the face of it: he would earn a commission on increased income only. Control did not come into it in the early stages of discussion. Furthermore, should he fail to turn the Beatles' affairs around, the band would owe him nothing.

The formula was by now second nature. Allen wasted little time on evaluating the sales potential of Billy Preston or a young James Taylor, both of whom were signed to Apple Records. The biggest band in the world should be getting the highest royalty, didn't EMI agree? Again, Klein's take it or leave it demands won the day; the new rate of 10% per album was unprecedented, more than two and a half times the royalty they had worked their way up to after several years of world-beating sales. However, Klein was willing to make concessions on repackaging and compilations upon which Brian Epstein had always taken a hard, uncompromising line. Where the old regime had seldom pulled a UK single from an album—"Hey Jude" for instance was a standalone release—Klein gave EMI permission to issue "Something" b/w "Come Together" from Abbey Road. In this regard, Allen was moving with the times; from the late '60s on, singles would always serve as aural trailers for the more profitable albums from which they came.

From the standpoint of history, Klein did the Beatles another (dubious) service by resurrecting the thought to be unsalvageable *Get Back* film and soundtrack project, turning it over to Phil Spector, who had credibility with both John and Paul and who was known to impose his wall of sound on everything he touched. And Klein transformed Apple Corps itself from a free-for-all, where even the delivery men were walking out with valuable souvenirs, into a tightly run ship whose employees now punched in and out if they wanted to keep their jobs.

Among the casualties were such key players as general manager Ron Kass and A&R executive Peter Asher. Anyone who had enjoyed Brian Epstein's confidence or friendship was suspect. Thirty years later, Paul McCartney's distaste for all things connected with Klein compelled him to release Let It Be . . . Naked, stripping bare even the rather grand "Long and Winding Road," whose orchestral arrangements, though perhaps a matter of taste, would be considered by most objective ears to be among the most outstanding achievements of Phil Spector's later years.

Those Apple staffers who liked the "all you need is love" vibe, resented this brash Yank coming in and imposing his capitalist money-grabbing schemes on what the Beatles themselves once described as an experiment in western communism. As friends were fired, projects were closed down and nice guys were cut loose. So, however improved the business might be, the personal stresses around and between the Beatles were aggravated, rather than alleviated, by Klein's activities. McCartney continued to insist that Klein could not be trusted as far as he could be thrown, yet even he was forced to concede, "If you are screwing us, I don't see how."

Nevertheless, "I used to have dreams in which Allen Klein was an evil dentist," McCartney told *Rolling Stone* some years later. He confessed to one of the biggest regrets of his life: when he read that Klein had renegotiated the Rolling Stones' contract, McCartney took the newspaper story to Epstein, waved it in his face, and demanded to know when the Beatles would ever share in similar largesse. The honest merchant in McCartney no doubt felt competitive with Klein and may have much preferred that he and his father-in-law were given credit for any improvement in the Beatles' finances.

The Beatles wound down in February 1970, by which time Klein's feet were firmly under the table. John and George in particular had cause to be thankful to him as he shepherded their dreams to fruition, projects that ranged from the Concert for Bangladesh and the *Imagine* movie, and onto the acquisition of John and Yoko's favorite film *El Topo*. More significantly from the standpoint of history, Allen was firmly identified with George's finest hour, All Things Must Pass, another Spector production. The first three-disc release by a solo artist, it was also the first to chart at Number One in the U.S. But bad blood could not help but swirl, first as Klein supported George's insistence that Yoko not perform at the Bangladesh concert (a decision that ultimately saw John, too, pull out), then when a series of apparent miscalculations saw much of the money raised by the Concert held back pending a U.S. tax investigation.

Allen's karma finally caught up with him in 1979 when he was convicted on charges of U.S. federal tax evasion. Klein had sold literally truckloads of albums that were accounted for on the books as "promos" (albums distributed free of charge to radio stations and the press for which the label is not obligated to pay artist royalties). His actual felony was pocketing the income from these sales without reporting it to the Internal Revenue Service. But let's tote up who Klein screwed in this affair: his country, which was entitled to tax him; the Beatles, both collectively and individually, from whom he stole royalties; UNICEF, the organization which should have received income from the sales of the Bangladesh concert LPs; and thousands of starving children in Asia. He was sentenced to two months imprisonment in one of those Federal facilities sometimes referred to as "country clubs" in contrast to state penitentiaries, and arguably deserved more. Though Allen's skills might have been put to better use eliminating waste in the prison's budget, his job, as he put it, was to prepare "twenty-four fruit salads a day," scarcely a sentence to hard labor.

The rest of the day Allen ran his empire from his cell, and if he had a spare moment he could shoot the breeze with music business professional and fellow inmate John Phillips. The man who wrote "California Dreamin'" and "Monday, Monday," helping to launch the folk rock revolution with the Mamas & the Papas, had drawn federal time of his own. The umbrella charge was "drug trafficking," which in detail encompassed the forgery of illegal prescriptions, money laundering and conspiracy to sell controlled substances. John and I shared a Bloody Mary not long after he came out of jail at Yellowfinger's on 62nd and 3rd, a then trendy spot on Manhattan's posh East Side. "Guess who was a few cells down from me, Andrew?" chortled John, smiling into the midday sun. "Your old pal, Allen Krime."

A falling out with Lennon followed (John would vent many of his feelings towards Klein in the song "Steel And Glass"), but the ultimate betrayal came when Klein sued his own former client, Harrison, for copyright infringement. To Allen, it was probably as simple as getting the attention of an artist he felt was off the reservation—a counter-insurgency, if you will. Like so many songs before it, George's "My Sweet Lord" was patently based on the spiritual "Oh Happy Day," a song long in the public domain and hence not subject to copyright. Unfortunately, another song derived from

"Oh Happy Day," the Chiffons' "He's So Fine," was still protected, prompting its publisher, Bright Tunes, to launch proceedings against Harrison.

Klein, naturally, was outraged, and happily assisted Harrison in preparing his defense. But as his relationship with the former Beatles crumbled, Klein looked for ways of bringing George back in line. He took himself out and purchased Bright Tunes for himself—and kept the lawsuit alive. A degree of justice prevailed, as the Judge slammed Klein for switching sides mid-suit, while Harrison was later able to purchase "He's So Fine" himself. But if any of Klein's manifold legal maneuverings was capable of leaving a really nasty taste in the mouth, that was the one.

Klein did not see it that way, of course. Asked about his less than spotless reputation in the rock industry, the wily old soul knew instinctively who to blame. "The press, you know. That's a Sixties thing: the good guys against the bad guys and I guess I became the bad guy. I was good copy and the public never wants to blame the artist."

While the vast majority of civil litigation is settled out of court, Allen never hesitated to take it all the way, whether he was the plaintiff or the defendant. Normally careless in his dress, he looked forward to trading his tennis shoes and pipe for the slimly reet petite Piaget wristwatch that classily accessorised artfully tailored single breasted suits, an appropriate amount of crisp shirt, and the ever-present red tie. In the courtroom, his immersion in the role of legal eagle reduced his highly paid attorneys to the supporting cast. It was the best kind of sport for Klein.

In the space of eight years, Allen Klein swept the rock 'n' roll Monopoly board, going to jail, true, but passing "Go" over and over while he acquired the most profitable properties and never failed to collect rent due from Sam Cooke, Mickie Most, Donovan, the Rolling Stones, and the Beatles. But now what? The publicity that flew around the Beatles break-up, in which he was painted second only to Yoko as the cause of their demise, ensured that it would be a very strange soul indeed who would consider taking him on in any capacity now. Allen, of course, saw it a different way, his way. He had already had the best; why should he go back to the buffet for seconds or thirds? He was already very full.

The Beatles with Maharishi Mahesh Yogi, 1967

I happened to be in London when McCartney pulled the rug from under Allen and the three other Beatles. I had not had much to do with Allen whilst he was busy with both the Beatles and the Stones. While walking only a stone's throw from where the Beatles were preparing to fight it out in court, I was taken aback by the tabloid placards on display outside the Holborn tube station: Allen Klein was the latest celebrity villain, variously headlined as a "gangster," a "thug," or a "crook." The most charitable sobriquet was "Yank." The times had changed so rapidly for both Allen Klein and the Beatles that all of them were overtaken by events: the artists wanted their freedom and the barracudas wanted respect. Neither side would fully achieve their aims; it was the beginning of the end of the '60s.

The Beatles got their freedom and as "solo artists" they now dominated the charts almost as often as they had as a band. Ringo's serial successes guided by the sure production of Richard Perry were particularly heartening. George got tired and retired; his hard-won peace had come at the cost of wars he never wanted. Paul McCartney has ever remained successful, proficient, enthusiastic and competitive even when hiding his brilliant light under the bushel of "Wings." John Lennon became the world's most famous house-husband and a doting father to second son Sean, notwithstanding occasional forays to the dark side with drug buddy Harry Nilsson. Mere weeks before his assassination, John was poised to become the most relevant ex-Beatle, with a new commitment to songwriting and recording.

As for Allen, he dabbled in movies and Broadway shows, but didn't bring to these efforts the killer instinct that fueled his pop music campaigns. Like many a piratical tycoon before him, Allen became a respected philanthropist and specialized in medical charities. In his own mind, his reputation required no rehabilitation and thus he was unsurprised to be regarded as a benefactor of his fellow man.

He spent a lot of time dithering on a large-scale Sam Cooke film project. But for Allen's indecision, the Oscars that went to director Taylor Hackford's *Ray* might well have gone to *The Sam Cooke Story*. I was enthusiastic about Hackford for the Cooke project; one of his earliest films remains a great favorite. *The Idolmaker*, from 1980, starred a completely genuine and doomed Ray Sharkey as a Simon Cowell type who eventually finds redemption as a singer/songwriter. Allen invited me to meetings with Hackford, who recognized both the historical and filmic merits of Sam's life, but ultimately Allen could not make up his mind and Taylor moved on. Klein no doubt realized that a director of Hackford's stature would not settle for a less than realistic portrayal of Allen himself and that may have been just enough to keep the project safely within the bosom of the ABKCO family.

Broadway, on the other hand, invited no such scrutiny. There was always room for one more would-be Schubert and his bank account. Unfortunately, Allen failed to hear the stampede of more experienced theatrical producers away from Edward Albee when the playwright insisted on directing his own *The Man Who Had Three Arms*. Klein produced it anyway. In his *New York Times* review, Frank Rich snarled, it "isn't a play—it's a temper tantrum in two acts . . . ." The play closed after only 16 performances and it would be another 11 years before Broadway took a chance on a new Albee play. Although a revival won an important award in a more avant garde setting a few years later, the show was a disaster on the Great White Way. Not that Allen cared much. By producing even a flop on Broadway he joined an elite club whose members provided each other with tickets for life.

Allen demanded I attend *The Man Who Had Three Arms* with him and would that three hours of my life I could never get back were all that were asked of me. Allen's favorite line was "Well, what do you think?" Allen was willing to entertain any opinion one might have as long as it confirmed his own. He immediately noted my lack of enthusiasm and treated me to a little dramatic critique of his own.

"I thought you'd understand it, Oldham, of all people I thought you would," he said with a sort of sigh.

"Why me?" I asked, already knowing I would not enjoy the answer.

Allen didn't miss a beat. "Well, the third arm represents talent and when the third arm starts to disappear it means that the man's talent has gone. I thought of all people, you'd get it." I cannot say I was disappointed when the production proved an expensive failure.

When I mentioned earlier that it would be a very strange soul who engaged Allen as a music manager after the Beatles broke up, I wasn't allowing for the boundless eccentricity of Phil Spector. Both Phil and Allen had been richly rewarded for their work on Let It Be and Imagine and until his death, they shared an attorney in Marty Machat. But Phil's own Philles catalog was in total disarray, with ragtag and spotty releases that came and went in various territories like bats in an attic.

The irony of the imperious Spector surrendering control of his precious masters to the likes of Klein, who had never shared nicely with others, leaves one agog. However, the ABKCO re-releases were professionally done and widely available, helping to restore Phil's reputation as a pioneer in the recording studio with a genius for hearing hits. Over time, however, Allen's prolonged battle with Alzheimer's and Phil's insatiable need for funds with which to pay for his two trials for murder, led Phil to look elsewhere for distribution. In October 2009, just three months after Allen's death, Sony's Legacy imprint announced they would be re-releasing the Philles catalog once again beginning with the iconic A Christmas Gift For You. Much good may it do Phil, who won't be eligible for parole until the age of 88.

It is fitting we end this tale of creativity bilked with perhaps the most poignant example of "they always fuck you for the first one" in recent years. The retribution Allen Klein wreaked on Richard Ashcroft and the Verve for their unauthorized sampling of my very own work, previously buried in the sands of time, is indeed one for the book. Ego and post-adolescent excess energy had led me in 1964 to form the studio only "Andrew Loog Oldham Orchestra." Between 1964 and 1966 I produced four albums for Decca, who humored me for bringing them the Stones: East Meets West, 16 Hip Hits, Lionel Bart's Maggie May, and The Rolling Stones Songbook.

It was from this last LP, never legitimately released on CD, that Ashcroft took the basis of his "Bitter Sweet Symphony," which in 1998 charted at 2 in the UK, 12 in the U.S. and in the Top Twenty in many territories internationally. My arrangement of "The Last Time," while typical of the ALO Orchestra, so departed from the Rolling Stones' own recording that I doubt that even the most devout Stones' fan would have recognized it once the Verve slipstreamed it into their own track. Indeed, my orchestral recording was a deliberate homage to Jack Nitzsche and his 1963 Reprise Records LP The Lonely Surfer and, in particular, Jack's version of the Jeff Barry-Ellie Greenwich-Phil Spector song "Da Doo Ron Ron," as re-arranged by David Sinclair Whitaker. From a purely musical standpoint, the Verve's lift was masterfully done and totally in keeping with the spirit of the original.

Secluded as I was at the time in Bogotá, I only learned of the Verve's potential legal problems when their manager Jazz Summers called to ask me to bring Allen Klein to the negotiating table in a reasonable manner. Arrangements are not generally subject to copyright so my recording was listed as a Jagger-Richards composition under the publishing control of ABKCO, as are all pre-1971 Stones' songs. Polygram had inherited the rights to my recording from Decca and were prepared to pay me appropriately.

Allen initially felt he was being more than fair by taking 50% of the publishing royalties due the Verve's own recording. When Klein learned of Summers's approach to me, he changed his mind or just as likely, he decided to punish the upstart by demanding 100% of the publishing, which meant that while he couldn't touch the recording royalties due the Verve from Virgin, he would wield significant power in licensing the recording to third parties in any manner he saw fit. Nike, Vauxhall and Opel were happy to exploit the song in their advertising, but far from appreciating the publicity, the Verve understandably resented their loss of control.

While this provided Mick and Keith with a nice little unexpected bonus, Richard Ashcroft was forced to accept a flat $1,000 for his lyrics. He later snarked, "This is the best song Jagger and Richards have written in 20 years." Ashcroft was not the only loser.

Indeed, the middle-aged Andrew Oldham was to be victimized by the fecklessness of the teenaged Loog. By aligning my interest with ABKCO's, the Verve, EMI/Virgin and Decca were able to argue successfully that I had legally approved the use of my track. But, more importantly, I was held to the terms of the original contract with Decca my mother had signed on my behalf in 1963 when I was 19 years old and not of legal age. That contract of course completely denied me any sort of artist approval, so that was that. I hired my own extravagantly expensive lawyers to get some of my own back and eventually there was an out of court settlement that enriched the lawyers far more than myself and left me utterly exhausted with the effort. I could now afford to fly in grand style to the nearest Rolls Royce showroom but I surely could not afford the car once I arrived.

Given that Allen Klein and I met when I was only 21, he has been an unavoidable influence on my entire adult life. Our business lives and our personal lives became inextricably entwined over the years and while we retained a timeworn fondness for each other, there was never any doubt as to who was the senior partner. Like Sam Cooke's widow Barbara, I depended on Allen for the food on my table. There were times, however, when Allen overlooked my inner turmoil and the addictions that fed it to take better care of me than I was taking of myself, even wishing for me in the worst of times better than I was wishing for myself.

The last time I saw him the Alzheimer's had set in. The four of us—Allen, his son Jody, Iris Keitel and myself—had lunch in his New York apartment. Allen studied me.

"I like your haircut, looks good on you," he said. He still knew how to get to me, even though he could not remember my name.

Iris put her hand on his. This was already a part of their life; it must have been awkward sharing it with me. Allen looked up at her, down at their hands and said, "I've got one of those as well."

Forever competitive, forever positive. I had to smile. I did, and so did Allen. Though damaged by the march of time, Allen Klein was still fighting to get out.

Twenty five years earlier, I had accompanied Allen to the musical review Your Arms Too Short to Box With God starring Al Green and Patti LaBelle. Depressed as my central nervous system was, I had difficulty staying awake through the performance, but

Allen insisted we go back stage to congratulate Al. Allen's agenda was never made clear to me but there had to have been one; Allen never did anything without reason. As Al Green and Allen Klein made small talk, I realized I was witnessing the age-old dance between black entertainer and white entrepreneur. With the possible exception of the great John Hammond, it was never difficult to ascertain which partner was leading.

As we left the theater and headed uptown, Allen was enjoying his end of the conversation when I excused myself, ducked behind a newsstand and lit a spliff (this was Ed Koch's New York, not Rudy Giuliani's). Allen kept talking and walking for some few feet before he suddenly realized I wasn't by his side. I took a luxuriant toke and grinned at Allen.

"What's the matter, Oldham?" he asked. "Am I boring you?"

Never, Allen, never . . . . You were a lot of things, but you were never boring.

IMMEDIATE RECORDS

"Don't have tears for the things that don't have tears for you."

— *Fernando Harker*

THOUGH IT'S SAFE to say that the Beatles and the Rolling Stones never intended to change the business of music as thoroughly as they did, "control" increasingly came to mean recording what they wanted where they wanted and when they wanted. Albums were no longer released purely on the basis of how many hit singles they contained; for the artists the notion of "concept" was replacing the record company's hunger for "product." It would be a while before artists became financial partners with their label lords and masters, but by the late Sixties the pop music fan was getting the political, social, sexual and pharmacological views of his faves more or less unadulterated.

    Those of us charged with encouraging and coddling this new creativity realized that until control of production and distribution was wrested from the labels, our independence would be token and perhaps short-lived, just as millions of parents hoped their children would outgrow the outlandish fashions they adopted to express their teenage "individuality." Youthful buying power was asserting itself on a breathtaking scale; how could the ratio of profits be reversed to favor the artist? Or at least not to favor the "major" record label?

    In America, the radio revolution kicked off by Alan Freed made room for dozens of truly independent labels that competed for airplay and sales with the established record companies, which were often smallish sub-divisions of huge conglomerates such as the Columbia Broadcasting System and the Radio Corporation of America. Nimble hustlers with an ear for tomorrow's hit today, the new entrepreneurs financed their own recordings, manufacturing and distribution, reaping large profits commensurate with the risks they took, although the artists themselves were seldom paid any better than they would have been by a major. (Keeping in mind that American indie artists were usually merely vocalists, while the label heads contributed the songs, the production and the image, not to mention the budget.) One cannot separate the creative achievements of pioneers like Phil Spector, Art Rupe, George Goldner, Leiber and Stoller, Bert Berns, Bob Crewe and Liberty Records from the highly personal and very aggressive manner in which they did their business.

When the Chess brothers wanted to serve the Chicago market for Delta blues, they bought their first masters from Sam Phillips' Sun Records and then signed the artists from down South directly. It was win win because before Atlantic Records the market for R&B was regional. It was the coordination and manipulation of American radio that made independent labels possible, and Alan Freed died for it in his way by letting the labels pay him, without shame. There was Starday from Beaumont Texas along with King out of Cincinnati who between them had George Jones and James Brown. It was a great business.

But the UK was as behind the US when it came to business practices as it had once been musically. In time, such independents as Track, Chrysalis, Stiff and Charisma would come to define the new British record industry as surely as their acts redefined the music, but in the early Sixties only Chris Blackwell's Island Records attempted to go it alone. Initially successful in his native Jamaica and among the Caribbean community in the UK, Blackwell somewhat compromised his indie purity when the potential success of Millie Small's crossover hit "My Boy Lollipop" forced him into an alliance with a larger, more established label partner. A wag once described the earliest Island Records as a "wheel barrow operation."

It remained for my own Immediate Records, the little bastard of a company inspired by the American producer-manager-moguls I admired, to change the rules of engagement and the UK record industry forever.

* * *

Our company began in mid-1965 in a phone booth between Baker Street and Wembley. It was all rather Superman. Tony Calder and I were being treated to yet another death-defying ride from our offices at Ivor Court, courtesy of my driver Reg King, who was by turns thuggish and boy crazy as it suited his mercurial nature. Tony was at the time my partner in the publicity firm ALO-Image, which represented Herman's Hermits, Freddie and the Dreamers, and Wayne Fontana and the Mindbenders via Kennedy Street Enterprises, along with the Beach Boys at such times as they graced our British shores.

We were moaning about what we had to put up with at Decca over the Rolling Stones, Marianne Faithfull (whom Calder had successfully produced after I was done with her), the Poets, and Vashti. Our promo man for ALO-Image and the early days at Immediate was Andy Wickham, thinner than any duke, more wired than thou, a tousle-haired wonder whose tacky silver ID bracelet contrasted with the tailored clobber he preferred.

The conversation between Calder and myself that fine spring day may have been about the lack of cooperation from Decca, the stagnant system, and the "they just don't care enough about us" syndrome. But, in truth, the problem on my part was aggravated by weed and prescription goodies from Doctor John on Harley Street. Calder largely resisted this temptation, but for me drugs were not purely recreational because without them, business itself wouldn't have got done. This made life somewhat unmanageable for Tony, as I was prone to fits of uncontrollable laughter during business conversations that were not meant to be hysterical and wouldn't have been had I not been stoned.

"We should have our own record company. That'd take care of everything, remove all of the shit," one of us would have said.

And the other one would have said, "We should, let's do it."

By now, our enormous white Lincoln Continental, with its elegant fins and rear-hinged doors, was rounding Marble Arch. Facing the Arch and Hyde Park, on the other side of the Edgware Road, stood Stanhope Place, white, splendid and understatedly opulent, home to Philips Records. Ironically, Philips was but third among the majors, after EMI and Decca and ahead of Pye. Stanhope Place was a palace compared to the dreary headquarters of its competitors.

EMI's building in Manchester Square was as unimaginative as its occupants, who resembled surveyors, architects, accountants and furniture makers with a workplace to suit. Memorialized on the cover of the first Beatles' album, there was little else to recommend it. David Bowie's first manager, Ken Pitt, lived around the corner, and I'm sure Ken found EMI House as uninspiring as I did.

Pye Records was a relatively minor division of mighty ATV television, itself a part of the Lew Grade network that ruled so much of British entertainment. In the basement of ATV House was a recording studio in which Petula Clark cut "Downtown" and Tony Hatch, "Downtown's" composer, churned out serial hits for the Searchers, who recovered quickly from Brian Epstein having rejected them for management. Pye's studio was available for hire and I used it for Vashti and the Poets while Mick Jagger produced Chris Farlowe there. The Stones and I would also finish Between the Buttons at Pye.

ATV's 'Oh Boy!'

Decca was housed in the greyest building of all on the Albert Embankment, and their studios in West Hampstead resembled a block that the Metropolitan Police had passed on as being too depressing. The Decca facilities really brought home the notion that in the late fifties the record business in Britain was a manufacturing enterprise rather than a show business upstart.

There was, and hopefully still is, a phone box on the corner that takes you from the park into Bayswater Road. The wily Calder hopped out of the car, borrowed a few pence from a passer-by, and called Leslie Gould at Philips Records. Within minutes, he had made a pressing and distribution deal for a non-existent Immediate Records.

Tony and I nursed a vision we brought back with us from our first visits to America. The real deal was even more impressive, inspiring and awesome than our cherished vinyl and celluloid dreams. We met people who were unabashedly buzzed to be part of the music business. Twenty-four hours a day, 7 days a week, our American counterparts happily hustled without checking their watches to see if it was time to go home. Where Tony and I came from, passion for something so trivial as pop music was considered to be unbusinesslike and, if expressed, enthusiasm verged on bad taste. We wanted the Americans' sense of purpose and abandon to be our daily mantra, and the very idea of Immediate Records seemed like a good start.

Our motto, "Happy to be a Part of the Industry of Human Happiness," artfully expressed our hopes and schemes. Forty-five years on, it is better and more fondly remembered than some of our artists and their records.

ALO-Image wound down, to be replaced by Immediate. We lost Andy Wickham to Lou Adler's Hollywood-based Dunhill, and later, a long and eventful career at Warner Brothers Records. From 1965 to 1970, Immediate happily embodied Britain's innocent pursuit of money and pleasure. We were as mod and swinging as our times, pilled up and pussy driven. British blues and blatant materialism provided the soundtrack for a new class of street hustlers and hippies, flush with disposable income.

Immediate was always, however, two parts romance to one part capitalism. I don't think it's widely understood to what extent I was the label's "angel investor," funneling my earnings from the Rolling Stones into sometimes commercially successful and often eccentric recordings that were released and unleashed via my personal license. The irreverence of Immediate's record output was more than matched by the label's flair for zany social promotion. I still get asked about the Nice advertisements that drew attention to the war in Biafra and the futility of American military might, as well as the banned David Bailey ads for Fleetwood Mac that showed stoned British bobbies enjoying a tea time spliff.

Immediate kicked off with three singles. Our first release proved to be inspired and a huge international hit: on a visit to New York's Brill Building in June 1965, we acquired the extra-US rights to "Hang On Sloopy" by the McCoys on license from Bert Berns' Bang label. Jimmy Page and I co-produced the other two initial Immediate singles. Eurotemptress Nico's "I'm Not Sayin'" scored a lot of publicity for the fledgling label and her white hot image plastered over the music rags established our image as edgy, to say the least. The third single, by a group called "Fifth Avenue," disappeared without a trace. Recorded before the launch of Immediate, I'd have done better to license the master to Decca or Pye, as I'd originally intended.

With the departure of Andy Wickham, Tony King became Immediate's promo man and glad we were of it. Tony, at the tender age of 18, had toiled within the Decca factory as an assistant to Tony Hall, then Decca's Head of Promotion, probably very happy his job required him to move about town promoting rather than breathe the dusty air of HQ on the Albert Embankment. We had a lot in common in that regard.

Tony was also very, very good looking and seemingly uncomplicated, which gave him an air of availability that was as much a ruse as that of any adopted by Laurence Harvey or Dirk Bogarde in their various roles on film. One sensed that there had been some kind of makeover there, but Tony was such a good actor that it was only some slight mannerism of speech that ever betrayed from whence he had come.

He had taken elocution lessons, so to speak, but could not resist leaving in a little of the old tart. Eventually, he became a fixture in the Rolling Stones' rock and roll circus, serving for many years until quite recently in the demanding capacity of Mick Jagger's factotum. But it's a credit to Tony's versatility and command of the music biz that in the mid-'70s he was highly successful as RCA Records' disco promotion man, his evenings spent working Studio 54 as Queen of the Hop, all expenses paid.

I first met Tony King when the Rolling Stones were signed to Decca and, on our days off, we used to go around to the Great Marlborough Street offices for a free drink and a chat. It was a big place with four offices and a huge reception area where we could stage cocktail parties and receptions for visiting US artists, some of whom I either represented in the UK or wished to. Tony Hall's wife, Malfalda, chose the building and decorated it. It was certainly an improvement over the Albert Embankment building.

Tony left Decca and went to work for Roy Orbison in Nashville. When Roy and his wife Claudette broke up, King went to Spain and worked as a bartender, where he caught hepatitis. Tony was always an early bird. While he was in hospital, I sent him a note asking him to come work for me at Immediate when he was better. And so he did.

Interviewed by Dave Thompson in 1994, Tony recalled, "We weren't in it for the money; it was just sheer fun. I did all the mailings myself, all the packing of the envelopes, everybody was hands-on. I had a tiny office next to Andrew's and I was just furiously stuffing envelopes full of 45s, sticking on stamps, taking them to the post office and running around town delivering them to the BBC. I loved doing it; I would do it some nights until midnight or two in the morning.

"Work was fun. I'd come into the office some mornings and Keith would be in the spare bed; it was a good bed to stay in when you'd been out or working late. Charlie Watts had a flat on the same floor; he and Shirley lived along the corridor. Kit Lambert and Chris Stamp took an office in the same building, Pete Townshend used to stay there and write, and all of a sudden Ivor Court was a happening music building, which was quite something, as it was supposed to be completely residential."

"What we were up to had never been done before, at least not in staid jolly old England. Like the idea of Andrew and the Stones controlling their own recordings, or the very idea of Immediate Records. None of us knew where pop music was going to lead us, so Andrew was taking every opportunity and often made a big mess of everything, but he would learn from the mess and the chaos and maybe that would give him his next idea. The only thing that was predictable about Andrew was how he ended up at the end of the sixties, drugged and crazy."

I could not have put it better, apart from the last line—I was drugged perhaps, but to be to be described as "crazy" by a promo person is another of those pot meets kettle moments.

Tony recalled, "There was a lot of pot around, and I was the official pot holder. I'd go around the corner to these two call girls who always had really good stuff. I'd keep different types of grass in different drawers in the office."

One time, "Andrew and his wife Sheila, Mick and Chrissie Shrimpton, and Donovan and I were going to this film premiere. Eddie Reed, Andrew's latest chauffeur, was driving us in Andrew's new Rolls. At the theatre, this cop opened the door and a great cloud of marijuana smoke wafted into his face. We rolled out totally stoned onto the pavement, just as the cameras were flashing. I learned that the police didn't actually know what pot smelled like; they probably thought we were just smoking foreign cigarettes. Another time we motored to Scotland to attend a Philips sales conference, smoking dope all the way. Andrew and I were joined by Nico and Greg Phillips (who had recently covered Billy Joe Royal's 'Down in the Boondocks')."

Gregory was a former child star I had met through either Lionel Bart or Reg King. While I enjoyed hanging out with him, our recording of Royal's American pop classic was a stretch that showed we often did things at Immediate simply because we could. We were ambitious, but our bottom line was often obscured by a cloud of marijuana smoke.

Gary Glitter (or Paul Raven as he was known following a nowhere career highlighted by his cover of Gene McDaniel's "Tower of Strength") produced my Scottish band the Poets, with whom I had had some success at Decca at the end of 1964. We released some more Bang Records 45s. We bought a record by Donovan's roadie, Mick Softley, and even had Tony Meehan produce our engineer Glyn Johns doing his best Jim Reeves by way of Epsom.

The quality of our output was uneven, to say the least, and many of our acts were better drinking companions than recording "artists." I made an atrocious record, amongst many, with the comedian Jimmy Tarbuck. Jimmy gamely rambled through the Ricky Nelson song "Someday," backed by a big band arrangement I nicked from Cher's American TV show. But despite Jimmy's performance on Sunday Night At The London Palladium, where he was compere, the record stiffed.

Apart from the stunning success of "Hang On Sloopy," which in truth was big enough to justify our existence if not our free spending, Chris Farlowe was the only other bright spark Immediate had to show in year one. I had worked as a teenaged gofer for Chris' managers Rik and John Gunnell when they booked jazz into the Flamingo on Wardour Street way back in 1960. Eric Burdon had produced a very decent recording of "The Fool" with Farlowe, so unlike many of our artists, we had some idea of Chris' potential. "The Fool" was good enough that we didn't mind that it wasn't actually a hit.

Our release schedule was prolific for such a new enterprise, but Tony Calder and I rarely paused to consider if our records were hits in the sense that people bought them. I recorded according to my whims of the moment, while Tony kept busy leasing masters from a growing network of people he had befriended in the States. Despite my having poached the Stones out from under Giorgio Gomelsky, we were all happy to have him in the family as a producer. Some of our records were little more than inside jokes. For example, our one-off single by the "Marquis of Kensington," an appropriately fruity nom de plume of Robert Wace, a pal of Calder's and co-manager of the Kinks. None of it was great and none of them were hits.

We continued to put a little something extra into Chris Farlowe, whose career looked like it might have legs. Mick and Keith joined me at the IBC studios with arranger Arthur Greenslade and engineer Glyn Johns, where we tried to Stax Farlowe up. It did not quite come off, but it was a good beginning for things Farlowe.

1966 would turn out better, and cost a whole lot more.

Tony Calder, Brian Jones, Bill Wyman, Mick Jagger

Tony King left to work for George Martin at his newly formed AIR Productions, where they were joined by producers Peter Sullivan, John Burgess and Ron Richards. AIR was surely a much more stable enterprise for the slimly opinionated Tony than was Immediate. He wanted a bit of grounding; every time you had a conversation with him, you realized after a few turns that you were standing at the check-out counter chatting a bit too long with the cashier. Just before he left I had brought in the formidable Cynthia

Dillane whom Tony may have justly regarded as competition for the number two spot. Cynthia stayed the course during Immediate's subsequent wild ride, and went on to marry sixth Stone, the displaced Ian Stewart.

But swinging London was a small world after all in those days, so that when Immediate moved to New Oxford Street, we found Tony officed there as our new neighbor and old friend. Though no longer on the payroll, Tony was perfectly placed to assist me in dodging the bailiffs when I'd take a runner over the rooftops into King's office and out his front door. I'm sure he enjoyed the view from his window as my ex-partner Eric Easton banged on my Rolls with a writ while shouting, "Andy, you'll have to come out and face the music sooner or later."

Ridding ourselves of Eric Easton worked out to be very expensive for me and the Stones, straining a relationship that was both financial and creative during the band's explosively successful mid-'60s run. In theory, our new business manager Allen Klein had shut Easton out of any further earnings from the Stones, but Eric proved to have time on his side and took a sizable pound of flesh from my own income while accruing to himself many copyrights that had been procured under false pretenses. Adding financial insult to Eric's injury was Allen's decision to move the Stones from their first US booking agent GAC to the William Morris Agency, where Klein hoped to compensate his man of the hour Jerry Brandt for having cut Jerry out of a promised deal over Sam Cooke. Life was getting very complicated and costly; the GAC settlement alone put us out $50,000. That year the devil looked after his own, and the Stones would have to wait a while longer for his sympathy.

In 1966, I spent £40,000 on two LPs at a time when you could have bought a troika of Rolls Royces "nicely equipped," as they say in the States, for the same money. In retrospect, albums by Twice As Much and Chris Farlowe represent the alpha and omega of my Immediate dreams and the beginning of the end of my honeymoon with the Rolling Stones.

Twice As Much were a folk rock duo in the manner of Peter and Gordon or Chad and Jeremy. David Skinner and Andrew Rose were more than willing to be the vehicle for my Brian Wilson-inspired aspirations. But their very malleability was against them enjoying any sustained success despite the warm reception accorded to their first single, a cover of Mick and Keith's "Sittin' On a Fence."

Increasingly Immediate was becoming a topiary garden of my own imagining where I would take a relatively innocuous group like Twice As Much and shape a sound that might or might not have suited them, but which at the time seemed to fill various holes in my own soul. I had been hanging out in New York with the Brooklyn-born songwriter Mort Shuman. Shuman was an idol of mine, having written "A Teenager in Love" with Doc Pomus for Dion and the Belmonts as well as "Save the Last Dance for Me" and "This Magic Moment" for the Drifters. Mort's tunes were eminently coverable, as exemplified by Marty Wilde's version of "Teenager" and Jay and the Americans' cover of "This Magic Moment."

One enchanted evening, Mort and I fell in love with the idea of a pop opera version of Leonard Bernstein's West Side Story. We got as far as "I Have A Love," which we arranged a la the Beach Boys, doubtlessly going out into the Manhattan night humming the melody of our latest creation. "I Have A Love" then became the cornerstone of the Twice As Much album, and the whole thing was a disaster, an expensive disaster, and that was basically what I was turning into that year.

My friendship with Mort Shuman had at least one other consequence for the history of pop: his involvement with the musical *Jacques Brel Is Alive and Well And Living In Paris* led me to expose Scott Walker to the Belgian composer for the first time. Despite the strong sales of Walker's Brel-inspired solo albums, I felt self-indulgence had ruined a perfectly fine pop singer. Given Tony Calder's enthusiasm for Scott, we might have had the records on Immediate, but they weren't really in my line.

Thus was ruined a perfectly fine pop singer who thereafter would lose himself and much of his audience in the pursuit of an angst that was often just as painful to listen to as it must have been for Scott to live through. Tony Calder wanted very much to represent Scott but given Walker's surrender to malaise we were lucky to have him get away. Immediate would probably have closed a lot sooner!

My marriage had failed and I was taking it personally. I was having disastrous affairs, and a lot of what I was listening to and wishing to produce was just plain soppy. But at least, in my madness, I was venting where it wouldn't touch the Rolling Stones. The Twice as Much period was just that, with absolutely no slight on the talents or ambitions on the duo, who gave it their best shot in the game of Russian roulette I was playing. I spent a lot of time with David Skinner, and felt very safe in his company. We listened to music, drove around England and played golf together, none of which pleased either his girlfriend or my soon-to-be ex-wife.

The Mick Jagger LP with Chris Farlowe cost a few grand more, but it was worth it. We never got my money back, because "Out of Time" was our only Number One—for the rest we had to resort to my old trick of buying our singles at retail in order for them to chart. The problem there, of course, is that the artist wants to be paid on those records as if they'd actually been bought by the public. Immediate, at its best, was a candy store full of kids with very sweet teeth, permanent munchies and a never ending supply of rolling papers.

Immediate had nothing to do with the real world and yet we did produce some great music. Humble Pie, Fleetwood Mac and the Amen Corner made their mark via Immediate. It was also first home for stars of a later day, among them Rod Stewart, Eric Clapton, Jimmy Page and Nico. Our producers included Mick Jagger and Keith Richards, Steve Marriott and Ronnie Lane, Michael D'Abo, Eric Burdon, Mike Hurst and Jimmy Page. In addition to these artists/producers, we also fielded discs produced by Shel Talmy and Glyn Johns.

And of them all, I still think that Mick Jagger's Chris Farlowe album was Immediate's finest hour. He was meticulous and professional, getting an "American" feel from the musicians that they weren't capable of ordinarily. Farlowe's success on purely musical terms allowed me to fantasize about a label built on productions by Mick and Keith, an early Glimmer Twins, if you will. Whatever we achieved later with Steve and Ronnie and the Small Faces, as successful and satisfying as it was, it was not the same, nor could it have been, as it would have been had I done it with Mick and Keith. Unfortunately, once Mick had a number one, he lost interest, while Keith never really leaped at the opportunity to begin with, beyond the three of us producing a pre-Mick Chris Farlowe, and him holding my hand for three days while we put together his Aranbee Pop Symphony Orchestra album.

The Immediate dream was over before it began, and when I say that the label helped me lose the Rolling Stones, that's what I mean. My intention was for a mini Motown, the three of us presiding over a vast pre-Apple empire of talent that we would bring to fruition together. Nobody else. Mick, Keith and I. That was Immediate. I'd helped them find their ability to write; through the creation of Immediate, I wanted to help them to produce. This is what we were about. When they turned their back on that, I felt they turned their back on everything we ever stood for, or against. And suddenly Immediate was the competition, because every hour I spent on the label was an hour less spent on the act.

Frankly, it would have been better for Mick's growth as an artist if he had not lost interest because he still had a great deal to learn. For instance, he asked us to sign P.P. Arnold to Immediate after her tour of England with the Ikettes in 1966, but there was no follow through. He produced a half-hearted duet between P.P. and Rod Stewart, a few b-sides with other artists and a single of "Backstreet Girl," which he and I co-produced for the waifish Nicky Scott. That was it. Which, given what was about to happen to the Rolling Stones over the next year, was understandable if you accept Mick was psychic, but it certainly brought an end to my own ambitions for a sweeping epic and gave me a b-movie instead.

With our overt singles mentality, Immediate did not subscribe to the old Hollywood axiom that messages should be sent by Western Union. To launch the Nice, who had been backing P.P. Arnold, we took front page ads proclaiming that "it's taken America 475 years to find itself and it's still looking—it took the Nice 7 minutes and 40 seconds." We shamelessly exploited images of Robert and John Kennedy along with

Martin Luther King to promote another West Side Story remake/remodel. You got it: "America."

While guitarist Davy O'List was nominally the leader of the Nice, organist Keith Emerson's over the top performances were the draw. The same week our print ads set tongues to wagging, the flamboyant stage designer Sean Kenny and I encouraged Emerson to set fire to an American flag on stage at the Royal Albert Hall. That Keith's pyrotechnics were for the benefit of Biafra was considered no mitigation by the Albert Hall management, who subsequently banned pop music for the next few years. Emerson, of course, went on to found Emerson, Lake and Palmer, who never met an excess they didn't like.

More hits flew, but my own behavior wasn't helping to put Immediate on an even footing. Our distributor EMI banned me from their Manchester Square headquarters after I threatened a sales rep with a two by four. Did they realize that I also dropped some Tuinol into the soup at a reception there? Still, we could be proud of my co-production with John Cokell of P.P. Arnold's "Angel of the Morning" as well as her version of Cat Stevens' "First Cut Is the Deepest" (produced by Mike Hurst). Shel Talmy gave us the Amen Corner national anthem "(If Paradise Is) Half as Nice" and the Small Faces, who had come to us from Decca, had two very good years between 1967 and 1969.

"Itchycoo Park," "Lazy Sunday," "Here Comes the Nice" and so on even opened the door a bit for Immediate in America, despite the fact that Clive Davis, who was running our distributor, CBS, personally disliked me. And why not? The Small Faces at their best captured the zeitgeist as well or better than Yank purveyors of psychedelic pop like the Cowsills and the Monkees. Unfortunately, the band never recovered from their imagined ill treatment at the hands of former manager Don Arden and previous label Decca.

At first, their demands seemed reasonable, at least by the artist dominated standards of the late '60s: a house in the country to write in, a studio in town presided over by Glyn Johns, and all the hash they could smoke, eat or otherwise consume. These conditions met, they promised to deliver a commercial masterpiece. And that they did. But unlike the Stones who thrived on endless world tours, the Small Faces felt they'd paid their dues under Don's strict work ethic and refused to tour America. I disagreed and our relationship suffered.

Immediate was more than 45s and hoopla. The Immediate Anthology of British Blues, though a pub and bed-sitter recording, provides an early testament to the roots of Eric Clapton, Jeff Beck, Jimmy Page, John Mayall and the early London R'n'B scene. If you had "chops," Immediate was the place to be. When Immediate was in New Oxford Street next door to the Dick James company, a young Elton John used to pop next door to our office for sandwiches and use of the piano.

While Immediate may have uniquely captured the spirit of its time, our leadership was short-lived. Years later, Terry Ellis acknowledged the path that had been cut for his own successful independent Chrysalis: "In England, some companies believed in records, Immediate believed in people . . . and records. They were ahead of their time."

I do not recall that much about the creditors' meeting held at the accounting firm of Stoy, Hayward on Wigmore Street. Nor do I care to. I do remember being pleased that it was close to Harley Street, where the lovely Dr. John dispensed tea and sympathy by hypodermic, and a kindly "You'll be alright now, Andrew." Turned out to be the kindest thing said to me all day. Drugs and drink before noon were the least of my problems.

Ken East, the blunt, friendly Aussie who headed EMI, quieted the jackals circling Immediate's carcass, among them envious managers such as Tony Stratton-Smith. Ken understood that the gathering was something other than a business meeting; the room was full of dandruff-brained vultures with bad teeth who had come not so much to acquire a potentially valuable catalog but to witness the bloody downfall of Andrew Loog Oldham.

Duncan Browne's superb Give Me Take You notwithstanding, we spent the last year milking what we had already sucked dry. What was left of my money we threw away trying to break free of CBS, our distributor in the US, so that we could go fully independent. In my typically breezy fashion, I once said that everybody should have an orchestra at the age of nineteen. I'm not that sure I'd say the same about having a label at the age of twenty-one.

Still, I would not have missed it for the world, because I had no choice. I didn't know about family, about investment, about putting something away for the rainy day. Immediate was my family and so I supported it.

As we staggered to the finish line, an ulcer-ridden Calder fled to Antigua, leaving behind an hysterical wife who considered my death by a thousand cuts to be inadequate revenge. She blindsided me at an EMI reception and had to be restrained from scratching my eyes out as she shrieked that I had stolen some preposterous amount of money from Tony.

Mrs. Calder was far from the sharpest barb in my crown of thorns. I had lost the Stones and my marriage in particularly disturbing fashion while what little money I thought I had went to bailing out the little label I loved. Suffice it to say that the weekends I spent undergoing electric shock therapy were comparatively restful. As David Bowie would declare only a couple of years later in describing the generation that came after ours, "Speed jive who wants to stay alive . . . when you're 25." Between the age of 19, when I met the Stones, and 25, when I lost Immediate, I had led several lives and no longer was certain which of them I wanted to keep.

To make matters worse, our tax situation would remain nightmarish for years to come. Had Mick actually graduated from the London School of Economics and employed the entrepreneurial gifts for which he is now celebrated, I doubt he could have saved us from a financial quagmire compounded by income derived globally and marginal tax rates in our country of residence approaching 100%. We would pay the Internal Revenue Service in the US a third off the top of what we earned there, only to find that the British Inland Revenue considered itself entitled to tax us on our gross. It took three years for them to send us a bill, and by that time there wasn't anything left to pay it.

We were left with only one option, according to British tax law at the time. If we all of us left England and didn't return for three years, our debt would be forgiven. My own remove to Connecticut in 1970 wasn't too hard to take, given the state of my personal life at "home." Keith was and is a gypsy regardless of where he hangs his hat so life on the Riviera didn't prove to be that much of a hardship. Had he not been forced to use a mobile studio, Exile on Main Street might not have become the masterpiece it is. But for Charlie Watts, British to the core, exile was a bitter pill indeed. Mick, true to form, was quite ready to lay this mess at my feet, but ironically, the accountant who should have been looking out for us was an Allen Klein appointee, so Bob's your uncle.

In 1975, Immediate Records In Liquidation was sold to NEMS Records Limited. This was not the NEMS of Brian Epstein and Liverpool reputation and fame, this was a nasty name-alike foisted upon a still unsuspecting industry by a host of city slicker wide boys and flush young spivs, in the shape and malice of Hemdale.

Brian Jones, Allen Klein, Road Manager Bob Bonis, Mick Jagger, ALO and Keith Richards

This particular Immediate, the second version, was run by Patrick Meehan and, for a brief while, by my ex-partner Tony Calder, who had made a remarkable recovery from his ulcer episode. Unfortunately, NEMS Records acquired only some of the Immediate copyrights, and no commitment whatsoever to honor the contracts that the original Immediate had entered into with its artists—meaning, in effect, that they could release the music without paying any royalties to the acts.

This is hardly fair trade, and another mark against, in addition to whatever I may have placed there, the image of Immediate and its inability to have kept to its original goals and slogan. Now it was not happy to be a part of the industry of human happiness, it was part of the general malaise. And, while Castle, the poor label's next caretaker, claimed to be above this fray, it is well known that the majority of former Immediate artistes remain unpaid to this day by the "chain of title" that runs from NEMS to Castle and Sanctuary.

Apart from these shenanigans, I continued to control the post-liquidation Immediate Records outside the UK, but I fared no better in my choice of bedfellows than the liquidators. Also in 1975, I allowed a fledgling French record company, Charly Records, to distribute Immediate in France and Belgium. Charly promptly assumed this to mean that they could release them wherever they wanted. So they did, and eventually they assumed control of the rest of Europe for the next five years.

I liked label chief Jean Luc Young from the moment I first met him in Paris, admiring the street spirit that so reminded me of what Immediate might have gone on to become. But I was also intrigued by the rumor that the Charly founder was financed by certain Corsican Mafia connections of the French actor Alain Delon. In 1968, Delon's chauffeur/bodyguard, Stevan Marcovic, was found shot in the head in a dumpster outside Delon's home. Delon's friend, alleged Corsican gangster Francois Marcantoni, was charged with accessory to murder. Delon himself was held by police for questioning, despite the fact that the murder took place in Paris, and Delon was filming in St. Tropez. Delon's then-wife, Nathalie, was also questioned.

My new buddy Jean Luc did nothing to confirm or deny the story, except to imply that maybe he, like Delon, had served in the French Army or French Foreign Legion, perhaps in Cuba or Indochina. The Mafia and movie star connections were fascinating to me, although even I wondered how it was I could loathe the mob in England and love it in France. Giorgio Gomelsky has also dealt with Jean Luc over the years, and when we discussed "Kid Cash," as we call him, Giorgio cautioned, "Beware the collector."

While in France to see Jean Luc, I was also visiting my soon-to-be bride, Esther Farfan, who was filming there. On one such visit, Esther had a weekend off and we went to stay at a house Jean Luc owned with his wife Heidi in a rural area on the far side of Charles de Gaulle airport. We all arrived at night with my American minder/driver, Josh Brando, at the wheel of a white Mercedes 450 I had shipped into France from Connecticut for the summer.

Jean Luc and I were trashed; he had this quite amazing amber liqueur that proved the perfect accompaniment to the sounds of Nina Simone, Serge Gainsbourg, Sidney Bechet, John Lennon and Harry Nilsson. He was, as Giorgio said, quite the collector. The next day as we left a local café, we passed a rather rowdy bunch of youths who were miffed at being honked out of the way by a gleaming white Mercedes, its darkened windows protecting the privacy of those within. They jeered and whistled and booed as we drove on. We thought nothing of it at the time and retired to Jean Luc's home expecting to catch up on our sleep.

Esther and I were asleep in the guest room, when we were suddenly awakened by a commotion downstairs. I made my way down the creaky stairs to find Jean Luc, slim, raffish, black haired, black hearted and tazzed standing guard with a shotgun. "Grab zer machete from ze garage, Aanndreww," he commanded calmly, "or anytheeng that is een there, a weapon, we need something to fight."

I picked up a huge scythe that was lying against a tractor. Now the night was still and our presumed attackers were silent and invisible. Suddenly headlights glared from out of the pitch dark and a howling arose as if from a pack of wolves.

"The local football team must have lost tonight and their fans are pissed off. I think it's the same guys your chauffeur honked at this afternoon."

I crept to the end of the garden wall away from the gates where some uneven stone work allowed me to climb a few steps and look outside. As I did, I saw the silhouettes of Esther and Heidi peering out of the darkened second floor window. Behind Esther and their mother, Jean Luc's children yawned and rubbed the sleep from their eyes. With not a Jean-Claude Brialy in sight, this was turning into Straw Dogs.

Lights from a couple of old Renaults played cinematically off the front gates, while a gaggle of sweaty, wasted French teens argued ferociously about who would lead the assault on the house.

The pack found a leader and followed by two or three of his first infantry, he attempted to clamber over the gates, supported from below by rebel yells in alarmingly violent French.

Jean Luc fired his shotgun directly through the gates, careless as to whether or not his bullet found a target. I'm not sure who was more shocked, me or the rebels. I saw a grubby hand trying to get a grip on the wall and when it was joined by its partner, I jumped into the air and brought my scimitar down on the wrist of the offending hand. It was quite crouching tiger, I can tell you.

I will always remember the intruder's scream as he dropped back down off the wall leaving a stream of blood from his deep wound. Jean Luc fired the other barrel into the air. Tires squealed, engines roared, Frenchmen swore and moaned with pain and indignation. And then they were gone.

In my world, a violent attack shared and overcome stands for something. The bond Jean Luc and I forged that night survived all the continuing adventures of Immediate that followed.

* * *

One year into this century I had been well for a while and wrote on my website: "The Immediate saga is not so clean. As of this writing, Oldham is at issue with Charly Records over fraud, non-payment, and the alleged backdating of agreements, created by Charly to extend any time and territorial rights they may have obtained from Immediate Records Inc. In addition, Oldham is objecting to any chain of title Castle records may have acquired from NEMS Records Ltd.

"Oldham is quoted as saying in a forthcoming article, 'I am in the business of clearing my universe and hope that that mission can be recognized by law. I allowed criminal acts to taint my Immediate legacy in the Seventies, which resulted in artistes unpaid and the reputation of Immediate soiled by masqueraders. I'm sending my laundry to the High Court cleaners and hoping for a clean bill of health.'"

War had been declared, and suddenly, as elegant, I thought, as Terence Stamp in the opening of Stephen Frear's *The Hit*, I was standing in front of m'lud in the High Court. The day the proceedings were due to commence, I let my lawyer go . . . not a good thing on the first day of a High Court case in which you have two opponents, Charly Acquisitions Ltd and Sanctuary Music Ltd. But my lawyer had conflicts of interest I could not live with. I had not realized that Jean Luc Young was a former client of his and, by all accounts, the two of them were still far too close for comfort. Justice Pumfrey, sitting light years above me, told me not to worry, he wanted this case and would explain any issues to me that I might not understand. I was now representing myself.

I cannot say I did not enjoy the battle. It was as exciting as any drug. I took off my earrings and combed my hair, but I forgot the most important injunction of all—"A gentleman does not wear brown in town," as Nicky Haslam's father used to say. I might have done better to leave the earrings on as well according to the very attractive female attorney sent by Allen Klein to protect me from myself. Quite stylish she was, too, long legged and bespectacled a la Hank B. Marvin. Instinct told her the Judge might have asked me where I'd gotten my own jewelry.

"Malibu, m'lud. California," I would have said.

"Oh, yes? Did they cost much?" He might have replied.

Let us now return to the beginning of the long and winding road that lead from the aforementioned creditors' meeting on Wigmore Street back in 1970 to my day of reckoning in 2001. For all our flair for publicity, Immediate sputtered out not with a bang but a whimper. Don Arden received the gold eagle lectern he had admired from our

Gloucester Place offices, but no other furnishings were salvaged. They couldn't even get the chandeliers down.

Don and I had just one more profitable prank left in us before I quit the UK for good. EMI, a company that never seems to learn from its mistakes, advanced us £10,000 for a single, no less, by a group that didn't exist. Even in 1970, someone might have sussed that the group's name, Grunt Futtock, was a piss take.

Tony Calder and I lost control of Immediate Music publishing to United Artists Records in 1968. UA was taken over by EMI in the late Seventies, and EMI controls the Immediate Music copyrights to this day. My co-writing contributions to Immediate Music earn me about £26 a year. Some of those songs I actually wrote, and some of them I share with the composer who actually wrote them. The Morris Levy template is a gift that keeps on giving. It took a while for the British record industry to become as corrupt as its American counterpart, but there you are.

I sit on a reasonably high floor compared to many, but even I am not paid for the Del Shannon recordings I made for Liberty/EMI in 1967. I may have some old royalty statements, dated 1970 or so, to prove that I was once entitled to remuneration, but as I no longer possess the original contract, they no longer pay me, and I let them get away with it because life is too short and the jungle is so near. But it's a terrible state to be in for an artist who would depend on these derisory sums for the very food on the table. Ironically, a new Allen Klein, were such a thing possible, could go after the lot of them, but what sort of door would that open? Karma, as they say, is a bitch.

While Immediate Records Ltd. was no more in the UK, I'd had the foresight to transfer the rights for the catalog outside of Britain to Immediate Records Inc., a US corporation, in 1969. I bought out Tony Calder to become sole proprietor and once the distribution deal with CBS ran out in mid-1970, I had free rein to find new partners.

There had been no satisfactory conclusion to the $7 million court case we brought against CBS. We protested that CBS was killing competition with their home grown product by paying a high 12% licensing royalty but failing to work the act after the first hit. Artists signed directly to CBS could expect no more than a two or three percent royalty and thus were more profitable.

From 1968 to 1975, EMI licensed the catalogue (through my company Immediate Inc.) for Europe and Canada. There were small but steady returns to be earned from rereleasing compilations or early albums by artists who had moved on to greater success. Steve Marriott's band after the Small Faces did particularly well as a live act in the US, and a 1972 repackaging of Humble Pie's two Immediate albums sold surprisingly well.

In the US, I licensed Immediate's back catalogue to A&M and then Seymour Stein's new label Sire. Throughout this period, advances from US deals and royalties from EMI earned me approximately $250,000—and none of the Immediate acts received any royalties. Nor were any due since not one of the acts had recouped their advances. Up to that point, we were fairly scrupulous in our accounting to the artists, who understood the concept of recoupment even if they didn't like it.

Artists from the Small Faces on down the scale to P.P. Arnold and Billy Nicholls were all on wages during their Immediate years, and, in most cases, had rent paid. The gonorrhea tabs were definitely covered. £40 a week sounds like nothing now, but it was a lot when you sold anywhere between zero and 180,000 singles, and no Immediate act, bar the Small Faces with Ogden's Nut Gone Flake, sold any considerable amount of albums. And even that only sold 65,000 copies in Britain.

As said, I had poured vast sums of my own money into Immediate, notably £25,000 advances to the Small Faces and Amen Corner, along with £12,500 on a buyout of Peter Frampton's contract. Frampton was becoming the draw in Humble Pie, then my best bet in the States, so the money had to be spent.

The Amen Corner were another tragedy, despite starring Andy Fairweather-Low, a teenybopper idol with blues ambitions. How could I, let alone the public, be expected to remember the names of everybody in a group with seven members? I had broken the rule I established with the "Rollin' Stones": five is more than enough.

True enough, the Amen Corner started out well for us. Like the Small Faces, they were sold to us by Don Arden, who was happy to make their Decca contract disappear for a large advance. Our reward was a number one single with "(If Paradise Is) Half As Nice," a slice of divine pop served up by producer Shel Talmy after the song had won at some European song contest or other. It just sent chills down your spine and turned yer Adam's apple into a drag act.

But Fairweather-Low was one of those artists who just can't leave well enough alone. As seriously as he took himself, it came as no surprise that he felt we didn't take him seriously enough. While most Immediate artists were quite happy to be on our dole, Andy seemed to feel he was an indentured servant (as if we didn't all have to serve somebody, as Dylan reminds us). Talmy gave us a perfectly good follow up to "Paradise" with "At Last I've Got Someone to Love" but Fairweather-Low's ill-advised persistence paid off for him, if not us, and we went with a lackluster version of Roy Wood's "Hello Suzie" and an even worse cover of the Beatles' "Get Back" instead.

Andy was in Bogotá, Colombia, a few years ago along with P.P. Arnold when they were backing up Roger Waters. I picked Pat up at the airport, and we had a time catching up. She asked me if I had seen Andy at the airport. I had no idea he was there.

"Why didn't he say hallo?" I asked.

Pat just gave me a look that seemed to suggest the lad was still bitter.

Sorry Andy. Sorry world . . . .

Which brings us full circle back to my 1975 deal with Jean Luc Young and his Charly Records. Charly had just completed the purchase of back-product from the Sun, Red Bird and Blue Cat record labels, and his capture of Immediate made the front cover of UK trade magazine, *Music Week*. I said at the time that I was more than happy to do it. "He was independent, he cared about things, and it was perfect for the kind of figures the Immediate stuff was going to do. It was a respectable home for that time."

Paul Mozian, one of Allen Klein's men, was now working for me. He told Simon Dudfield years later, "Jean Luc was a scallywag, a street ruffian that had some money, but we could never really figure out where his money came from. He wanted to establish a record label, he really had the hots for the Immediate thing. He was so delighted to be able to get the licensing for Europe."

Kid Cash came up with $10,000 and I was actually able to go to his bank account in Geneva and cash the check. Mozian continued, "Then Kid Cash brought the [Immediate] stuff to the UK and that's when the trouble began, between the Meehans, Charly and Andrew: 'What did you really license and how can you license something you don't own?' We had to go sort it out. I met Don Arden in England, who was gonna help Andrew against Patrick and Tony. I guess Andrew figured Don Arden would be a good powerhouse at the time. He was wrong."

Calder had been lured back from Antigua to run OPAL records, the black music subsidiary of NEMS, and found himself piggy-in-the-middle of the Meehans' plans for Immediate Records Ltd. NEMS had already signed Marianne Faithfull and planned to reform the Small Faces, make a video for "Itchycoo Park," re-release it and get a new LP out of the group. Needless to say, Meehan had not taken kindly to Jean Luc Young's decision to make what NEMS claimed was mischief on their turf with the rights he had acquired from Immediate Inc.

The Stones in concert

Since the collapse of Immediate, I had produced albums by Jimmy Cliff, Donovan and Humble Pie, as well as Motown. Now I was approached by Calder to join the NEMS group as "director of special projects" or "executive catalyst." There was talk of an "Immediate II" with everyone working together. I agreed to meet them at the Midem Music Festival in Cannes for a clear-the-air discussion. I liked the idea of playing David Geffen for a while, although the thought of being back in business with Calder was not heartwarming, due to a singularly unpleasant encounter at the Royal Albert Hall a couple of years before.

When Esther and I arranged to meet Meehan Jr. and Calder for some concert or other, I little suspected Tony's consort would be my ex-wife Sheila in all her brittle and disingenuous glory. Both of them knew that I had no inkling of what was obviously an intimate relationship, and if fucking your friend's ex-wife is in poor taste, surprising him with it is assault. I could see Sheila enjoying my discomfort; a consideration for other's feelings was never her strong suit. But Calder, bastard though I knew he could be, should not have shown me, let alone Esther, such disrespect. Esther and I turned and walked back down the red carpet with as much dignity and as little violence as I could muster, hoping we had seen the last of both Sheila and Tony. They deserved every bit of hell I had no doubt they would put each other through.

Tony indeed had a special gift for turning erstwhile friends into deadly enemies, and so it was that once we got to Midem for our meeting of reconciliation, old pal Don Arden had his own bone to pick with the troublesome Calder. Don was furious with Tony for his involvement with the Meehans, who had in Don's mind stolen the management of Black Sabbath from him. Don resolved his annoyance in straightforward fashion: he stuck a pistol in Tony Calder's mouth, muttering something about an unpaid light bill he claimed Calder had skipped out on. So much for "Immediate II." This was a great way to introduce Esther to my world, but she was from Colombia and nary batted an exotic eyelid.

Between 1976 and 1983, Charly and NEMS managed to stay out of each other's way by carving up territories in a manner similar to that of the Allies dividing the Middle East between them after the first World War. Profitability was somewhat ensured by the fact that neither company felt legally or morally responsible to pay artist royalties. It had somehow slipped the British liquidator's mind to stipulate that sort of thing in the sale to NEMS, and Jean Luc, even assuming you could track him down, never had any intention of paying royalties, as a matter of "principle." Giorgio Gomelsky has him declaiming, "I'm the one who does the work and puts the records out. Why should I pay royalties?" After MCA finally nailed him for $7,000,000 over unauthorized releases of the Chess catalogue, Jean Luc made himself scarcer than ever.

Meanwhile, Meehan Jr. had parted with Calder and in 1983, just as CDs came along and jump-started the next twenty-year boom, he sold NEMS to Castle Music for what was described as a very substantial sum of money, and so Castle, and later Sanctuary, would inherit the undertaking not to pay royalties.

I liked Patrick. There was nothing not to like, as long as you kept it social. As far as business went, he was just too bright and bent for me, but I did enjoy his company. He was a one-man Guy Ritchie movie. He had immense charisma and was slyly dashing and always a good host. I pictured myself playing David Geffen to Patrick's Mo Ostin and Tony Calder's Joe Smith, but all Patrick really wanted from me was my signature as he tightened his global grip on Immediate.

Over the next 17 years, Castle put out on CD almost anything and everything Immediate had ever recorded and made pony deals with the acts they needed for PR for £5,000 or £10,000 amounts. They paid more for the Small Faces, giving drummer Kenney Jones the wherewithal to start demanding his royalties in earnest. Though this amounted to something like £250,000, Jones continued to maintain that he was short-changed.

And while Castle kept their Immediate operations to the UK, Charly continued to exploit the Immediate back catalogue world-wide—the dispute over who owned what being resolved via some sort of private joint-ownership agreement. I was out of the picture altogether.

Early crowd control

In 2000, Castle was acquired by Sanctuary Records, who splashed out on lavishly packaged CD box sets, as well as straight up album re-issues. Royalties, unless you had the kind of legal help Kenney Jones invested in, were still not being paid, and that was the biggest crime, bigger than any others in this chapter, alleged or actual. It was enough to drive a penniless act whose fifteen minutes on Immediate were a distant memory to drink, drugs, depression or death. Is it possible that by perpetuating 35 years of greed, Sanctuary inherited Immediate's karma as well as its catalogue? Within years of going public with the kind of ambitions now being realized by Live Nation, Sanctuary itself went up, up and away. Be careful of what you acquire, you may become it.

So, as a result of my confusing "being well" in body and mind with "being right" legally, in 2001, Immediate Records Inc. and I were plaintiffs in a High Court case against Sanctuary and Charly. To my mind, I was entitled to the rights and royalties on master recordings I had paid for and leased to Immediate as well as rights in such acts as the Small Faces and the Amen Corner for whom I, rather than the label, had paid.

As stated earlier, I ended up representing myself at the Old Bailey. I had run low on funds and did not trust my lawyer, Nick Kanaar, who I suspected of colluding with Jean Luc Young to defeat me. Jean Luc had already sent a different lawyer around to buy me off and drop the case, but I was convinced that I held the high ground in the matter and decided to proceed on my own.

As luck would have it, Justice Pumfrey turned a friendly ear to yours truly when he learned I had produced one of his favorites, Alma Cogan, begging the question that Alma was probably the only artist named in the action with whom he was familiar. He promised he would walk me through the legalities and make sure I understood everything. Yes, thank you, m'lud; though the Rolling Stones were about not being patronized, your patronage is needed, so thank you, sir.

Alas, the finer points of English law are not something you can pick up overnight, and really it is only in movies that the good, decent man representing himself takes on highly trained and highly paid legal counsel and wins. But as you would expect, I was game. I rocked a striped brown DKNY four button suit, and for eight days did my best Mr. Smith Goes to Washington.

Sanctuary called on Kenney Jones, Mike Hurst and Jerry Shirley. I was very disappointed at Jerry Shirley turning up for the other side, and dumbfounded by his inability to speak the truth. I had Paul Banes (Immediate's US General Manager from 1968-1970) and former Poet's singer George Gallagher in my corner. A willing, but not first division, team.

But my star witness, Stan Blackbourne, the old Rolling Stones/Immediate accountant, the man who knew the books better than anyone, had died a few months prior; and Tony Calder was forbidden from testifying on my behalf as the Judge decided he would be an unreliable witness—given, I suppose, the number of Immediates he had been involved with. Knowing that Tony could blow holes in Castle/Sanctuary's chain of title, Charly succeeded in continuing the case in another domain. There was also some evidence that the entity under which Jean Luc was appearing had been struck off the Irish registrar's list for non-payment of taxes but that blow to Charly's credibility was never brought out.

I was also forbidden from referring to the MCA case against Charly. Therefore I was no match for Charly's barrister, nor Sanctuary's QC, who slipped and slid their way around any claims I made. The Sanctuary solicitor, however, caught my eye with his very smart Jerry Garcia tie and went on to become a pal after the trial.

When the Judge scolded me because "Mr. Oldham did not get a receipt from Don Arden when he gave him £25,000 in cash for the Small Faces," I knew the gig was up. I gave Don money and he gave me the Small Faces; the group was my receipt. While Sanctuary's QC generally acted fairly in defending their rights to what they had bought, Charly's barrister wanted my head on a pike. He tried to make the case that because my primary residence was in Bo-ga-ta, Colooooombiayaaa I had no right to pursue justice in Britain.

I was kept on the stand for an utterly exhausting four days, during which I made fatal concessions and foolish mistakes. My inexperience showed at every turn. Opposing counsel deliberately dragged my testimony out over a weekend, knowing that I would fret all the more about Monday's appearance. I was worried about my mother who was elderly and very ill, and I learned to my regret that the appropriate diet for a litigant is cakes and espresso and not the steak and potatoes I'd been eating.

In my favor, Paul Banes noted that original label copy produced during the trial showed I was the owner of many Immediate recordings that had been privately financed by me, and that Immediate was contracted to pay royalties to me as the owner. Banes felt at worst there would be a guaranteed payment of the royalties that were allocated in 1965 to all artists and to me, even if the amount was paltry, because the better selling records would not thus be included.

As a point of honor, I looked forward to sending Mick and Keith a check for the work we had done together on Chris Farlowe, no matter how small the amount. If anything, it was even more important to me morally to send Mick some payment for the work he had done on his own. But despite the distinction I tried to make between records financed by ALO Ltd. and those financed by Immediate Records Ltd., the Judge ruled that it was my fiduciary duty to put the ALO Ltd. rights into Immediate Records Ltd. So much for my crash course in British jurisprudence.

I was very shaken by Mr. Justice Pumfrey's final verdict—an "indisputable" paper trail led to copyright ownership remaining with Charly and Sanctuary.

It had been a strange and quixotic experience and, in part, I felt some slight relief that I'd lost. Imagine having to account for a few pounds here and there to artists like Farlowe and P.P. and the Faces, who thought they had sold millions and were owed the same. Imagine having to deal with them again, especially without mother's little helpers. You cannot go back; it's true.

The fact of the matter was that such paper trails as still existed were not helpful to my cause, and I'd made myself an easy target for double-dealing solicitors and disgruntled artists. Once I'd decided to represent myself, just about the only supporter I had in the case was the presiding justice, who nevertheless watched me die a death of a thousand cuts. In retrospect, I think I was trying, as an outcome of my newly achieved sobriety, to work a kind of 12-step program of my own, in which the complex karma of Immediate's ancient history would somehow be purified and turned to the benefit of all. If there had ever been any doubt that I was more of a romantic idealist than a killer shark, those doubts were laid dramatically to rest.

* * *

The following appeared as a legal bulletin in 2002. "Charly Music Ltd founder Jean Luc Young has lost his appeal of the High Court ruling that he was personally liable for copyright infringement by issuing Chess recordings dating from 1947-1975. In the High Court in London last year, Mr. Justice Rimer upheld MCA's claim that it was entitled, as assignee, to the copyright in all sound recordings listed in a monograph The Chess Labels—a Discography compiled by Michel Ruppli and published by Greenwood Press in 1983... The recordings, originally produced by brothers Leonard and Philip Chess, include thousands of jazz, blues, R&B, and rock 'n' roll tracks by Bo Diddley, Chuck Berry, Muddy Waters, and others."

I had not been allowed to bring this matter before the court. Neither was Tony Calder allowed to explain the Immediate chain of title and contracts that he, as a partner and officer, had signed. Sanctuary was taken over by Universal in 2007. Jean Luc Young remains out of MCA's reach, rumored to be in Thailand, but no doubt still bopping around Bayswater Road. Nobody in the record business, or what is left of it, really cares, not even those minding the Universal store. They have problems enough just keeping their jobs. Justice Pumfrey has no such problem. He passed away a few Christmas Eves ago, at the tender age of 56. *Ars longa vita brevis*—which happens to have been the name of the Nice's second Immediate album.

PHIL SPECTOR

I'VE OFTEN WONDERED how deeply Phil Spector got stuck in the word-play Tom Wolfe created around him in his 1965 essay, "The First Tycoon of Teen."

"Spector," he wrote, "while still in his teens, seemed to comprehend the proletariat vitality of rock and roll that has made it the darling holy beast of intellectuals in the United States, England and France. There have been teenagers who have made a million dollars before, but invariably they are entertainers, they are steered by older people, such as the good Colonel Tom Parker steers Elvis Presley. But Phil Spector is a bona-fide Genius of Teen. Every baroque period has a flowering genius who rises up as the most glorious expression of its style of life—in latter-day Rome, the Emperor Commodus; in Renaissance Italy, Benvenuto Cellini; in late Augustan England, the Earl of Chesterfield; in the sal volatile Victorian age, Dante Gabriel Rossetti; in late-fancy neo-Greek Federal America, Thomas Jefferson; and in Teen America, Phil Spector is the bona-fide Genius of Teen."

You have to hope that Wolfe is taking the piss and that this fawning portrait was not the reason Spector named one of his children Dante. It's not unlikely, however, that Phil took Wolfe literally and thus never got over being a "teen tycoon," let alone a "flowering genius." Had Phil Spector the adult lived up to Wolfe's purple prose, he'd have self-destructed long before his fatal tryst with Lana Clarkson. But although perhaps younger than his peers, mentors and rivals in the early days of rock 'n' roll, Phil was not as uniquely talented as Wolfe might have had it. Even allowing that he may have been first among equals in company with Jerry Leiber and Mike Stoller, Doc Pomus and Mort

Shuman, and Ahmet Ertegun, Wolfe's essay did him far more harm than good in New York's close-knit pop community. I don't think Ahmet, Jerry or Mike ever forgave him for what was, after all, Wolfe's original sin.

Wolfe's piece gave Phil Spector a kind of legitimacy that hits alone couldn't buy. And despite his diplomatic pedigree, Ahmet Ertegun longed for the acknowledgment a *New Yorker* profile eventually provided. Leiber and Stoller created a legacy fully as important as Phil's, with considerably more sanity in the process, but they never really got over their protégé upstaging them. Doc and Mort not so much; they got Phil and they were never threatened by him.

Wolfe gave Phil wings of wax and his essay encouraged the tycoon of teen to fly too close to the sun. Too much attention was now being paid to this fledgling psychotic and it was corrosive. Phil, of course, was always an artist first and a businessman mainly because he liked to win and for others to lose. He'd have done better if the proportions had been reversed: Lou Adler, Albert Grossman and Shep Gordon, for example, were able to have their cake and eat it too, without being drawn to walk through the looking glass.

The last time I saw Phil pretty well convinced me that the rabbit hole was pretty much his natural habitat.

I arrived in LA in the second week of June 2008, and stopped by the Warner Brothers offices in Burbank to see Seymour Stein, the head of Sire Records and an important part of our musical life since 1964. Keith Richards and I first met Seymour while scouting material for the Stones to cover in the Brill Building, home (with 1650 Broadway) to New York's most happening publishers. Keith and I went to Trio Music without an appointment and Jerry Leiber refused to see us. We were just getting into the elevator when a young plugger, the aforementioned Seymour Stein, rushed on out and dragged us back in. He was flustered and apologetic over the Leiber brush off, although Keith and I didn't mind; it happened in England all the time. Seymour sat us down and got down to music. Thirty minutes later, Keith and I left with more than a few 45-RPMs, among them Alvin Robinson's "Down Home Girl," written by Jerry Leiber and Artie Butler, which the Stones would record rather well the next time they hit the studio.

The Warner Brothers offices in which I reunited with Seymour were not those I remembered from the glory days of Mo Ostin, Joe Smith, Lenny Waronker and Elektra Mark III under Bob Krasnow. Even the artists on the walls seemed to look upon us with dead eyes. In fact, the 21st Century version of Warner Brothers resembled too much the Decca's and EMI's of the early '60s before the likes of Seymour and yours truly got their turn at bat. More than ever, the record companies assumed their random successes confirmed their personal talent.

Artist/producer Brian Eno was recently blunt about the sea change that is sinking the industry: "I think records were just a little bubble through time and those who made a living from them for a while were lucky. There is no reason why anyone should have made so much money from selling records except that everything was right for this period of time. I always knew it would run out sooner or later. It couldn't last, and now it's running out. I don't particularly care that it is and like the way things are going. The record age was just a blip. It was a bit like if you had a source of whale blubber in the 1840s and it could be used as fuel. Before gas came along, if you traded in whale blubber, you were the richest man on Earth. Then gas came along and you'd be stuck with your whale blubber. Sorry mate—history's moving along. Recorded music equals whale blubber. Eventually, something else will replace it."

As I watched Seymour greet the visitors that came and went from the beautiful office he was squatting in, I felt as if I were at a wake without food. I recalled that Warner Brothers Records as we once knew it had evolved from Frank Sinatra's vision of an artist centered label. He called it Reprise and recruited Verve Records executive Mo Ostin to run it. Sinatra had been drawn to Capitol Records in the early '50s for the same reasons, but by 1960 old blues eyes was restless once again.

The original founders of Capitol were Buddy DeSylva, of the songwriting team DeSylva, Brown and Henderson; fellow songwriter Johnny Mercer; and Glenn Wallichs, owner of Hollywood's hot record shop, Music City, located on the corner of Sunset and Vine. There was not a suit in sight, but an awful lot of talent. De Sylva had enjoyed a long career on Tin Pan Alley, writing a scrumptious amount of hit songs for Broadway musicals and movies. Mercer wrote or co-wrote "Fools Rush In," "Jeepers Creepers" "The Shadow of your Smile" and "I Remember You" (supposedly written about Judy Garland, with whom he had an affair when she was 18 years old). My own particular favorite was "Satin Doll" which, as an instrumental, was a standout track on the classic George Shearing Quintet-Peggy Lee Capitol album, Beauty and the Beat.

Back at the wake, Seymour sat at a desk across from Andy Paley and myself, making himself temporarily at home in star producer David Foster's office. Andy Paley used to be a Sire Records artist and now is an arranger/writer who has collaborated with Brian Wilson, Debbie Harry and the Ramones, and more recently scored The L Word. Andy was hustling Seymour on a girl group Jonathan Richman has either used or raved about. Just like Seymour hustled Keith and I back in '64. This is what we do. It is Seymour who once said, "You can be wrong most of the time in this business and still be successful."

The girl group left. They had been nice to listen to. Their repertoire took us back to the Angels, the Shangri-La's and the Brill Building. We felt at home with the memory as opposed to the moment. Andy Paley had been nice to watch. He sat on David Foster's couch with an electronic keyboard on his lap and a strange homemade mini-kick drum and tambourine attached to his left foot that he stomped enthusiastically in a Lovin' Spoonful jug band kind of way as he played the keyboard and urged his trio of singing fillies to realize this was their one and only shot, and to please remove the humility and find some kill.

"I told you, didn't I?" said Seymour, after he had emerged from this sani-wrapped old-tyme lackluster harmonic sandwich, "We can't have lunch."

Food and music . . . Music and food . . . That was Seymour.

If WC Fields had been younger, better looking and not anti-Semitic, he might have been Seymour Stein.

"Okay," I said, "we can't have lunch."

I had arrived the night before from Bogotá, eaten too much on the eight-hour flight, and then eaten again at the sushi house next door to 9000 Sunset Boulevard opposite On the Rox. Given all that, and given that it was 93 degrees, I was not that hungry.

"We have to go and see Phil Spector. He's expecting us," Seymour said. "I told him you were here, he said to bring you."

My first reaction was that I was glad not to have had forewarning about a Phil Spector meet. It was not something I wanted too much time to think about. If you have read my previous books, or comments elsewhere, you will know of the huge influence Phil Spector has had upon my life. Above and beyond the music, which has touched and moved most of our lives, there was the very idea of Phil. "To Know Him Is to Love Him" (the original "Love Garage" record), the Crystals, the Ronettes, the Righteous Brothers, and Bobb B. Soxx and the Bluejeans defined the Wall of Sound. But even when unrewarded by the charts, Phil could work magic. For instance, the virtually unknown Sonny Charles and the Checkmates Ltd. and their spellbinding "Love Is All I Have To Give" and "Black Pearl."

And then when "River Deep Mountain High" failed to get to Number One, Phil eventually overcame his bitterness and disappointment to produce the Beatles, collectively and individually, after George Martin. *Let It Be*, *John Lennon/Plastic Ono Band*, *Imagine*, and *All Things Must Pass* were among the biggest selling and critically acclaimed albums of their time, and it's hard to imagine them sounding like they do without Phil's contribution. Thanks to Phil, the "quiet" Beatle finally received his due, while John Lennon's primal scream reamed its way into the world's conscience, almost every tune a prayer for peace from a soul in pain. As for *All Things Must Pass*, I had to take two days off the hook to take it all in.

Phil was difficult, so much so that Paul McCartney had no use for him. After the early successes with Lennon and Harrison, many of his projects began with so much promise only to die crib deaths. Diverse talents would hope to be touched by greatness

Phil Spector

only to leave the studio shaking their heads, among them the Ramones (courtesy of Seymour), Dion, Leonard Cohen and Celine Dion. There were long periods of time between these setbacks for Phil to brood alone in his house on the top of the hill, too much time for his own good. It wasn't so much "Back to Mono" as back to darkness as guns, wigs, gates and guard dogs not so much kept the world out as they kept the tycoon of teen in a prison of his own devise. The lights were out on Casa Phil.

However, after years of disorganization and shoddy remasters, Phil's Philles catalogue was made available once again in fine digital fashion, oddly enough via Allen Klein's ABKCO Records. A week after Phil's manager Marty Machat died, Klein had talked Phil into letting him handle the Spector Legacy. A first-tier legal eagle that had worked for Klein as well but fallen out with him, Machat went on to manage Phil and Leonard Cohen. Marty's appetite for strange must have been enormous. It so happened I was in New York staying with Allen when we got news of Marty's passing. Allen insisted we sit shiva, though it had been years since he had anything good to say about his former attorney. Surrounded by the old guard of Jewish entertainment, I felt like an accidental tourist. Didn't feel too bad, actually.

In 1989, Phil overcame his paranoia long enough to allow himself to be inducted into the Rock and Roll Hall of Fame. Bodyguarded everywhere he went, he fell out with Ahmet Ertegun in public, much to the discomfiture of Jann Wenner, chairman of the Hall's Board of Directors. Caught in the middle of a clash of titans, Wenner resembled the Sunday driver who keeps to the right lane on a six-lane freeway. Didn't keep him from being jolted by the bumpy ride that was par for Spector's course.

We sang Phil Och's "Outside A Small Circle of Friends" as Phil swayed on stage, and Ahmet silently hoped Phil would fall off it. Phil's acceptance speech had the bitter humor of Lenny Bruce without the lovable eccentricity of Ernie Kovacs. As publisher of Hunter Thompson, Jann Wenner should have been accustomed to fear and loathing but the sour smell of success in the room was hard to take.

In *Rock Dreams*, and again in *20th Century Dreams*, author Nik Cohn wrote especially well about Phil: "Phil came to class with problems. He'd grown up in the

Bronx and his father was dead and, to be perfectly honest, he had picked up some quite unappetizing habits. Also, he was undersized and Jewish and spoke in a funny squeaky voice. Although he showed undoubted promise, he never really fitted in and, when he dropped out of class after only one semester, the rest of the kids were secretly relieved. Baby Phil, the High School drop-out; arriving in New York he slept in offices, on floors and benches and desktops, until finally he was let loose to produce a record. Then, at a single shot, he paid back twenty years' accumulation of rage. Out poured torrents of pent-up energy; invention; insanity, malice, fantasy, grotesquery; and when the smoke cleared, he stood revealed in Hollywood technorama, a colossus; true inheritor of Cecil B. de Mille; ultimate rock 'n' roll showman, teen-dreamer and bullshitter, genius and freak."

Freak . . . .

In 1997, I brought my family to another Hall of Fame induction ceremony which honored the Mamas & the Papas. After a run-in with a thoroughly Manischewitzed and medicated Phil, my son Max looked at me with bewilderment.

"Papi," he said, "you used to idolize this man?"

Yes I did, son, and now as part of a convoy led by Seymour Stein, I was about to find out if I still did. It occurred to me now that he had always treated me about as well as I was treating myself at the time of our occasional encounters. When I had been anything less than together, he had been alpha, predatory, a male wolf siccing his pack on a weakened creature that had been left behind by the herd to die.

One night at a Songwriters Hall of Fame event, he eviscerated Darlene Love's manager for daring to sue him over unpaid royalties. In Phil's mind, the singers were never the artists despite what was printed on the record label; he was the artist, a solo artist at that. He surely agreed with Alfred Hitchcock, who corrected a famous quote attributed to him: "I never said all actors are cattle; what I said was all actors should be treated like cattle."

Now, in most cases, when a producer, manager, or record label is asked about underpayment, they simply lie. They are innocent of stealing from the artist until proven guilty by a very expensive and/or very clever accountant and/or lawyer. Who probably is stealing from the artist as well. But Phil was a genius. As a matter of business practice, he never used a recording by the A-side artist as the B-side of the singles he produced. That way he only had to pay the artist for one side. Since the B-side paid exactly the same as the A-side, he saved himself 50% automatically.

Sometimes, Phil worked himself into such a frenzy he was more amusing than frightening, though one would have been wise not to let him know you were laughing at him. One evening after yet another Rock and Roll Hall of Fame ceremony, Phil, our mutual friend, arranger Jack Nitzsche, and I strolled over to Foreigner Mick Jones' Central Park West apartment. There, before his son Dante, Phil threatened to kill me if he ever saw me take drugs. Thank God we were both so high he didn't notice I was.

Back on the road again, Seymour, Andy Paley and I made our way onto the San Bernadino Freeway en route to Alhambra, where Phil was doubtlessly working himself into a tizzy of anticipation. I have mentioned it was oppressively hot, and I was reminded of one of my favorite American TV shows from my childhood, Broderick Crawford's Highway Patrol. We did not have deserts in the UK. It also occurred to me that in all the over forty years I had known Phil, this was the first time we had met when the sun was still shining.

As we made our way from Los Angeles to Alhambra, I wondered if we were retracing the route that Phil took with Lana Clarkson. It crossed my mind that it was a hell of a long way to go for a nightcap, not that either Phil or Lana needed one at that point, according to the testimony of witnesses at the various restaurants where Phil had been self-medicating. At the time Phil wandered into the House of Blues VIP room, he was not in good shape. He had recently taken the British buzz band Starsailor into Abbey Road studios and produced only a few tracks as weeks stretched into months. To the band, it didn't matter that one of them became a Top Ten single in the UK. With the arrogance and self-importance of youth, they fired Phil Spector.

Now insanity was certainly waiting in the wings of his vast empty mansion, a spiritual predator that knew Phil would eventually crack. Four years of sobriety were discarded in an instant and Phil was sick again. An alcoholic may stop drinking for a day, a month or a year, but his body never stops wanting a drink and the moment he slips and drinks again, he's a drunk again because the body never stops drinking, even if you have.

I had a personal reason to remember the date on which Phil met Lana Clarkson. Esther and I had accompanied our son to Los Angeles where Max was enrolled in Santa Monica College. We opened the newspaper the morning after we arrived to read some terrible news: our club in Bogotá had been bombed and forty-three people were dead and hundreds injured. It was a professional job and an act of insane political protest. You really have to have lived in Colombia to appreciate that collaboration between the native rebel forces and the IRA was not a bad joke. The Irish were training FARC thugs in terrorism in exchange for drugs they were selling back home in Belfast. The point is that the attack came on a Friday at a time when Max habitually visited the club to plan his evening. Had we not been in LA, he would in all likelihood have been there. Friends of ours were.

Still in shock, we turned the page to more bad news: legendary rock and roll producer Phil Spector had been arrested on suspicion of murder.

Alhambra is weird. Maybe it's the heat. As we waited for security to clear us through, I squinted up at Phil's Pyrenean mansion on a hill and made a movie in my mind. Dennis Hopper played Murry Wilson, father to three of the Beach Boys, while Timothy Hutton played Brian and whoever it was that laid Brooke Shields in Blue Lagoon played Dennis. I think the gate opened before I got around to casting Carl Wilson. Then my mind went unwillingly to another stately home in the hills where Sharon Tate met her grisly fate at the hands of another California madman. I shivered in spite of the hot sun.

Phil is at the front door when we arrive. Our first daylight meeting. All of a sudden, I'm happy, I'm impressed, he is obviously still Phil Spector. I don't even check out the foyer. His hair is brown, quasi long and curly. He is dressed in various shades of grey. And blue. It works. His braces are adorned by a large button supporting the U.S. Democratic nominee for President, Barack Obama. The Beatle boots are gone, so is the Ahmet Ertegun imitative mode of speaking. The shoes are two-tone, and his voice is quieter, less shrill, less hysterical. The man has a trial, or rather a re-trial, at the end of September and Tom Cruise, who once did, doesn't want to play him anymore.

We talk about the trials. We discuss my books; Phil has read one and enjoyed it. I am pleased. We discuss New Orleans and the Bush administration's failure to take care of its own. We talk about mutual friends, we recall our past together. It turns out that the reason Seymour has been summoned concerns the possible recording career of Phil's spanking new wife. Rachelle Spector is a former Playboy model who is 28 years old to Spector's 69. She and Phil were married after his arrest while he was awaiting his first trial. I cannot wait to hear how Seymour will handle this request from a man we have both admired our entire adult lives, who is likely to be incarcerated for the rest of his life within the next few months.

Seymour tells Phil that Warner Brothers is just not signing anybody new. Phil takes it sitting down, he does not say much, he just looks Seymour over with a long, enquiring look. Phil has seen it all before. Rejection. I have to wonder if this is why I had been invited, to cushion what Seymour knows will be unwelcome news. To make the conversation harmless, a neutral player around whom everybody will behave.

This is not as strange as it may seem; it has happened to me before. I recognize the moment, and I am familiar with the game. As it was with the band Starsailor, Phil is being told he is not required. But this time his smile goes on forever. He takes it, almost, like a man. I say almost because I know that the pain of rejection is never limited to the snub at hand. It comes in waves, reverberates like a chord with all the other disappointments in a life. Perhaps, finally, this makes it okay. Rejection is an old friend who can only hurt you if you are foolish enough to let it. Phil has at last started to look his age. Well, sort of, not quite. He will never quite look like an adult; he will always be the teen tycoon.

If my presence made an awkward situation a bit easier for Phil and Seymour, I was glad because I am really quite fond of both of them and realized that they had to play out their parts, Phil as the aging king who can no longer have whatever he wants just by asking and Seymour as the superannuated music mogul who would prefer not to admit he no longer has the power to perform certain services even for an old friend. I'd been in this position before under even more stressful circumstances, although I didn't appreciate just how stressful until the incident was over.

When I moved to Colombia in the mid-'80s, I was taken in hand by the black sheep nephew of a former president who taught me the protocol to be followed while indulging my then bad habit with the celebrated local product. One evening I joined my "Godfather" at his home for an evening on the town to find him deep in conversation with his father, the brother of the former president. The Spanish they were speaking was deliberately pitched in such a way that an Anglo such as I would not be able to follow.

After a while, we three got into a Mercedes and headed uptown where we drew up to an imposing mock Tudor McMansion, Bogotá style. Think Richard III dubbed in Spanish and played by the cast of the Sopranos. The foyer was filled with swarthy Indian Scarface types who held gold-rimmed briefcases on their laps with rather obvious bulges in their suits. Under the armpits. I was nervous, but I trusted my Godfather, and, besides, what the other guests were up to had nothing to do with me.

The owner of the house nodded to me wordlessly and waved my friends into his office. While I waited for them I fidgeted a bit, eager to get on with my evening and its mind altering pleasures. So far as I was concerned, the sooner this pit-stop was over, the better.

About ten minutes later, our immaculate host ushered father and son out of his inner sanctum, now all smiles, charm and elbow rubs. I was introduced and we left quickly. Back in the Mercedes, the conversation was pitched so that I could understand it.

My Godfather and his father had visited the immaculate one to discuss a large outstanding debt. I had been taken along to neutralize the situation so that if things went south, the Indians in the foyer would think twice about killing all three of us. I gathered that their creditor did not object; he was sophisticated enough to know that in the event he wasn't paid, there would be another occasion to exact his revenge.

Back at Phil's, we get up to leave, we hug. As regards his wife's prospects of becoming a Warner Brothers artist, no slight has been given and no slight has been perceived. I wish him strength for his future. Have I been talking to a man who would rather kill himself than go to jail? I don't know.

A few days before the second jury delivered the verdict that would leave Spector contemplating the rest of his life behind bars, publicist and A&R man Andy Wickham visited Phil in the courtroom. Andy mentioned that he had worked for me back in 1964 when Phil and Gene Pitney crashed a Rolling Stones recording session and taught the boys a good deal about how to have fun getting it done. After weeks of staring into the void as he heard himself described day after day (for the second time) as a misogynistic monster, Phil's eyes brightened with interest.

He beamed and asked how I was, and was I well?

I was pleased to hear that with everything in his life hanging by the most precarious of threads, Phil had the energy to care about another person's well-being and the enthusiasm to express it. When the gloves are off, you know who your friends are.

Though I have no insight into Phil's guilt or innocence, and I certainly wish Lana Clarkson were alive, for everyone's sake, it's too bad Phil couldn't have been sentenced to "time served." Because whether he was rich or reviled, producing "Stand By Me" with

John Lennon or packing his bags after Starsailor said "au revoir," shaking maracas while Brian Jones grinned from ear to ear or tapping his foot while Seymour Stein told him his wife needed to look elsewhere for her big break, Phil Spector was for too many years in his eventful life a prisoner. A prisoner who had locked himself into a very luxurious cell, perhaps, but a prisoner nevertheless.

That visit to the castle in the Valley brought a certain closure to my friendship with Phil that I cherish. He knew me when I could scarcely afford to leave my mother's home, he knew me when "Satisfaction" became the kind of number one we could all be proud of, and he knew me throughout all those years when both of us sort of wandered in a wilderness of painful memories of past glories.

To know him is still to love him. And yes, Maximillian, I guess I do idolize this man. His music inspired me and his friendship gave me the courage to enter the ring and fight for myself and my dreams. He dared me to take off the gloves and punch it out with a world that at first could have cared less. And as for loving him, yes I do, and I do, and I do....

GOD ONLY KNOWS

SO GREAT AND globally influential was the so-called "British Invasion" on America's music, mores, fashion and film, that the influence of America on we creative Britons is often underestimated. Besotted as we were with American music from the Everly Brothers to Howlin' Wolf, it did not escape us that no British pop artist had ever made so much as a dent on the US Top Ten, pace Acker Bilk. Cliff Richard, our once and future home-grown Elvis, and Billy Fury, an incandescent talent with few peers, were equally disregarded. By the time the Beatles and the Stones cáme around it was remarkable enough to have snagged a recording deal; the dream of success in the States was all but unthinkable. Seen from an objective business-like point of view, this negligence of British "stars" was perfectly understandable.

In the late Fifties and early Sixties, much of the ready cash generated by the music business came from juke boxes, which were a textbook case of vertical integration before such matters were taken up by MBAs. A rather small circle of connected gentlemen controlled the entire "industry": the machines themselves, the restaurants, bars and amusement arcades that provided them with a home, the record labels and music publishers who provided them with product, the contracts of the artists who actually made the music, and the "independent" distributors who placed the records at retail. Retail sales and radio airplay were nice adjuncts to the juke boxes since they provided mechanical royalties and broadcast licensing fees in addition to the profit from vinyl sales. But the real money and the opportunity to move money around came from the thousands of quarters dropped into slots all across the land, from the greasiest spoon diner to the lounges frequented by call girls during happy hour. It was an avalanche of untraceable cash equalled only by the numbers racket.

And it was all "legitimate," as comic Phil Silvers crowed in the Broadway musical about the pre-Invasion music business, *Do Re Mi*. Sales may have been fudged and artists stiffed, but undoubtedly taxes were paid, and for a while the record business and its handmaiden the juke box and cigarette machine business competed for the connected gentlemen's attention with construction and garbage hauling. Their Achilles heel would prove to be radio and the greed of its DJs with their huge following of eager to spend teenagers. The connected gentlemen no doubt saw the cash they paid DJs to play certain records as the same kind of payment they had always made to cops to look the other way. But once the Feds got their hooks into the likes of Alan Freed for "commercial bribery," the business was never really the same. Would that the Murdoch family suffer such a fate.

The point being that even if the wise guys thought the Beatles were the next Frank Sinatra, they wouldn't have been interested. Since they didn't manage the English acts and didn't control their publishing, there wasn't enough money in it for them. Ironically, indie label Vee-Jay, already raking it in with the very Italian Four Seasons, was the first company in America to release a Beatles record. Probably because they got it for free. But once Capitol and Ed Sullivan realized what they had in the Beatles, the business changed forever. Yet the old ways were only temporarily stymied. A few short years later, Allen Klein would take a couple of pages from the Mo Levy songbook and tie the best of us up in expensive knots.

But in 1964, '65 and '66, the Beatles and the Stones were simply too busy enjoying their success in America to be reading their merchandising and publishing contracts very closely. The colonies loved them and they loved America back. The Stones' image as bad boys may have been largely fabricated, but the frisson of recording illegally in Chicago and LA inspired their first really great records. And while the Beatles remained the biggest concert draw in the world, the non-stop touring the Stones did back and forth across the US was their equivalent of the six shows a night the Beatles played for months at a time in Hamburg's Star Club. It made them the world's greatest rock and roll band.

Years since my last tour with the Rolling Stones, my love affair with America is undiminished. And a few years ago, my conversations with another Brit, of more or less my generation but a world apart professionally, brought home to me what a large part America had played in who we had become. Christopher Hitchens, the brilliant intellectual and essayist, famously became a naturalized American citizen after the 9/11 attacks and moved his family to Washington DC. I was, of course, most attracted to this "talented hater" with "impeccable manners," and it was our shared love of the US that I found most fascinating. I had always felt I was meant to find my fate in the States. Hitchens was once asked by his friend James Fenton if he felt that "in England there was always something holding him back." Hitchens agreed and so do I.

"Life in Britain had seemed like one long antechamber to a room that had too many barriers to entry," Hitchens tells us of his decision to move to America in 1981. In an astute commentary in the *New York Times,* Timothy Egan compares Christopher Hitchens and Keith Richards, why I'm not really sure, calling them "The Junkie and the Atheist." Egan suggests that "both men, on paper at least, are hard to love, but impossible to dislike. In the United States, they got what so many from other shores have obtained—renewal." When the world I'd built up for myself in the UK from 1962 to 1969 fell apart, I too relocated to the US, to a rather nice and green part of Connecticut not far from Keith's principal home for the past many years.

I later moved with my wife and son to her native Colombia and now feel rather more like an American émigré than an expatriate Briton. But it is one of my pleasures to visit with my countrymen when they find themselves in Colombia, and it is fascinating to see what a diverse club it is.

In 2006, I had a call from photographer Jonathan Becker asking me if I would like to meet Christopher Hitchens, who was speaking at the Hay Festival of Literature and the Arts, Colombia's major contribution to the world's intellectual discourse. Self-educated and compulsively literary as I am, I naturally found the opportunity and its context most welcome. Though somewhat self-conscious about my lack of formal education, I thought I might well be as unusual an acquaintance for Hitchens as he would be for me. I doubted he had seen much exposure to the Johnny Jacksons of the world.

We arranged to meet in the garden of his hotel, and when I arrived he was finishing an interview. He acknowledged me with a wave that showed me I'd been recognized. He has a remarkably innocent face for one who has subjected himself to years of intellectual torment in search of a truth that should he ever find it would probably only resonate with a relatively small minority of the public. He looks well-fed; I imagine him to have been "pretty" in school and perhaps suffered for it. I can tell from a distance that his conversation is animated and enthusiastic. Mannered, perhaps, but spontaneous. I am guessing he travels light.

He politely refuses our offer of a good Colombian breakfast, which at that hour would be our second of the day. "I don't really eat breakfast," he says. "A double scotch and half a banana will do." He was known to call the cigarettes and booze that may have contributed to his premature death a source of "junk energy," and, until he fell ill at the age of 60, required at least one bottle of wine and two drinks of "Mr. Walker's amber restorative" as a daily minimum. Compared to the intake of either of the Rolling Stones' guitarists, this seems quite moderate, and he had been notably drug free all his life, condemning them as a "weak-minded escapism almost as contemptible as religion." I smile inwardly at the Iraqi flag pin he is wearing in his lapel, not so different after all from all those "I Love Mick" buttons we were never paid for.

Our first conversation with Hitch, which skirts the edges of our different experience of the Sixties, goes well enough that we meet him on two more consecutive mornings. I let him set the conversational agenda. He was more likely to bring up his children than his strongly held political beliefs. I gather he found our company something of a respite from his reason for being in Colombia, to bring the full-on Hitchens experience to life for his fans. We traded anecdotes about our lives as we walked around Cartagena's old town, where I pointed out Gabriel Garcia Marquez's house. Both of us were experienced hands at the gringo in Latin America routine, but we both enjoyed pretending to be film directors scouting out locations abroad.

On the last day, Hitchens finally acknowledged that he appreciated that I was always sober and he often was not. I had given up cigarettes by that time as well, while he was seldom without one in his hand, helping him to make points as he spoke. He had the kind of grudging admiration many drinkers do for anyone who had it bad and quit, but it was clear he had no intention of stopping . . . yet. He quietly admitted that he couldn't go on abusing his body indefinitely and not pay a price. But he felt he had a few more years to work it out.

Christopher Hitchens felt that the booze and tobacco were part of his creative essence, much as I'm sure that Keith has over the years in a very different way from Mick. His goal had always been to have a "life instead of a career or a job." He was a devoted and loyal friend, although those close to him were often the targets of his most scathing intellectual criticism. Ever relishing the ironic, he once called friendship "life's apology for relations." Our brief acquaintance was invigorating and made my favorite quote of his come to life: "Take the risk of thinking for yourself, much more happiness, truth, beauty, and wisdom will come to you that way." Rest in peace.

* * *

Spring 2012 found me back on the road in the US en route to join the Bruce Springsteen tour in Philadelphia. I was on the New Jersey Turnpike, enjoying the excessive power of the Jaguar XJ12 I'd borrowed from Little Steven Van Zandt back in Manhattan. Though I haven't owned a Jaguar in years, driving Steven's late model I was reminded about why the big Jag had been the saloon car of choice for both the long Good Friday types and ministers of the Queen's cabinet.

Little Steven Van Zandt and ALO. New York, 2012

Let me repeat, I love being on the road, in the States most of all. Unlike travel by plane or train, a road trip by automobile tells you who you are. I just love bunging the bags in the trunk and hitting the American asphalt. I find it a kind of mediation and purifying to the mind.

It occurs to me while listening to some recent tracks for my Andrew Loog Oldham Orchestra plays the Rolling Stones Songbook Vol. 2 that I am pleased after all these years to be remembered as a record man. Not just as a producer of some excellent tracks but as a connoisseur of recorded entertainment, to the point where at one time I ran trade ads at my personal expense for "You've Lost That Lovin' Feeling," and today I am a radio disc jockey with no small following on Little Steven's Underground Garage Sirius Radio channel.

But anticipating the Springsteen lollapalooza before me, it comes over me that my own personal milestones in music have always come with live public performances, performances I generally don't even have any responsibility for. Back to my earliest youth I had been lucky to catch a wave on quite a few occasions. When I was thirteen, I learned why "The Girl Can't Help It" at the Ionic Cinema in Golders Green. With Gene Vincent and the Bluecaps, Fats Domino, Eddie Cochran and Little Richard rocking her world, who could blame her? I went to see The Girl Can't Help It every day of its week-long run, taking in both the afternoon and early evening shows.

All of the featured artists were Yanks, of course, and it never crossed my mind that in a very few years I would be earning my small keep as a PR for the tour Don Arden promoted with Little Richard. Yes, after that first celluloid introduction to rock 'n' roll heaven, it all came together pretty quickly, my last few years at school notwithstanding.

In 1960, at another venerable London cinema, the New Victoria, the Everly Brothers were backed by Buddy Holly's band, the Crickets. The boys broke my teenage heart and then gave me rock 'n' roll to put it back together again. If The Girl Can't Help It was a sort of baptism, then the Everly Brothers live were my christening. Their records had filled my dreams, sleeping and waking, but to hear the records performed to perfection and then some on stage set the bar of my expectations very high. Not for the Everlys a musicians' union-dictated accompaniment; they had borrowed the equivalent of a Jaguar XKE and brought it to my neighborhood.

After school, I spent the summer of 1961 living by my wits in the south of France. Though a somewhat amoral little twat, I was far from lazy when it came to earning my independence. I dressed the windows of a men's boutique in Juan Les Pins and served tea and scones to the British tourists at Butler's Tea Rooms. On the way to and from my two jobs, I wasn't above hustling for spare change, pitching the passersby on holiday with whatever unlikely story of ill fortune came to hand. And, quite by happenstance, I got a graduate level course in American jazz courtesy of the famous festival at Antibes. It wasn't enough for me to take in a few days of Ray Charles, Count Basie and Lambert, Hendricks and Ross. I became Les McCann's gofer, and over the sandwiches I brought him, he gave me a nickname, "Sea Breeze." "'Cause you always coming and going and your feet don't touch the floor."

When it came to the best pop music, I was an equal opportunity idolator; the jazz I heard in Antibes was just as thrilling as what I'd heard in the movie theaters, and different, because it was both adult and hip. Whatever racism these performers may have faced back home, in France, they were aristocrats based on merit and talent and treated as such. A boy accustomed to the gloom and rationing of Fifties Britain was dazzled as Harlem and the Mediterranean merged in a musical Eden. One can easily understand the enduring charm of the music for jazz raised and reared Charlie Watts.

Back in London, I checked out the radical comedy routines taking over tiny stages in Soho. Peter Cook compared his Establishment Club in Greek Street to the Berlin cabarets where the performers made fun of Hitler for as long as they were allowed. It was a members only club, and packed the night in 1962 Lenny Bruce held forth, but I somehow managed to find a spot in the corridor in which to remain inconspicuous, but all ears. The blues weren't really my cup of tea, but I understood enough about America's many conflicts and contradictions to feel the anger, pain, and frustration in Bruce's riffs, so influenced by jazz and an influence upon it.

For anyone who might describe me as an opportunist in those days, I'd remind them that I was indeed "present at the birth." I stumbled upon so many historical events I might have been Woody Allen's Zelig. By early 1963, Brian Epstein hired me to PR for the Beatles on a tour of the UK. The teenage passions violently unleashed at the Granada, Bedford was like a siege out of a more primitive time. The kids' banshee wailing never let up for a moment as they broke every window they could reach, and would have driven a stolen car through the back stage doors could they have gotten one. It was much more than a scream. It was a roar, both magnificent and dangerous, and I knew that soon the entire world would be roaring along.

When I wasn't risking blindness from shards of glass in the Beatles' dressing room, I sometimes took myself to the lobby of the Cumberland Hotel in London, where visiting American artists and their managers often stayed. They were occasionally in need of a PR for the day or week and someone to show them around. There I met Albert Grossman, who had brought his artist Bob Dylan over to London for the first time. I knew by then I would never sing a note or play an instrument, but I now saw before me in the form of Grossman's relationship to Dylan a path to my future. A month later, I introduced myself to the Rolling Stones, having just seen them perform for the first time. It so happened they were available for management. You might say preparation had met opportunity.

And, at that very moment, I changed from being merely a fan trying to avoid a 9 to 5 job and became a man who learned afresh everyday thereafter that the responsibilities that come with independence never let up. And those musical moments of serendipity and revelation became even more precious.

There was the time that Keith and I slipped into the studio to hear Frank Sinatra record. Monterey Pop, of course, which brought home just how big and brave the world of rock music had become globally. Flawed but fabulous performances as diverse yet memorable as Brian Wilson performing Pet Sounds after decades in retirement, or the Clash committing to ten days of performances at New York's Bond's in order not to disappoint their fans. Some newer acts like Razorlight and Franz Ferdinand, who surprised and touched me with their presence.

And so I was very much looking forward to Bruce that evening. Anyone who had seen his historic run at New York's Bottom Line in 1975 knew that Springsteen was a force of nature and would bring together an enormous international audience, which was being fragmented into fans of David Bowie vs. fans of Styx. In the many years since, Springsteen has grown older in a way that exemplifies the dignity he would wish for everyone who admires him. The British Invasion of almost fifty years ago kicked open a lot of doors for rock 'n' roll. But in this second decade of the 21st Century, the really great music is being made in the country that created it. Because of rock 'n' roll, everyone can say with some justification, "We are all Americans."

I accelerated to pass a Prius with an Obama sticker on the bumper, and through the hybrid's open window I heard for just a second "Satisfaction."

Another highway. Another overlook at the top of the mountain.

ACKNOWLEDGEMENTS

TOTAL THANKS TO Dave Thompson for the first all-important round. Johnny Rogan for the last inspection and suggestions. Pete Fowler for cover design and illustration. Special thanks to Terence Stamp for his mind's eye on Kit Lambert & Chris Stamp, and Lou Adler. Mucho thanks for the work, the care and the opportunity.

"Anyone who limits his/her vision to memories of yesterday is already dead."

~ Lily Langtry

The author and publisher are grateful to the following for permission to reproduce illustrative material which appears in the chapters indicated. Photographs other than those listed below are from the Andrew Loog Oldham Collection or are of unknown origin. Information regarding copyright holders or copyright material will be gratefully received by the publishers, and any errors rectified in future editions.

PROLOGUE: *ALO*—Photo by Jonathan Becker; INTRODUCTION: *First photo session with the newly formed Stones*—Photo by Philip Townsend; ALEC MORRIS: *Alec Morris*—Photo courtesy Pat Benians; KIT LAMBERT AND CHRIS STAMP: *Terence Stamp and Chris Stamp with Rolls Royce*—Photo by Terry O'Neill; DON ARDEN: *Saturn Returns, with Ruby, Max and Esther*—Photo by Jonathan Becker; ALLEN KLEIN: *The Beatles with Maharishi Mahesh Yogi, 1967*—Photo by Philip Townsend; IMMEDIATE RECORDS: *Tony Calder, Brian Jones, Bill*

Wyman, Mick Jagger; Brian Jones, Allen Klein, Road Manager Bob Bonis, Mick Jagger, ALO and Keith Richards; The Stones in concert—Photos by Gered Mankowitz; GOD ONLY KNOWS: Little Steven Van Zandt and ALO, New York, 2012—Photo by Betina La Plante; LOVING THE ALIENS: *Ian Stewart, Keith Richards & ALO*—Photos by Gered Mankowitz; ABOUT THE AUTHOR—Photo by Betina La Plante.

ABOUT THE AUTHOR

BY THE AGE of 19, when he discovered the Rolling Stones and became their first manager and producer, Andrew Loog Oldham was already a force to be reckoned with. Besides managing the Stones and producing their first ten albums, Andrew Loog Oldham founded England's first indie label, signing and helping to launch the careers of Rod Stewart, Fleetwood Mac, Marianne Faithfull, Nico, and the Small Faces. Andrew currently divides his time between Bogotá, Colombia and Vancouver BC.

Printed in Great Britain
by Amazon.co.uk, Ltd.,
Marston Gate.